Land of Tomorrow

Land of Tomorrow

POSTWAR FICTION AND THE CRISIS OF AMERICAN LIBERALISM

Benjamin Mangrum

OXFORD
UNIVERSITY PRESS

OXFORD
UNIVERSITY PRESS

Oxford University Press is a department of the University of Oxford. It furthers
the University's objective of excellence in research, scholarship, and education
by publishing worldwide. Oxford is a registered trade mark of Oxford University
Press in the UK and certain other countries.

Published in the United States of America by Oxford University Press
198 Madison Avenue, New York, NY 10016, United States of America.

Library of Congress Cataloging-in-Publication Data
Names: Mangrum, Benjamin, author.
Title: Land of tomorrow : postwar fiction and the crisis of American liberalism /
Benjamin Mangrum.
Description: New York, NY : Oxford University Press, [2019] |
Includes bibliographical references and index.
Identifiers: LCCN 2018012099 (print) | LCCN 2018035692 (ebook) |
ISBN 9780190909383 (updf) | ISBN 9780190909390 (epub) |
ISBN 9780190909406 (online content) | ISBN 9780190909376 (cloth :alk. paper)
Subjects: LCSH: American fiction—20th century—History and criticism. |
Liberalism in literature. | Liberalism—United States—History—20th century.
Classification: LCC PS374.L42 (ebook) | LCC PS374.L42 M36 2018 (print) |
DDC 810.9/3587392—dc23
LC record available at https://lccn.loc.gov/2018012099

9 8 7 6 5 4 3 2 1

Printed by Sheridan Books, Inc., United States of America

It seems so easy for America to inspire and express the most expansive and humane spirit; new-born, free, healthful, strong, the land of the laborer, of the democrat, of the philanthropist, of the believer, of the saint, she should speak for the human race. It is the country of the Future. From Washington, proverbially "the city of magnificent distances," through all its cities, states, and territories, it is a country of beginnings, of projects, of designs, and expectations.

—Ralph Waldo Emerson

The Founding Fathers dreamed America before it was. The pioneers dreamed of great cities on the wilderness that they crossed. Our tomorrow is on its way. It can be a shape of darkness or it can be a thing of beauty. The choice is ours, it is yours, for it will be the dream that we dare to dream.

—Lyndon B. Johnson

Emerson was right. We are the country of tomorrow. Our revolution did not end at Yorktown. More than two centuries later, America remains on a voyage of discovery, a land that has never become, but is always in the act of becoming.

—Ronald Reagan

CONTENTS

ACKNOWLEDGMENTS

The process of writing this book has been a study in the generosity of others. This generosity has included fellowships at the University of North Carolina at Chapel Hill and the Society of Fellows at the University of Michigan. I'm grateful to these institutions for supporting my work. I'd also like to thank Sarah Humphreville at Oxford University Press for championing this project.

It's an honor to have been supported by so many talented and generous people. Foremost among them is John McGowan, who read multiple iterations of the chapters, offered both regular advice and free therapy, and has been a wellspring of liberalism, both intellectually and personally. Matt Taylor was unflinchingly generous through his advice and even more with his time. Suzanna Geiser read so much and so often—including an early draft of the fifth chapter—and with each new piece of writing provided extensive feedback. Katie Walker read multiple drafts and has been an invaluable colleague. Florence Dore intervened in early versions of the fourth chapter and then the entire manuscript. Sean McCann also read an early draft of the manuscript and raised questions that have been influential for the argument's framing. Suzanne Churchill, Gabriel Ford, and Randy Ingram read a draft of the introduction and have encouraged this work in many other ways. Ben Murphy invited me to present part of the fifth chapter in the Americanist Speakers Series in Durham, NC. Priscilla Wald was a generous host and interlocutor during this talk. I'd also like to thank India Gray for her keen eye as a copyeditor.

I'm grateful for the support and intelligence of many others: Neel Ahuja, Kathy Barton, Pam Betts, Susan Bickford, Shireen Campbell, Scott Denham, Eric Downing, Adam Engel, Laura Finch, Rebecka Rutledge Fisher, Mary Floyd-Wilson, Ann Fox, Cynthia Gerlein-Safdi, Linda Gosner, Jennifer Ho, Thomas Kelly, Heidi Kim, Kevin Ko, Zoran Kuzmanovich, Don Lopez, James Macmillen, Andrea Mangrum, Joel Mangrum, Rick Mangrum, Adam McCune, Brendan McMahon, Annie Merrill, Mandy Neese, Mary Neese, Shelby Neese, Tim Neese, Rachel Norman, Alan Michael Parker, Scotti Parrish, Barbara Petroff, Les Petroff, David Porter, Richard Russell, Ben Sammons, Lynette Shaw, Mike Stroope, Linda Turner, and Marlous van Waijenburg.

Grady and Ivy Mangrum have been the source of so much joy during the life of this book. They were on my mind during the writing of every paragraph.

What I've said about the indispensable place of others is eclipsed by Ashley Neese Mangrum's love and support. She's been an eager interlocutor, caring friend, and constant advocate. I cherish Ashley, her companionship, and the life we've made together. It's to her that this book is dedicated.

Land of Tomorrow

Introduction

What happened to American liberalism?

After the Democratic Party's loss in the 1968 general election, historians of the liberal tradition have looked to the fractious four years preceding Richard Nixon's victory to provide answers to this question. Prior to the splintering of the Democrats' base between 1964 and 1968, American liberalism had seemed to be the only show in town.[1] Through the popularity of President Roosevelt and his New Deal programs during the 1930s, the Democratic Party forged the longest running political coalition in American history, winning control of both houses of Congress since 1932, interrupted only by small Republican majorities in 1946 and 1952. Yet a contentious 1968 Convention in Chicago, and then Hubert Humphrey's loss to Nixon, made it abundantly clear that the Democrats' liberal base had splintered. The party that billed itself as the institutional caretaker of American liberalism was fracturing in very public ways over the Vietnam War and the civil rights movement.

An established body of scholarship—including work by Alan Brinkley, Allen J. Matusow, Dan T. Carter, Glenn Feldman, and Wendy L. Wall—has identified many of the institutional and political causes leading to the end of New Deal reform and the later collapse of the Democratic coalition.[2] As Michael Schaller and George Rising explain, the trials that beset American liberalism allowed for the subsequent "Republican ascendancy," a return to the pre-Depression era dominance of conservative Republican politics, which would culminate in the electoral triumphs of Ronald Reagan in the 1980s.[3] Prior to this ascendancy, the postwar caretakers of liberalism preserved the New Deal's coalition of "interest blocks," including labor unions, racial and religious minorities, white Southerners, urban political bosses, intellectuals, and a collection of farm groups. This coalition exerted so much influence at the national level that even President Eisenhower took the American welfare state as a given.[4] Indeed, because this coalition was so influential in national politics, many scholars characterize the postwar decades (the 1940s, 50s, and 60s) as the "apex of American liberalism."[5] Similarly, in a recent book that

1

recalls the autobiography of Henry S. Reuss, a Democratic US representative from Wisconsin, the historian David Goldfield describes the postwar generation as sharing a "commonwealth ideal" that governments "should enhance opportunities for all Americans."[6] These descriptions of the robust dominance of postwar liberalism have remained the standard historical narrative about the postwar decades since the 1960s. After Johnson's defeat of Barry Goldwater in the 1964 general election, the distinguished presidential scholar James MacGregor Burns declared, "By every test we have, this is as surely a liberal epoch as the late 19th Century was a conservative one."[7]

Land of Tomorrow reexamines this standard account of postwar liberalism's dominance by showing that the period of "apex" was in fact rife with tumultuous changes within American intellectual culture. These changes transformed the character of liberal thought and contributed to the many pressures challenging the tradition of social-democratic reform established during the New Deal era. To explain this transformation, *Land of Tomorrow* examines the routes through which the literary life of the nation conferred cultural prestige on a cluster of new political sentiments within American liberal thought. This confluence of intellectual and literary history explains the drift in postwar liberalism away from the progressive experimentation and regulatory commitments of the 1930s. As Sheldon Wolin puts it, American liberalism shifted "from 'social conscience liberalism' to 'neo-liberalism'; from a New Deal ideology—emphasizing social welfare, civil liberties, and a modest degree of governmental planning and regulation of industry—to an expansionist ideology" that fueled Cold War anxieties, regulatory concessions to a consumer economy, and an imperialistic foreign policy.[8] While the established explanations for the Democratic Party's fracturing in 1968 rightly looks to the Dixiecrat rebellion, Cold War containment, and disagreements over the Vietnam War, political theorists like Wolin and literary historians like Thomas Schaub have suggested that other disruptive changes were afoot within the intellectual climate of American liberalism. Schaub describes these changes as "revisionist liberalism," and he argues that intellectuals and writers felt their liberal commitments had been chastened by the dawn of the nuclear age, the rise of fascism in Europe, and emerging revelations about state-sponsored atrocities in the Soviet Union. As Schaub explains, these postwar developments tarnished idealizations of statist social democracy.[9] The postwar "inheritors" of New Deal liberalism were consequently beset not only by external and international pressures but also internal change.[10] The political culture of postwar liberalism was a house being rebuilt on shifting intellectual sands.

In order to examine these changes within the substrate of postwar political culture, this book analyzes liberal thought on two layers: underappreciated trends in the history of ideas and, through the work of postwar writers, the granular features of those broader trends. This book's attention to both broad movements and particular texts shows that new forms of political affect began to enjoy cultural prestige during the postwar era. These new political sensibilities circulated in works by Ralph Ellison, Saul Bellow, Patricia Highsmith, Vladimir Nabokov, Chester Himes, Richard Wright, Walker Percy, Flannery O'Connor, and Lionel Trilling, among many others. In addition to these writers, the genealogy of twentieth-century liberalism's transformation also includes the postwar American reception and interpretation of modern European fiction and philosophy, particularly work by Friedrich Nietzsche, Jean-Paul Sartre, Albert Camus, Hannah Arendt, Fyodor Dostoevsky, and Franz Kafka.

This genealogy of cultural ideas uncovers the reorganization of American liberal thought prior to the crises of 1967–1968 and the Republican resurgence in the following decades. These changes in the structures of liberal thought and feeling were not the sine qua non of the eroding support for what some postwar thinkers called "organizational liberalism" and the activist-managerial state it supported; nonetheless, the cultural prestige conferred on these sensibilities justified a politics that was inadequate for the substantial resurgence of free-enterprise conservatism.[11] By looking to fiction that garnered prestige during this period, this book shows that many of liberalism's literary standard-bearers legitimized and circulated an intellectual culture opposed to the reform agenda established during the "active phase" of the New Deal (1933–1938). Studying the literary scene from 1945 to 1968 thus provides a crucial cultural prehistory to the failures of American liberalism in the face of the Republican ascendancy.

Postwar Prestige and the Moment of Fiction

Land of Tomorrow takes literary fiction as both the particular expression of public sensibilities and as conduits for the circulation of political affect. In other words, postwar fiction did more than reflect wider changes in liberal thinking. By giving cultural confirmation to new political sentiments, and by helping particular forms of political affect gain literary prestige, I argue that certain domains of the literary arena would aid in the many political and cultural pressures undercutting the maintenance of a social-democratic political order in the United States. Literary fiction didn't just embody a revised liberalism; writers encouraged its revision. Several prominent schools of postwar fiction legitimated cultural attitudes that ran counter to the activist-managerial state established during the New Deal era. The postwar fiction analyzed in this book helped give articulate form to animus against the political idea of an interventionist welfare state, often by providing literary clarification to anxieties already in public circulation, but also by offering alternative political sentiments that emphasized the life of the self as an antidote to the felt crises of the moment.

On the one hand, then, postwar fiction provides its own form of access to intellectual history, which relies on, in Michael Edwards's phrasing, an "extended notion of context as a series of ripples (doubtless in deep intellectual waters), moving from the texts at the centre of the inquiry to cultural, political, and social structures and beyond."[12] This book similarly views literary fiction as, among other things, evidence of the ripples of intellectual history. Literary fiction thus functions, in many respects, as political philosophy expressed in narrative form. Or, in a different metaphor employed throughout the following chapters, literary fiction allows us to trace threads across a web of intellectual culture and institutional structures. These threads show how American liberalism was being reconstituted in ways that would delegitimize federal reform and progressive collective action.

On the other hand, *Land of Tomorrow* also shows that the literary arena was an active feature of the eroding legacy of a pragmatic and social-democratic reform agenda. The ideas of the literary arena had political and social consequences through their contributions to the shape of liberal discourse. Work by postwar writers had the public effect of being, to borrow Raymond Williams's phrasing, a "confirmation" of "a pressing and varied experience which was not yet history."[13] The mantle of this body of literary thought was therefore a variegated one: some literary texts were clarificatory, others were representative of wider trends, many circulated new ideas, a few registered thoroughgoing dissent from a political or cultural order, and so on. This variability makes postwar fiction all the more important for understanding not just the sweep but also the granular complexity of the history of ideas. More than ancillary phenomena added on top of the more fundamental "base" of the nation's political economy, these texts helped reimagine the intellectual substrate—the structures and sentiments of cultural legitimacy—within the liberal tradition.

As I've already intimated, one of the principal mediums for postwar fiction's contributions to American intellectual life was the "prestige" that texts, writers, and cultural institutions conferred on certain cultural trends and political sentiments. At the beginning of the postwar era, a burgeoning publishing industry disseminated fiction on an unprecedented scale, even outpacing the growth of the American population.[14] While selling books became increasingly lucrative for publishers, literacy and public reading also grew exponentially during the 1950s.[15] As James English shows, the marked growth in the publishing industry during the 1950s corresponded to the expanding economic weight of reading and the proliferation of markers of prestige.[16] Prizes such as the National Book Award garnered public and economic value, and these markers of prestige in turn bestowed a cultural imprimatur upon certain ideas and narratives. Therefore, two interconnected trends occurred at the same moment in the life of the nation: novel reading garnered a new scale of importance, while the markers of cultural prestige began to multiply. In short, what may broadly be called "novel culture" became a more prominent feature of American life.

Yet the rise of novel culture wasn't spontaneous. The expanding significance of novels during this era was, as Evan Brier argues, partially a result of successful marketing strategies by the book trade, which often presented novels in particular as embattled holdouts against ostensibly vulgar mass culture.[17] According to Brier, shrewd editors and a burgeoning mass-publishing industry found the novel-as-cultural-bastion to be a widely marketable branding of fiction. As a result, postwar fiction accumulated unprecedented leverage in determining which structures of thought and feeling—which sensibilities about the self, its status in collective space, and about the value of public institutions—attained wider public legitimacy. Americans turned to the novel to diagnose their present moment because, as Mark Greif says, this literary form "attained its one permanent high-water mark in the years of midcentury" and thus became the genre that "sustained obligations of national and moral import."[18]

While many of the writers studied in the following chapters enjoyed the markers of prestige bestowed by the institutions of the literary marketplace, I also analyze work that enjoyed a different sort of prestige in the arenas of popular culture, including novels by Patricia Highsmith and Sloan Wilson. My claim is that many of these "literary" and "best-selling" writers expressed political sentiments tuned to the affective pitch of an anti-organizational liberalism, which in turn weakened the fledgling social-democratic order in the US. All the writers considered in this study understood themselves to be on the spectrum of liberal thought, at least during this period of their careers. Through this attention to the literary life of the nation, this book shows how the decline of a progressive reform agenda in the United States extended beyond conservative opposition in Congress or the mobilization of the business community and "free enterprise" sentiment in the American public.[19] The transformation of liberal thought itself played an important part in the drift away from "the reform impulse of the 1930s," to use Richard Pells's description.[20] The works from this period that scholars so often praise—works like *Invisible Man, Lolita,* and *The Adventures of Augie March*—were carriers of an intellectual crisis. Many of these standard-bearers of intellectual culture sowed the seeds of liberalism's discontents.

Steinbeck, Mailer, and the US Welfare State

The contrasts between the literary careers of John Steinbeck and Norman Mailer illustrate one of the patterns for the transformation of political sentiment in the middle decades of the twentieth century. When Steinbeck published *The Grapes of Wrath* (1939), the American economy had only barely begun to emerge from the 1937–1938 recession that stalled Roosevelt's recovery agenda. The Great Depression had by then been elevated to the status of a national myth. Steinbeck did not need to remind Americans of the national crisis, which still loomed over the late 1930s and its slowly improving economic fortunes. Rather than preaching to the dispossessed choir, then, *The Grapes of Wrath* draws on the shared experience of the Depression to respond to the economic crisis and political demands of a recession-hardened America. That is to say, instead of scorning New Deal reform, Steinbeck's novel is critical of its unfulfilled promises through the state's failures to attain the social and economic aspirations that had elevated the Democratic Party to political power in 1932–1933.

Roosevelt famously expressed the party's newly formed progressive aspirations in his address at the 1932 Democratic National Convention:

> These unhappy times call for the building of plans that rest upon the for-gotten, the unorganized but the indispensable units of economic power, for plans . . . that build from the bottom up and not from the top down, that put their faith once more in the forgotten man at the bottom of the economic pyramid.[21]

Roosevelt's vision of capitalism for the proletariat managed to coax GDP back to its pre-Depression level by 1939. Yet the high levels of unemployment during his administration—hovering around 25 percent in the mid-1930s and still as much as 15 percent by 1940—was at odds with the New Deal agenda of national restoration dedicated to providing economic security for the "forgotten man."[22] What's more, as Susan Edmunds observes, "the Roosevelt administration's adoption of a Keynesian economic vision" to address the recession "placed a federally supported order of private—and almost exclusively white—domestic consumption at the center of the nation's economic recovery plan."[23] In 1938 when Steinbeck was finishing the novel, the New Deal rhetoric about "the for-gotten man" was not only unfulfilled but also, despite the massive realignment of black voters in 1936, still plagued by racial discrimination.

This ongoing dearth of jobs and dignity during the 1930s provided some of the social urgency for Steinbeck's novel, which embeds that experience within the seemingly impassible fury of an Oklahoma landscape. The coincidence of social and economic forces drives the Joad family to California in search of security and employment. After several deaths and desertions, the beleaguered Joad family arrives out West to find an oversupply of labor. Law enforcement officers harass the unemployed, while large corporate farms collude to choke out smaller farmers and thus ensure a system of cheap labor. The Joads soon discover Weedpatch, a "gov'ment camp" built in 1936 for the purpose of pro-viding housing to migrant workers. Steinbeck's setting was based on an actual camp built by the New Deal's Farm Security Administration. Weedpatch, as one destitute woman puts it, offers "water right handy" and "no cops let to come look in your tent any time they want."[24]

Still, the Joads discover that this federal haven is an awning with too little cover. While the Joads eventually are given space in the government camp, they are consistently beleaguered with economic and political problems. Local police officers often try to break into or dissolve the camp, but, more importantly, the federal relief is insufficient. As Ma Joad says, the family only eats "fried dough" and "Tom had five days' work" in the one "month we been here" (478). After discovering that federal relief is spread thin, the Joads soon search for work elsewhere and become strikebreakers at a peach farm. Much like the winds of the Dust Bowl that swept them toward the promises of California, the members of the family are again caught up in the wider forces of a conflict between labor unions and corporate farms. A family friend, Jim Casy, becomes a casualty of this conflict, and Tom Joad murders the man responsible for his friend's death. In turn, Tom becomes a fugitive in the land of opportunity; he is yet another "vagrant" dispossessed within the life of the nation (456).

Despite the deficiencies of federal reform in the novel, *Grapes of Wrath* calls attention to precisely the confluence of social and political concerns underpinning Roosevelt's original reform agenda: the lack of protections for workers' rights and organized labor, a fundamental distrust of concentrated economic power, and the need for expanded relief programs to address poverty and unemployment. Not only was the novel consistent with these progressive political sentiments, but also, as Alan Wald explains, *The Grapes of Wrath* "popularized numerous conventions of the American labor narrative."[25] It baked political equality into the form of an especially influential cultural template. Steinbeck's novel provides an account of politics that, rather than spurning the New Deal, demands the fulfillment and even augmentation of the progressive federal management of the nation's welfare that many of Roosevelt's advisors had imagined. Indeed, government camps, such as Weedpatch, are the only refuge from local police and the exploitative system of labor created by large corporate farms—they are foretastes of things to come, harbingers of a more thoroughgoing and expansive welfare system.[26]

The political sentiment of the New Deal advocated precisely this sort of expansive regulatory system of managing the economic life of the nation. The reform agenda established in the early years of Roosevelt's presidency (1933–1938) is often described as the "progressive" or "active" phase of the New Deal. As Brinkley explains, this was a moment in American intellectual and political life "awash in ideas," some of which "were rooted in the progressive philosophies of the first decades of the twentieth century, others in the experience of World War I, still others in some of the generally unsuccessful reform initiatives of the 1920s."[27] There was no ideological core to the active phase of the New Deal: it was a constellation of political sentiments, regulatory institutions, and pragmatic programs that developed in response to the displacement and economic devastation of the Great Depression. The majority of Roosevelt's advisors explained this crisis as a consequence of concentrated economic power and a speculative financial sector. The New Deal reform agenda thus sought to control overweening monopolies, strengthen organized labor, and regulate the economic vicissitudes produced by American banks and industries.[28] While few in the administration were categorically opposed to capitalism, there was nonetheless a diversity of competing ideas about how to structure the national economy.[29] Some in the administration looked to centralized economic planning, while others simply advocated antimonopoly legislation. As Louis Menand puts it, "there was no master plan, no guiding philosophy, for the reforms that Roosevelt oversaw. Some were his idea; some were Congress's; some were left over from the Hoover Administration. Roosevelt was improvising."[30] The reform phase of the New Deal thus featured a "chaos of experimentation," as Richard Hofstadter recounted in 1955, an ad hoc pragmatism that aspired to mitigate the economic uncertainties and wage inequalities produced by industrial capitalism.[31]

From regulatory legislation such as the Banking Act of 1933 to compensatory welfare programs such as Social Security in 1935, the New Deal tried to reform the socioeconomic structures of American life through the regulatory mechanisms of an activist-managerial state and the expansion of federal welfare. The centralized programs designed to usher the nation out of the Depression also involved regional planning and agricultural reform, as exemplified by the Tennessee Valley Authority (TVA) and the Agricultural Adjustment Administration (AAA). One of the centerpieces of the early New Deal, the National Industrial Recovery Act of 1933 (NIRA), authorized the president to regulate industry, mandated a minimum wage, and established the Public Works Administration (PWA), which was led by Harold L. Ickes, a progressive Republican who had been a past president of the Chicago NAACP. Significant provisions of both the AAA and NIRA were later struck down or hamstrung by the Supreme Court, but their initial effects were momentous. The 73rd Congress and the executive branch limited deductions for capital depreciation, reorganized tax rates to remove the onus from the middle class, and ended the tax-exempt status of corporate dividends. During its short existence, the PWA—replaced by the Works Progress Administration (WPA) in 1935— also provided well-paying jobs through public construction projects.[32]

Perhaps most remarkably, Roosevelt's administration and a New Deal-friendly Congress courted labor unions, which formed a central faction of the Democratic Party's coalition. For example, the 1935 National Labor Relations Act (also known as the Wagner Act) strengthened the collective bargaining power of American unions by requiring businesses to bargain with any union supported by a majority of its employees. Sensing the favorable winds that this legislation signaled, the Congress of Industrial Organizations (CIO)—which was open both to communist union leaders and African American members— became more aggressive in organizing previously nonunion workers. During the 1930s and early 1940s, the CIO became one of Roosevelt's largest supporters.[33]

The reform phase of the New Deal era also featured the Glass-Steagall Act of 1933, which was a response to what many in the administration felt was the direct cause of the Great Depression: the conflation of commercial and investment banking.[34] A central provision of the Glass-Steagall Act established a rigid separation between these two forms of banking in an effort to protect citizens from speculative investments. At the same time, the 73rd Congress also authorized the president to promote free trade through tariff reductions. Thus, the patchwork policies of the New Deal's active phase crossed ideological lines for the sake of pragmatic political reform: aggressive regulation of concentrated economic power, a social-democratic commitment to the rights of laborers to organize, and a federal system of social security were matched by a commitment to antimonopoly free trade.

Steinbeck reiterates many of these Roosevelt-era demands for national institutions of protection and welfare on behalf of the rural poor. He frames the crisis of widespread poverty through the travails of a family whose name alludes to the biblical Job, a "righteous" man who nonetheless experiences catastrophe and whose suffering calls into question the goodness of God. Whereas Job functions as a narrative means for scrutinizing the principal authority of the ancient Mediterranean world, the suffering of the Joads teases out the injustice of national life without guaranteed economic security and greater social protections for the poor. Steinbeck puts this national mythologizing to political use most tellingly through Rose of Sharon, whose name is taken from the endearment given to one of the lovers in the biblical book Song of Songs. "I am the rose of Sharon," the woman of the poem proclaims, "the lily of the valleys" (2:1). Her assertion provides grounds for erotic linguistic play—her lover "feedeth among the lilies," for example. By way of contrast, Rose of Sharon's lover in Steinbeck's novel abandons her during the search for more secure social space. Steinbeck's Rose of Sharon is a deserted beloved, a figure for possibility gone awry and an inhabitant of a world without fulfillment or dignity.

The mythologizing in *Grapes of Wrath* elevates political ideas about the dignity of "man" alongside notions of collective welfare. These ideas are typified in another mythological aspect of Rose of Sharon's character. Many readers in the Judeo-Christian tradition interpret the beloved in Song of Songs as a communal allegory of God's relationship to a chosen people. In that religious tradition, "Rose of Sharon" more often than not signifies the beloved community, rather than a virginal beloved. In an adaptation of this tradition, Steinbeck's Rose of Sharon takes on secular allegorical status, much like his turn on the biblical Job calls into question the goodness of national life without public securities. This take is clearest during the novel's famed ending when Rose of Sharon and the remaining Joads encounter a nameless boy and his starving father. The Joad daughter, who has only recently given birth to a stillborn child, nurses the starved man: "Her hand moved behind his head and supported it. Her fingers moved gently in his hair. She looked up and across the barn, and her lips came together and smiled mysteriously" (619). Steinbeck's Rose of Sharon—who here also represents a Madonna figure—becomes an image of a mythic community, a surrogate family for the nameless masses who are otherwise destitute in the world. She provides for the well-being of the poor; she stands in for the aspiration of a secular family to welcome the dispossessed.

Steinbeck's image of a political community responsible for the welfare of the masses is replaced with a different set of cultural metaphors that came to prominence after the Second World War. In particular, in Norman Mailer's work from the 1950s and 1960s, progressive politics transforms into a new figure, which he describes as "the American existentialist—the hipster." Writing during the summer of 1957 in *Dissent*, one of the major postwar organs for progressive thought, Mailer argues that the Second World War of "super states" and the advent of "instant death by atomic war" have subjected the "psyche" of postwar Americans to a unique intellectual crisis. "One could hardly maintain the courage to be individual, to speak with one's own voice," Mailer says of this postwar milieu, "for the years in which one could complacently accept oneself as part of an elite by being radical were forever gone."[35] The collectivist politics of Steinbeck no longer seems plausible to Mailer, for a "stench of fear has come out of every pore of American life, and we suffer from a collective failure of nerve" (277). How can there be a political community—a secular order of welfare—when the collective itself is systemically sick?

The only hope under such dire circumstances, Mailer insists, "has been the isolated courage of isolated people." Mailer's despair at the conditions of postwar life prompts him to look toward the hipster because, he says, such a figure responds to the threat of "a slow death by conformity with every creative and rebellious instinct stifled" through "the only life-giving answer" available to him: "to live with death as immediate danger, to divorce oneself from society, to exist without roots, to set out on that uncharted journey into the rebellious imperatives of the self" (277). In short, the collective condition of postwar society is either to be swallowed up by the state and mass society or to be fractured from that collective. The self—the courage to be individual—becomes Mailer's haven from the bleak conditions of postwar collectivism.

Based on this diagnosis, Mailer says that Americans face a fundamental, existential dilemma: they may either retreat into mass conformity or turn toward countercultural scripts. For those who follow the latter route, Mailer argues that the "Negro" in particular has become a model for life amid the absurdities of postwar society. In Mailer's fantasized view of structural racism, black Americans either "live a life of constant humility or ever-threatening danger" (279). By simply expressing the self—rather than suppressing it, becoming a subservient shadow of a self—black Americans face the lynch mobs of Southerners and the bellicosity of urban policemen in the North. Their everyday situation, according to Mailer, is an existential crisis. As a result, he argues that a particular subculture of the postwar generation was "attracted to what the Negro had to offer," for the "existentialist synapses of the Negro" seemed to provide a universal pattern of existence that white, postwar Americans could appropriate (278, 279). From this nexus of racial fantasies and cultural idioms, Mailer imagines that the "language of Hip" is born, giving "expression to abstract states of feeling which all could share, at least all who were Hip" (279). The hipster, in other words, becomes Mailer's figure for correcting the existential threats and oppressive social structures of the 1950s.

Because this figure draws on the "existential" plight of black Americans, Mailer asserts that the hipster "for practical purposes could be considered a white Negro" (279). Mailer's inflection of existentialism through the aspiration of crossing the color line is, as Michael Szalay says, "a complex variant of the peculiarly American tradition of blackface minstrelsy." Szalay explains that notions of hip such as Mailer's derive from the anxieties of "white men [who] sought and found in black subculture a means of negotiating the conflicted ideological and organizational imperatives of postwar liberalism."[36] Because the Democratic coalition was fraught with internal disagreement and beset with external pressures, American existentialists like Mailer looked to black Americans to sort out their sense of political displacement. They objectified blackness in the search for a cure for the illnesses of mainstream liberalism. Mailer's existentialist turn in particular centers on a crisis between "the Hip and the Square," that is to say, a "primal battle" over whether "to open the limits of the possible for oneself, for oneself alone" (290). The collective becomes "Square," but affirming the self and its desires is the essence of "Hip." Whereas Steinbeck's leftism offers a script for collectivist political action, organized labor, a critique of concentrated economic power, and an urgent demand for socioeconomic security, Mailer's progressivism looks to "Hip" to "return us to ourselves, at no matter what price in individual violence" (290).

These differences between Steinbeck's and Mailer's sensibilities are indicative of one prominent pattern I trace throughout subsequent chapters. While marshaling crowds to protest the war in Vietnam was later his self-avowed métier, Mailer's turn toward existentialism in the 1950s displaced the locus of political action from the collective to the life of the self. The "heart of Hip," he says, is an "emphasis upon courage at the moment of crisis," the willingness to assert the self irrespective of social consequences (291). Mailer's notorious example in "The White Negro" is the *acte gratuit* of "two strong eighteen-year old hoodlums" who "beat in the brains of a candy-store keeper" (284). Such arbitrary acts of violence—"no matter how brutal"—offer something like a radical form of dissent from the social death of the self. Mailer thus elevates the singular—the daring of the unknown, an abandonment of premeditated behavior, and the refusal to conform—as the only viable alternative to the vast bureaucracies that order postwar life. As a result, the authentic life of the self becomes the touchstone for political action.

These differences between Steinbeck in the 1930s and Mailer in the 1950s represent one especially influential form of the new political affects that beset organizational liberalism. But of course, the crisis wasn't only affective and intellectual. Literary critics like Alan Nadel and the cultural historian Elaine Tyler May have shown that the shifts in political sentiments in postwar fiction were linked to the "containment culture" of the Cold War era.[37] For instance, as Walter Benn Michaels puts it, "the Cold War may be (and often was) described as universalizing, as involving every part of the world and potentially every part of the universe." The conflict between the United States and the Soviet Union was dominated by "difference" understood in terms of mutually exclusive ideological disagreement.[38] According to Michaels's account, that construal of difference as *disagreement* came to dominate American intellectual life until the late 1980s. Perhaps for this reason, as Landon R. Y. Storrs explains, the federal government during the postwar era cannibalized itself for the sake of the rigidities of ideological conflict through the Federal Employee Loyalty Program, which screened over 5 million of its employees from 1947 to 1956. The effect of the program, according to Storrs, was to drive the postwar heirs of New Deal progressivism underground or off government payrolls.[39] In essence, the ideological conflicts of the 1950s suppressed the spectrum of policies and political philosophies that characterized the reform phase of the New Deal.

But the sources of liberalism's transformation are not circumscribed by the Cold War. For one, they predate it. Despite Roosevelt's landside electoral victories in the 1930s, the New Deal reform agenda had been under significant pressure long before the contentious postwar decades. One of the principal sources of these challenges came from the Southern bloc of Roosevelt's coalition. The tensions within Congress regarding the Fair Labor Standards Act of 1938 (FLSA) is a telling example of the fact that the reformist impulses of Roosevelt's administration had begun to alienate significant portions of his original constituency. The FLSA established a forty-four-hour workweek, a minimum wage, and prohibited most forms of child labor. It also was particularly contentious for Southern Democrats, who began to worry that the federal dollars and employment initiatives of FDR's work programs came at the cost of greater equality for black laborers.[40] Prior to the FLSA, Democrats in the South had frequently been given racially motivated concessions during the early reform legislation of the New Deal era. For example, federal laws regulating the wages and working conditions of laborers were often passed with exceptions for farms, whose employees in the South were most often African American. In exchange for sustaining the racial structure of rural farming, Southerners supported the coalition's legislation regarding union activity.

However, as the National Labor Relations Board enforced the Wagner Act and, later, the FLSA, an environment conducive to labor organization slowly began to achieve in the South what progressives in Congress originally failed or neglected to do: a wave of often-effective strikes among industrial employees, many of whom were African American, began to eke out better working conditions for all laborers.[41] The gains were small but uncomfortable for the Dixiecrats in 1938. Thus, after the FLSA was passed, a segment of the New Deal coalition began to work actively to undermine the legal framework of the Wagner Act and inaugurated an era of tensions within the Democratic Party that would come to a head in 1948 and again, this time with partisan finality, in 1964. After 1938, though, the Southern bloc of the New Deal refused to pass any significant reform legislation because of these fears. The result was that, as Ira Katznelson puts it, the Fair Labor Standards Act became "the last law-making victory of the New Deal's radical moment."[42]

The reform agenda of the New Deal was often contradictory. And even as this reform agenda was challenged by conservative Republicans, the ad hoc quality to Roosevelt-era reform also underwent significant transformations in response to an economic recession during 1937–1938, the growing influence of Keynesian redistributive policy among Roosevelt's advisors, and the international pressures of the Second World War.[43] What's more, the legacy of the New Deal's active phase faced unique pressures following Roosevelt's death, as a less popular president took the reins of a powerful federal apparatus. By the mid-1960s, as I detail in the following chapters, the Democratic Party's vision was a fraught politics of redistribution and an uneasy commitment to social equality; it was not predominately a politics of activist regulation. The structural, regulatory, and reformist positions of the "active phase" of the New Deal had either been mitigated or entirely abandoned.

Mailer's "The White Negro" provides cultural and intellectual texture to these shifts. In fact, the essay is striking for how significantly it deviates from Mailer's earliest practices as a writer. Before Mailer's long dalliance with existentialism, he wrote the bestselling novel *The Naked and the Dead* (1948), which follows a platoon of soldiers during the fictional siege of the Japanese-held island of Anopopei. Mailer explores the ethnic and nationalist impulses of American soldiers during the Second World War and, more broadly, the justice of the US war effort itself. Mailer calls attention to the divisions that stratified the military along racial and class lines, and *The Naked and the Dead* was therefore hewn from the same cloth as Mailer's literary masters at the time—most notably, Tolstoy's social realism in *Anna Karenina* (1878), American naturalists like Steinbeck and James T. Farrell, and the early radicalism of John Dos Passos. In the vein of these literary predecessors, Mailer distributes the focus of the narrative across the lives and consciousness of over a dozen infantrymen and officers. The narration regularly blends with a Southern soldier's untutored dialect or an upper-class, East Coast officer's brooding meditations on mortality and the army. The narration also provides short accounts of the "life" and "education" of the soldiers, thus situating the siege of Anopopei within a wider account of social reality.[44] The dispersion of social reality across classes and characters in *The Naked and the Dead* embeds an awareness of class consciousness within literary form, if not also suggesting an outright political commitment to analyzing the markers of class distinctions. This brand of realism embeds within literary form a progressive commitment to evaluating the structures and consequences of inequality.

In contrast, Mailer's long *affaire de coeur* with existentialism had profound effects on his work. For instance, *The Armies of the Night* (1968), with its acerbity directed against liberal Democrats and their support for the Vietnam War, signals this intellectual shift by identifying the novel's narrative center with an absurd and self-reflexive comic hero—Mailer himself. The author becomes a character in his own novel and, as a result, Mailer presents self-reflexivity as the governing window for the narrative. Mailer argues that an "absurd" twentieth century makes certain demands upon literary form, and so the authorial attempt to represent social reality must emerge out of that absurdity:

> So if the event took place in one of the crazy mansions, or indeed *the* crazy house of history, it is fitting that any ambiguous comic hero of such history should be an egoist of the most startling misproportions, outrageously and often unhappily self-assertive, yet in command of a detachment classic in severity. . . . Such egotism being two-headed, thrusting itself forward the better to study itself, finds itself therefore at home in a house of mirrors, since it has habits, even the talent, to regard itself. Once History inhabits a crazy house, egotism may be the last tool left to History.[45]

Mailer's image of the progressive chronicler—a disproportionately large head, who is preoccupied with regarding itself and whose "home" is amid reflections of itself—departs sharply not only from the implicit demands for greater social-democratic intervention in *The Grapes of Wrath* but also from the literary strategies of *The Naked and the Dead*. For Mailer the existentialist, the global threats and social malaise of postwar America require the author to inflect political fiction through a "talent" for self-reflexivity. The life of the self, in other words, becomes the locus for political understanding.

The contrasts between Steinbeck's and Mailer's figures for progressive politics—and even Mailer's shift from realism to self-reflexivity—were features of the rising preference for modernist literary culture in the United States. In his analysis of the bestselling books of the 1950s, Gordon Hutner explains that fewer works of middle-class realism were published in the 1950s: "The critical debates about the death of the novel, or the loss of faith in mimesis in the face of the New Novel in France," Hutner says, "translate into questions about the capacity of Howellsian realism to give depth, texture, and meaning to everyday life."[46] Even among its postwar supporters, "the realist novel frequently seemed to be in its death throes, its aesthetics doomed and its political inertia and cultural exhaustion too profound to accommodate the changes within the culture."[47] The felt crises of the postwar moment—its absurdity, as Mailer put it—demanded new aesthetic templates, which most often borrowed from modernist texts that were enjoying new cultural weight in the United States. In other words, Mailer's career represents another changing structure of thought and feeling important to the genealogy of twentieth-century liberalism: the reception history of modernism and its postwar iterations in American fiction. As I argue in subsequent chapters, the postwar varieties of modernist literary culture confirmed opposition toward organizational politics in liberal and radical domains of US literary life. Indeed, as a political corollary to these literary shifts, Mailer suggests that the exigencies of avowedly absurd "history" now requires the writer to reform the self, not the structures of society or the programs and institutions of the welfare state.

This constellation of literary and aesthetic changes had consequences for the forms of political affect that enjoyed intellectual currency and cultural prestige in the postwar decades. In light of these new sensibilities, the social-democratic order established during the "active phase" of the New Deal era became increasingly construed as a political hazard, rather than a pragmatic institutional means for liberal ends. The following chapters detail how the legacy and institutional forms of this political order became numbered among the sources of alienation for many postwar writers. This reorientation of US literary culture was no doubt due to the fact that New Deal programs had substantial and often damning flaws.[48] As only one example, as the Agricultural Adjustment Administration (AAA) and the Fair Housing Administration (FHA) systematically weighted their interventions in favor of white Americans. The FHA, in particular, supported de facto segregation by refusing to guarantee mortgages to black homeowners, whether in the North or the South, when they applied to live in white neighborhoods. In short, the active phase of the New Deal was no halcyon era. There's no two ways about it: Roosevelt-era reform was also the institutionalization of American liberalism's support for racial discrimination.

From New Deal Reform to the Postwar Crisis

Subsequent chapters return often to the inequalities of New Deal reform as a feature of the social-democratic order instituted during the 1930s. This political order sedimented many prominent strains of the long Progressive era and its nascent ideas about a reformist welfare state, which arose in the midst of sprawling poverty throughout the United States. New Deal reform thus offers a complicated precedent for developing a more thoroughgoing commitment to social-democratic institutions. Yet the question of this book is why postwar liberals were increasingly reticent about this precedent for a reformist politics. The rhetoric of liberalism's partisan caretakers often gestured to reform, but their policies and programs exhibit a loss of confidence in regulatory institutions as either a bulwark against economic inequality or a solution for the problems of an American consumer economy.

Johnson's War on Poverty is a telling bellwether of these shifts. The Economic Opportunity Act of 1964 (EOA) attempted to eliminate poverty by providing job training, as well as loans and grants to small businesses through local Community Action Agencies (CAAs). Despite the Act's concern for the economically dispossessed, Mical Raz argues that a theory of poverty unique to the postwar moment underwrote the EOA: Johnson's "war" replaced the reformist New Deal explanation for poverty—that is, as a consequence of the structural inequities of concentrated economic power—with the notion that poverty is the "deprivation" of opportunity.[49] "Opportunity" became a euphemism that avoided the structural inequalities of consumer capitalism. This new political rhetoric within the postwar Democratic Party is peculiarly tautological: the cause of poverty is a lack of opportunity, while the causes of the lack of opportunity are the manifestation of poverty. Such circularity is apparent, for instance, during Johnson's State of the Union address in 1964, where he announces the War on Poverty:

> To help that one-fifth of all American families with income too small to even meet their basic needs, our chief weapons in a more pinpointed attack will be better schools and better health and better homes and better training and better job opportunities to help more Americans, especially young Americans, escape from squalor and misery and unemployment rolls, where other citizens help to carry them.
>
> Very often a lack of jobs and money is not the cause of poverty, but the symptom.
>
> The cause may lie deeper in our failure to give our fellow citizens a fair chance to develop their own capacities, in a lack of education and training, in a lack of medical care and housing, in a lack of decent communities in which to live and bring up their children.[50]

This vision contrasts sharply with Roosevelt's insistence that the socioeconomic troubles of the 1930s derive from the power of "organized wealth." For Roosevelt, at least during his first two terms, concentrated economic wealth was to blame not only for the Depression of 1929 but also the recession and spike in unemployment during 1937–1938.[51] In contrast to Johnson, FDR presented the cycle of poverty as a function of structural avarice, speculative banking, and unchecked industry. Indeed, the dismal 1936 presidential campaign of Alf Landon against Roosevelt failed in large part because of the public animus toward the support Landon's candidacy received from wealthy businessmen.[52] Johnson's commitment to alleviate the nation's "poverty crisis," on the other hand, had dropped the regulatory language of the early New Deal and its antipathy toward concentrated economic power, favoring instead the rhetorical and vaguely Keynesian frames of "supply" and "opportunity." In this version of postwar liberalism, the cycle of poverty becomes a self-enclosed and self-replicating crisis. Its causes are its effects.

Within Johnson's political vision, the welfare state became transmogrified into an engine of opportunity, not a system for regulating or dispersing economic power. Similarly, Mailer presents the welfare state as another bureaucracy in a long laundry list of alienating institutions. Iconoclastic egoism would, according to Mailer, become the salvation of the special type of existential poverty confronting the postwar self. The absence of an economic regulatory impulse in the figures presented by both Johnson and Mailer, as well as a nearly exclusive emphasis upon compensatory and "opportunity" programs in Johnson's War on Poverty, embody the turn that institutional liberalism had taken in the postwar decades. Following the planned wartime economy of 1940–1945—the period when the federal government's control over the economy reached its historical apex—the Democratic Party drifted toward an embrace of a form of political-economic organization known as "embedded liberalism," which refers to a state-sponsored economic and industrial strategy with a modest regulatory environment. The form of embedded liberalism dominant in the late 1940s and 1950s nurtured—often planned at a federal level—a web of industrial production and global trade. Yet those forms of central planning were, in effect, a tepid compromise between the expansion of a global marketplace and a domestic welfare state.[53] As *Land of Tomorrow* shows, the social and political pressures of the postwar era cultivated visions of American political (as well apolitical and antiregulatory) life that would slowly erode support for the restraints on capital established during the reform phase of the New Deal era. Embedded liberalism provided something like a historical border phase for this transformation.

Novel Developments in American Intellectual History

The struggle to define American liberalism during the postwar era took place on multiple fronts. Corporate interests, Dixiecrats opposed to civil rights, and anxieties about Soviet communism—juxtaposed with progressives like Henry Wallace, who had been one of Roosevelt's most prominent advisors and his second vice president (1941–1945)—contributed to the changing shape of the postwar Democratic Party. But beyond this well-documented tumult in U.S. institutional politics, this book examines several underappreciated phenomena that were central to the transformation of American political culture during this era: namely, the resurgence of forms of aestheticism as a bulwark against centralized state authority; the adaptation of European existential thought; the popularization of psychoanalysis and the professionalization of the therapeutic disciplines; the collusion between the postwar welfare order and American consumer culture; the reception of modernist literary culture; the emergence of an "independence regime" in partisan affiliation; and the articulation of a new philosophy of liberal management. The following chapters demonstrate how these trends changed American liberal thought. For their part, postwar writers augmented these trends by conferring literary prestige upon forms of liberal thinking that privileged self-possession, the burden of individual choice, and an aesthetic theory of the public sphere. These political sensibilities surfaced in a variety of ways, including among the "new" professional-managerial class that, as Stephen Schryer argues, gave up on "building institutions" during the postwar era in favor of other forms of professionalism.[54] Long before the "deregulation revolution" of the 1980s, then, liberal managerial authority had by the 1960s become its own worst enemy, recasting activist-managerial politics as the symptom of a malaise that liberalism now aspired to dispel.

To explain the development of this ouroboros in liberal political culture, I turn first to the work of Vladimir Nabokov, whose *Bend Sinister* (1947) and *Lolita* (1955) typify one of the ways the experience of European totalitarianism inflected postwar political sensibilities: that is, the resurgence of what I characterize as aestheticist responses to concentrated political power. Such responses appeared among several domains of public writing in the United States, including work by Hannah Arendt and Friedrich Hayek. These intellectuals feared that totalitarian oppression might take hold in the United States, and they consequently tried to shape policy and public sentiment against an activist-managerial state. In the first chapter, I trace how Arendt, Hayek, and Nabokov, as well as influential figures in American literary criticism, particularly the New Critics and Lionel Trilling, questioned the legitimacy of a robust social-democratic order. These disparate figures expressed their doubts about this political order, sometimes implicitly and sometimes directly, through their respective affirmations of aestheticism. In *Bend Sinister*, for instance, Nabokov rejects the tropes of the dystopian novel to separate the literary arena from politicized public life. This body of literary and critical work thus invoked forms of aestheticism—that is, existence ought to be governed by private judgments and pleasures—as a cultural strategy for dealing with the specter of totalitarianism looming over the United States. Within these segments of postwar intellectual life and literary sentiment, aesthetic domains became a haven from an increasingly politicized and state-managed world.

In the second chapter, I explore a different permutation of the waning legacy of the New Deal by examining the work of Richard Wright, Saul Bellow, Ann Petry, Carlos Bulosan, and Ralph Ellison. Fiction by Ellison and Bellow, in contrast to Petry, Bulosan, and Wright's work during the 1940s, were part of the reception and circulation of existentialist sensibilities within American public discourse. The development of an American idiom of existential thought contributed to the declining intellectual currency of social-democratic politics in the United States. In particular, the reinterpretation of European existentialism, as the sentiments underwriting Ellison's *Invisible Man* (1952) suggest, identifies the authentic life of the self as the locus for political action, rather than political coalitions or organizational reform. Ellison's invisible man responds to his estrangement from the Brotherhood and the liberal sensibilities of his college by retreating into the self as the last remaining site for authentic freedom. As the narrator puts it, his turn inward is "a covert preparation for a more overt action."[55] Books like *Invisible Man* and *The Adventures of Augie March* (1953) reveal how existential sensibilities had come to inflect the vocabulary of American political culture in ways that would change the terms for diagnosing societal problems and, in turn, would privilege authenticity as a governing democratic virtue.

Often in ways that were indebted to the place of existentialism within the changing political culture of the United States, the professionalization of psychology and increasing prevalence of the therapeutic disciplines had far-reaching implications for how Americans thought about the public sphere. I offer a frame for understanding this dimension of postwar intellectual life by analyzing Patricia Highsmith's fiction, which inflects American existentialism through what Nathan Hale describes as the "golden age" of psychoanalysis's popularization in the United States. This third chapter shows that the conjunction of professional psychology, popular psychoanalysis, and existentialism challenged the social and philosophical basis for a social-democratic order by widely disseminating psychological explanations for social phenomena. In contrast to the literature of the long Progressive era and certain strains of literary naturalism, the ego and its vicissitudes became the dominant template in the 1950s for understanding both society and the self. For instance, in *Strangers on a Train* (1950), Highsmith mimics the plot of Dreiser's *Sister Carrie* (1900) only to subordinate the markers of her characters' class to the psychological drama of self-invention. Highsmith's novels thus recast violence, murder, alienation, class envy, and social mobility as phenomena of the largely autonomous, internal arena of an existential psyche. As these literary artifacts suggest, postwar writers and intellectuals often reconfigured the products of socioeconomic inequality after the templates of the individual's psychological experience. This template undermined the presuppositions of structural reform in favor of therapeutic interventions.

The fourth chapter looks to several influential Southern writers, especially Walker Percy and Flannery O'Connor, to explore two other challenges to the postwar welfare order: the collusion between the welfare state and a consumer economy, on the one hand, and the development of what political scientists call an "independence regime" in the American electorate, on the other. This independence regime shares substantive affinities with the phenomena explored in preceding chapters, especially the resurgence of aestheticism and the development of an American strain of existential thought. Percy's and O'Connor's fiction further elucidate these developments, for they each criticize bureaucratic liberalism on the grounds that its programs and institutions trivialize the self and identify political life with economic consumption. For example, Binx Bolling, the protagonist in Percy's *The Moviegoer* (1961), explains that being a "model citizen" entails a glut of papers that ostensibly license his existence: "identity cards, library cards, credit cards . . . my birth certificate, college diploma, honorable discharge, G.I. insurance, a few stock certificates, and my inheritance."[56] Much like this satirical take on the bureaucratic contours of Binx's life, the novel suggests that a national welfare state impinges on the authentic life of the self by configuring it according to bureaucratic markers and tokens of exchange. According to this vein of Southern fiction, the procedural mechanisms of the welfare state are built on the model of a consumer economy. In contrast to what these writers identify as the alienating ethos of institutional liberalism, their fiction imagines an intellectual culture based on the individual's unmediated confrontation with reality, rather than the surfeit markers of a consumer economy.

The final chapter analyzes postwar fiction on American corporate life and managerial authority, including bestsellers like Sloan Wilson's *The Man in the Gray Flannel Suit* (1955) and the countercultural work of Jack Kerouac, J. D. Salinger, and Ken Kesey, among others. I argue that this fiction conveys a philosophy of liberal management distinctive to the postwar era—a philosophy that also received its articulation in the theories of corporate management by Abraham Maslow, Peter F. Drucker, and Kurt Lewin. The new philosophy of liberal management rejected Frederick Winslow Taylor's earlier views, which promoted "scientific efficiency" and guaranteed high wages. Postwar organizational thought and literary corporate fictions, in contrast, presented personal development, self-direction, and private satisfaction as preeminent virtues in a democratic society. Individual authenticity, rather than the organizational efficiency and wage incentives of an earlier era, became central to the calculus of the managerial sciences. At the same time, postwar theories of management and novelistic corporate fictions elevated the self-legislating manager to the status of a cultural paragon.

By looking to the literary arena of the postwar era, this book examines a constellation of ideas that transformed American liberal thought. This constellation of ideas reveals postwar liberalism to be wrought after the image of angst. The new forms of political affect among liberals attest to their failures—and often even their unwillingness—to justify a robust social-democratic order for postwar America. The Vietnam War and resistance to civil rights clearly provoked the fracturing of the Democratic Party, but the intellectual culture embraced by many postwar liberals also hastened and justified the drift from an earlier commitment to activist-managerial institutions. This book thus reframes the literary prestige so often attributed to many of the canonical writers of the postwar era, situating such prestige as a feature within the crisis and transformation of American liberalism. As a result, many of the revered fiction writers and intellectuals of the postwar decades established a center of gravity within liberal political thinking that privileged authenticity, aesthetic judgments, and self-management. *Land of Tomorrow* aspires to grapple with the assumptions, debts, and consequences of this moment in American liberalism's genealogy.

1 }

Aestheticism, Civil Society, and the Origins of Totalitarianism

After reading the representation of the incompetent, bureaucratic, and often-violent police state in Vladimir Nabokov's *Bend Sinister* (1947), the prominent literary critic Edmund Wilson wrote in a letter to the author, dated January 30, 1947, "You aren't good at this kind of subject, which involves questions of politics and social change, because you are totally uninterested in these matters and have never taken the trouble to understand them."[1] Yet Nabokov would suggest over a year and a half later in a subtle taunt to his friend that it was Wilson who'd failed to understand. In a letter dated September 3, 1948, Nabokov updates Wilson on his affairs, mentioning, "[I] [h]ave had some lively correspondence with the Army in regard to a hideous transl[ation] of *Bend Sinister* (a novel I published a couple of years ago,—you should read it some day) into German."[2] The implication is that Wilson had not actually read the novel—or at least not closely enough to understand it. Nabokov chides "Bunny" (as he often called the irritable Wilson) for viewing the novel as failed political fiction.

That the police state of *Bend Sinister* is at once foolish and bureaucratically incompetent lends credence to Wilson's complaint that Nabokov had written a simplistic version of Kafka's or Orwell's narratives.[3] However, Nabokov's novel is more complicated than this dismissive view allows. Instead, *Bend Sinister* is a parody of the tradition of political fiction—a rejection of the anti-utopian subgenre.[4] As a parody, Nabokov's novel represents more than the liberal anti-communism of books like Richard Crossman's *The God That Failed* (1949) and Arthur Schlesinger Jr.'s *The Vital Center* (1949). *Bend Sinister* instead offers a pattern of thought—later reiterated in *Lolita* (1955) and *Pale Fire* (1962)—in which organizational and social imperatives are overcome by an affirmation of literary pleasure. This gesture in Nabokov's first "American" novel is important, I argue, for the type of opposition to an activist-managerial state it exemplifies within American intellectual history. Much like other accounts of totalitarianism by Erich Fromm and Hannah Arendt, Nabokov depicts the subjects of totalitarian states as suffering the deprivation of their individuality. Many such accounts worried that the bureaucratic and nationalistic precursors to European totalitarianism had begun to surface in the United States, not least in the programs of the welfare state. Yet this chapter identifies an important subtext in the literature on totalitarianism: the invocation of aestheticism as a bulwark against the threat of political tyranny.

Nabokov's fiction articulates one variety of aestheticism closely related to other postwar critics and intellectuals. Nabokov's aestheticism maintains that existence ought to be governed by subjective pleasures and private judgments of value rather than a unifying concept of rationality, materialism, or history. Nabokov's parody in *Bend Sinister* is a clarifying instance of the wider phenomenon of the resurgence of aestheticism, particularly as the novel dissolves the "political" dimensions of the narrative within the horizon of literary pleasure. In turn, Nabokov's aestheticism provides a window on related varieties of aestheticism in work by the economist and political philosopher Friedrich Hayek, the New York intellectual and writer Lionel Trilling, the prominence of the New Critics in the US academy, and also the conditions for the revival of Friedrich Nietzsche's philosophy during the postwar era. Each of these important figures in postwar intellectual life relied on varieties of aestheticism. Hayek, for instance, imagines economic liberalism as a prophylactic to tyranny, but his influential views were based on an underlying commitment to private judgments of value. Before pursuing these ideas across Nabokov's fiction and its connections with postwar political philosophy, this chapter begins by setting the scene for the resurgence of aestheticism through the work of Lionel Trilling.

Aestheticism and Trilling's Liberal Imagination

Much like the protean forms of Nabokov's fiction, aestheticism took on different guises as it enjoyed an intellectual renaissance among the cultural tastes and critical registers of postwar America. While the writings of the New Critics in the 1930s and 1940s would shape the postwar disciplinary contours of literary studies—a point I take up later in this chapter—a coterie of intellectuals and critics congregating in New York rejected the New Critics' distinction between literature and politics. These included Philip Rahv, Sidney Hook, Harvey Swados, Hannah Arendt, Edmund Wilson, and Dwight Macdonald, among others. At first blush, they appear to be exceptions to the sort of aestheticism that concerns this chapter. However, as an implicit corollary of their explicitly political commitments, many of these intellectuals held a deep-seated distrust of the programmatic commitments of liberal bureaucracy. This distrust came in part from the New York intellectuals' debts to Leon Trotsky and his critique of the Soviet Union's Stalinist bureaucracy.[5] They were allergic to most types of organizational authority.

This front in the challenges to an activist-managerial state found something of a clarion call in Lionel Trilling's *The Liberal Imagination* (1950). Trilling maintained that "at this time liberalism is not only the dominant but even the sole intellectual tradition" in the United States, but the book's essays nonetheless offer certain correctives to the liberal thought of the day. Indeed, Trilling describes many of liberalism's "particular expressions" as "useless and mistaken."[6] Observing that the contemporary spectrum of liberalism "moves toward organization," he worries that such a tendency in American political thinking "unconsciously limits its view of the world to what it can deal with, and it unconsciously tends to develop theories and principles, particularly in relation to the nature of the human mind, that justify its limitation."[7] In other words, one "tendency" of postwar liberalism takes the reduction of human experience to be a constituent element of its philosophical underpinnings. Based on such a reduction, liberalism often resorts to bureaucratic political forms. While there is value to such an "organizational impulse," Trilling warns with the air of a lay preacher that the liberal intellectuals of the postwar era "must understand that organization means delegation, and bureaus, and technicians, and that the ideas that can survive delegation, that can be passed on to agencies and bureaus and technicians, incline to be the ideas of a certain kind and of a certain simplicity."[8] The bureaucratic liberalism centering on an activist-managerial state, as Trilling presents it, passes on a facile intellectual inheritance; it cultivates reductionist bureaucrats who order the world according to shallow ideas.

The answer to the reductionist "impulse to organization" behind the liberal welfare state of Trilling's day is to "recall liberalism to its first essential imagination of variousness and possibility, which implies the awareness of complexity and difficulty."[9] Trilling glosses the crisis confronting postwar liberalism as the sedimentation of an abiding tendency to elide individual interiority, contingency, and possibility. Literary critics and intellectuals are tasked with subordinating organizational authority to a reinvigorated moral imagination, one that liberals should disseminate to an educated reading public. Thus, as Stephen Schryer argues, Trilling urges intellectuals to abandon "their technocratic pretensions toward social reform in favor of a different, humanistic model of cultural education oriented toward the educated middle class."[10] To invest one's critical energies in structural or institutional reform may not only be a misplaced expression within liberalism but may also distort its imaginative and cultural foundations. For Trilling, organizational authority poisons the well of an ostensibly life-giving moral and cultural authority. This sensibility was a closely related expression of the reticence toward organized labor among other intellectuals in Trilling's orbit.[11] While this view of liberalism's postwar imperatives differs from the image of a self-contained work of art that the New Critics advanced in the preceding decades, both forms of critical sentiment present organizational politics as an imposition upon the pleasure, meaning, and possibility of private judgments of value.

Nabokov's fiction helps clarify the stakes for these critical sensibilities by showing how an anti-managerial liberalism ennobles private judgments of value as the final measure of the political imagination.[12] These literary and critical sentiments licensed opposition to the pragmatic institutional commitments that New Deal liberalism established before the Second World War. Even as the distinction between domestic and global realms of life collapsed under the weight of the war against European fascism, the specter of authoritarian organizations hovered over postwar writers, intellectuals, and a reading public to such a degree that it aroused a form of liberal mistrust—and often even antipathy—toward the activist-managerial state. The novels of Nabokov's "American" period (1947–1969) participated in this wider phenomenon by giving a literary experimentalist's cast to the animus toward organizational liberalism. Emerging from the conflict with totalitarian regimes, these anxieties construed reformist liberalism as vulgarizing, enfeebling, or undermining the aesthetic conditions of human life.

Totalitarianism, the New Deal, and the Politicization of Life

Nabokov twice fled violent regimes in his lifetime. As an adolescent, he escaped the Bolsheviks after the October Revolution of 1917. His father, Vladimir Dmitrievich Nabokov, was a "classical liberal" and prominent member of the Constitutional Democratic Party that came into power after the February Revolution of 1917. V. D. Nabokov became secretary to the Provisional Government, yet the Bolshevik Revolution a few months later forced the elder Nabokov and his family to flee, eventually settling in Berlin. His son became a well-known poet in the émigré circles of Berlin and settled in the city, remaining even after V. D. Nabokov's assassination in 1922. In 1925, Nabokov the writer married Vera Evseyevna Slonim, a Russian-Jewish émigré, but the couple was eventually forced to leave Berlin in 1937 because of the city's growing anti-Semitic environment. The Nabokovs traveled throughout France until they were forced yet again to flee the German army in 1940, eventually settling in the United States.

As Nabokov puts it, he "brushed against" "Fascists and Bolshevists" in his lifetime, dismissing such regimes as simultaneously "idiotic and despicable."[13] Nabokov explains that his rancor for these powers centers less on their ideology than the ways they violate and encroach upon the individual's interior life. For example, in his autobiography, *Speak, Memory* (1967), Nabokov recalls that the Bolsheviks appropriated and nationalized his inheritance, an expansive estate, not long after the October Revolution. Instead of commiserating with "the particular idiot who, because he lost a fortune in some crash, thinks he understands me," Nabokov explains that his

> old (since 1917) quarrel with the Soviet dictatorship is wholly unrelated to any question of property. My contempt for the émigré who "hates the Reds" because they "stole" his money and land is complete. The nostalgia I have been cherishing all these years is a hypertrophied sense of lost childhood, not sorrow for lost banknotes.[14]

Nabokov's "quarrel," he explains, is not an ideological disagreement about private property but rather that the Soviet nationalizing policies violated the site of his memories. They encroached upon the space of his soul. Like an enlarged or "hypertrophied" heart, the sixty-eight-year-old Nabokov's longing for the world of his youth swelled to painful proportions as the material anchor for his memory had been seized and then transformed into collective property. Violated by dictators and political revolutions, Nabokov instead retains only the "right to yearn after an ecological niche" (*Speak* 73). Nabokov's ecological metaphor again suggests that the object of his longing is not his material inheritance but a lost world, one seemingly prior to the political turmoil of his adult life. His "brush" with communism and fascism, in other words, becomes representative of the politicization of life, the collective seizure of an arena of private existence.

Each of Nabokov's fictional explorations of political life bears the imprint of this sense of violation. In *Invitation to a Beheading* (1935–1936), for example, Cincinnatus C. awaits his execution for committing "gnostical turpitude," or the refusal to conform to his society's absurd groupthink.[15] As Cincinnatus is led away to be executed, he refuses to believe in the reality of the prison, his executioners, or their rule, and the narrative world is upended: the upwards stairs lead downward, the prison crumbles around him as he exits. The crowd awaiting the execution becomes "quite transparent," and the figures of the regime shrink to a diminutive size (222). The platform for Cincinnatus's execution "had long since collapsed in a cloud of reddish dust," while everything else "was coming apart. Everything was falling" (223). The narrative world dissolves just as Cincinnatus is executed. Politics steps aside to make room for the verbal capacities of literary representation.

While *Invitation to a Beheading* bears the imprint of the aestheticism that informs *Bend Sinister*, Nabokov's story "Tyrants Destroyed" signals an earlier evolution in the author's handling of politics.[16] Written in Menton during "spring or early summer 1938" as a Nazi invasion was looming, "Tyrants Destroyed" features a nameless narrator who plots to kill the dictator of an unidentified European country. Nabokov admits in a note that prefaces the story that this unnamed tyrant—along with his sources, "Hitler, Lenin, and Stalin"—resurfaces again in *Bend Sinister* under a different guise.[17] In the earlier story, much like in *Bend Sinister*, the nameless protagonist is a childhood friend of the dictator. But as the ruler's grip tightens upon the country, the narrator finds that the tyrant is "penetrating everywhere, infecting with his presence the way of thinking and the everyday life of every person" (9). The absence of individual names in the story mirrors this infection: there are no more *persons*, only vague and anonymous *figures*. Yet even as the narrator objects to the individuality that the tyrant steals from the country's citizens, he discovers that the ruler's disconcerting "penetration" has even begun to affect his own consciousness. At first, the signs of this "penetration" are minor: "I must have achieved a certain secret liaison with him," the narrator recounts, "for around eleven o'clock, when he goes to bed, my entire being senses a collapse, a void, a weakening, and a melancholy relief" (31). Soon, though, the narrator believes that the tyrant has seeped into his "entire being" (32). As a result, the narrator cannot imagine existence outside this politicized state of mind: his subjectivity has begun to take on the contours of tyranny.

Both *Invitation to a Beheading* and "Tyrants Destroyed" exemplify concerns that Nabokov returns to in *Bend Sinister*. In contrast to the anxious narrator of "Tyrants Destroyed," though, Nabokov's protagonist in *Bend Sinister*, a philosopher named Adam Krug, exhibits unabashed indifference toward the political regime. This posture is clearest during Krug's first interview with Paduk, the regime's dictator. When they were children, Krug was accustomed to bullying the young tyrant by sitting on his head. As adults, the tyrant has requested to see Krug because, as the latter puts it, the philosopher is "the only person who can stand on the other end of the seesaw and make [Paduk's] end rise" (145). Krug knows how to throw his weight around, but he never does so in a way that is advantageous to Paduk. Krug's apolitical refusal to support the regime prevents the tyrant from obtaining legitimacy outside the borders of his coerced country. In turn, Paduk refuses to confirm the safety or location of Krug's arrested friends. Paduk finally declares, "All we want of you is that little part where the handle is." Krug bellows, "There is none," and then the two men get to the heart of their disagreement:

> "If," said Krug, "you cannot leave me and my friends in peace, then let them and me go abroad. It would save you a world of trouble."
> "What is it exactly you have against my government?" [Paduk asks.]
> "I am not the least interested in your government. What I resent is your attempt to make me interested in it. Leave me alone." (146–47)

In contrast to the consumed "being" of the narrator in "Tyrants Destroyed," Krug hardly thinks about the regime. He wants to enjoy the life of the mind, and he wants to experience his private grief and pleasures without the surveillance or intervention of the state.

What's important about Krug's response is that Nabokov inscribes this same indifference in the very form of the novel, particularly in later moments when the narrator questions whether the narrative representations of the political events are accurate or "real." For example, as the exchange between Paduk and Krug becomes heated, the narrator interrupts the dialogue: "No, it did not go on quite like that. In the first place Paduk was silent during the interview. What he did say amounted to a few curt platitudes . . . " (147). The exchange in which Krug expresses his political apathy is negated, undermined by the narrator's uncertainty about the story he tells. These doubts about the interview call into question whether the scene itself is of any importance, as if even the narrator, who otherwise saturates the novel with detail and attentive word play, does not pay much attention to a scene of political disagreement.[18] The narrator's intervention also presents Paduk's political and ideological "platitudes" as conspicuous artifice, as if they were a fiction built for a literary purpose. In other words, the conflict between the tyrant and the philosopher becomes of less interest than the art and play of the novel's language. What matters is the scene's status as *art* and not the staging of *politics*.

Nabokov's parody of a political narrative evokes the aestheticized suspicions of political existence among other varieties of postwar liberalism. Trilling, for example, expresses this worry when he claims, "Unless we insist that politics is imagination and mind, we will learn that imagination and mind are politics, and of a kind that we will not like."[19] According to Nabokov's version of this sensibility, even the literature analyzing totalitarianism succumbs to the selfsame politicization of existence that underwrites tyrannical authority. Commenting on this idea, Brian Boyd says that *Bend Sinister* should be understood in relation to the anxieties of Nabokov's newly adopted but war-haunted home:

> [Nabokov] detested the mass mobilization of minds that war required, the air of crisis everyone was supposed to breathe. No, he instinctively responded, it is in the very nature of dictatorship, as it deprives its citizens of their freedom of choice, to inculcate in them a sense of crisis and unite them against some designated opponents: the Jews, the bourgeoisie, the Communists, the kulaks, the Fascists. I will simultaneously attack dictatorship *and* the notion that all good citizens should rally around to attack it—which itself would be just another form of social dictate.[20]

Bend Sinister simultaneously renounces what Nabokov saw as dictatorial about the politics of wartime America and the long shadow of totalitarianism stretching from across the Atlantic. Roosevelt's description in December 1940 of America as the "Arsenal of Democracy"—an appellation recalling the industrial-scale weapons production preceding US entry into the war— seemed to Nabokov to be a close cousin to the "Nazi masters of Germany" who, as Roosevelt says, "dominate all life and thought in their own country."[21] Movements that configure life in terms of the "mass mobilization of minds" for any political cause become institutionalizations of collective compliance. The metafictive play of Nabokov's first American novel, then, isn't merely a form of opposition to fascism or totalitarian regimes; it is an attempt to reject politicization of all stripes.

Civil Society, the Welfare State, and Mid-Century Political Philosophy

The prospect that organizational politics could propagate tyranny animated a variety of attempts to secure cultural and philosophical safeguards for the postwar political order. Indeed, the contest to define the relationship between American democratic liberalism and the origins of European totalitarianism became a staple of the book trade in the United States. For example, as early as 1935, Ethan Colton noted the similarities between the New Deal and "Fascist politics in Italy and those of the Nazis in Germany." Colton observes, "All three adhere to the institution of private property. They are alike in requiring its uses to be adapted to the national welfare in contrast to that of the owning class primarily. . . . A planned economy is the goal."[22] While the Roosevelt administration would later deemphasize central economic planning in favor of Keynesian deficit spending to respond to a recession in 1938, the legacy of its activist phase (during which Colton wrote) would feed later comparisons with fascism and National Socialism during the postwar moment.

In the widely read *The Road to Serfdom* (1944), Friedrich Hayek similarly asserts that the "experimentation of the New Deal" lies on the political spectrum that had provided the economic mechanisms for the rise of totalitarianism.[23] Hayek argues that the "great utopia of the last few generations," the democratic socialist state, "is not only unachievable," but "to strive for it produces something so utterly different that few of those who now wish it would be prepared to accept the consequences" (82). Hayek says that socialist-progressive policy and centralized economic planning are a road "on which it becomes more difficult to turn back as one advances," eventually reaching a tipping point not just to the collectivization of a nation's economic activity but also to totalitarian control over the everyday behavior of the citizenry (58). Hayek thus conflates democratic socialism and fascism as "merely variants of the same totalitarianism which central control of all economic activity tends to produce" (43). Hayek's argument was widely read, frequently condensed, and often misrepresented for partisan purposes, but its account of the political economy of democratic socialism gave more definite shape to the fear that the economic programs and regulatory activity of the New Deal would chart a path for the development of totalitarianism in the United States.[24]

The intellectuals who offered cultural and philosophical safeguards against this threat often drew on the concept of civil society, which has a long and protean history within practical and philosophical thinking about collective life. The importance of the postwar resurgence of the civil-society concept is the uses to which it is put by thinkers as diverse as Hayek and Hannah Arendt—usages that, I argue, shaped postwar political culture in ways inimical to an interventionist and bureaucratic welfare state. These mid-century revisions of the concept are intellectual precursors to what Robert Putnam describes as the aggregate losses in membership within civic organizations, volunteer groups, labor unions, and even voter turnout since the 1960s.[25] For Putnam, the decline of American civil society is largely the result of technological changes in the postwar era. Yet many (though not all) versions of the idea put forward in the wake of the Second World War notably reconfigured collective affiliation in paradoxically aestheticized terms—that is to say, in ways that used the idea of civil society to carve out domains of experience that privilege individual spontaneity, possibility, and contingency.

The term *societas civilis* was first developed by the Roman jurist Cicero, who adapted it from the political philosophy of Aristotle. Cicero uses *societas civilis* as a technical term with limited applications to the legal arena of the polis. Picking up on Cicero's usage, Augustine similarly employs the notion to refer to "an assemblage (of men) associated by a common acknowledgment of right and by a community of interests."[26] While later medieval philosophers would also occasionally refer to Cicero's *societas civilis*, writers during the seventeenth century—most notably Thomas Hobbes, John Locke, and the Dutch jurist Hugo Grotius—revived the idea and gave it a more prominent place within early modern philosophical thought. Bhikhu Parekh explains that, for Hobbes and Locke in particular, civil society was "not separate from the state nor one of its institutions; rather it was a way . . . of constituting the state."[27] In effect, for these seventeenth-century theorists, civil society refers to the associational underpinnings that justify the need for a formal edifice of government.[28]

Following significant revisions to the early modern tradition by G. W. F. Hegel and Karl Marx, Alexis de Tocqueville establishes the predominant American tradition of maintaining some theoretical degree of independence between civil society and the state.[29] For Tocqueville, arenas of "civic association" are so widespread in the United States that they are central to the character of the equality and political participation at the heart of nineteenth-century American democracy. Societies of voluntary association are, according to Tocqueville, independent from the government, but he nonetheless describes such groups as "political associations." While they are not supported by partisan groups and remain institutionally and financially autonomous from the government, these civic associations come together for explicitly political ends.[30] Tocqueville argues that these associations make democracy in America unique from its European counterparts:

> The Americans have introduced a form of government *within* associations which is, if I may put it so, a civil administration. Individual independence

is recognized in it [i.e., the network of associations comprising civil society]. . . . No one has sacrificed his will or his reason but they exert them for the success of a common enterprise.[31]

Inaugurating a tradition within American political philosophy that would later be picked up by Putnam and Michael Walzer, Tocqueville insists that "independent" civic associations constitute the primary avenue through which Americans curb tyranny and the power of rapacious business interests.[32] They are a "civil administration" because these "political associations" exert pressure on American democratic life despite the fact they are not tied directly to the edifice of the government. As Tocqueville describes the nineteenth-century phenomenon, civil society is independent from *state* authority, but individuals nonetheless form such associations in order to achieve a more just form of democratic governance. The "Tocquevillean" idea of civil society, then, refers to *politically motivated* associations of citizens who are independent from government and powerful businesses.

One consequence of Tocqueville's framing is that he presents the civic arena as a third sphere of collective life, as if it were *to some degree* separate from "the market" and "the state." The importance of this framing is that the idea of civil society—in contrast to Hegel, Marx, and the early modern philosophers—begins to signify an arena defined both by the struggle for political liberty and by an antagonistic opposition toward oppressive economic and statist interests. Many intellectuals and political philosophers after World War I similarly looked to the "public sphere" to reinvigorate American liberal democracy. Particularly in the work of John Dewey, this discourse adapted the legacy of the civil-society concept in influential ways.[33] Dewey maintains that a "public" or nongovernmental civic arena is the source of both the structure and the problems of American political life. Dewey explains, "American democratic polity was developed out of genuine community life, that is, association in local and small centres" in New England and the frontier wilderness. Dewey explains that the conditions for this associational existence were "mobile and migratory," and thus the demand for democratic governance across such a diverse terrain developed into the Electoral College system.[34]

However, Dewey felt the associational model for democracy was quickly eclipsed by the realities of territorial expansion. In turn, expansionism created a paradox within the political and public lives of modern Americans:

> We have inherited, in short, local town-meeting practices and ideas. But we live and act and have our being in a continental national state. We are held together by non-political bonds, and the political forms are stretched and legal institutions patched in an *ad hoc* and improvised manner to do the work they have to do. Political structures fix the channels in which non-political, industrialized currents flow.[35]

While American democracy is predicated on associational life, the geographical expanse of the US government's territory makes such "public" conditions extremely difficult. According to Dewey, the associational origins and subsequent national expansion of democracy create a paradox at the heart of American "public" or civic life: our political system presupposes shared social experiences, but the social, economic, and physical conditions for that public life often distort collective deliberation rather than being conducive to genuine democratic debate.

Dewey argues that the commercialization of nineteenth-century technologies—including railways, the telegraph, and, later, the telephone—allowed for the manipulation of the public sphere for economic interests. Control over the mechanisms that facilitate public association, Dewey argues, amounts to disproportionate influence over the government: "bosses with their political machines fill the void between government and the public."[36] The technological mechanisms for civic association create an increasing "remoteness" between the public and the state—a gap filled by private economic interests. Nonetheless, Dewey insists that the recuperation of American democratic life depends upon a richer and more expansive civic life, rather than the enlargement of an impersonal "government which is nominally [the public's] organ."[37] Dewey thus sets a precedent among twentieth-century liberals who sound the alarm against the expansion of a bureaucratic state on the grounds that it violates the associational life necessary for democratic freedom.

While the idea of civil society or an associational "public sphere" has a complicated and protean history, the concept's relationship to the political sensibilities underwriting the welfare state is equally complex.[38] Frederick Powell charts the various ways that networks of independent civic association have been integral to the historical rise and decline of the modern welfare state. Beginning in the eighteenth century, Powell argues, European and American political reform movements wrested authority from aristocratic privilege. As these civic movements subverted the entrenched interests of the elite classes, social questions of collective welfare became one of the primary *political* objectives in Western Europe and the United Kingdom, while political representation itself took center stage in the United States. Powell argues that the bureaucratic edifice of the modern nation-state—a form of government united by ethnic or national identity—slowly became reoriented during the nineteenth century toward the greater good of society, thus giving birth to the European *Sozialstaat* (welfare state). Social democracy is thus the distant child of anti-aristocratic civic associations. This transformation in the forms of Western governance amounts to the increasing entanglement of the state and society.[39] In other words, Powell concludes that civil society provides the origins for the modern welfare state.

The paradox of this convergence is that "the more successful civil society proved at socialising the state, the more imperilled its own autonomy became."[40] Not unlike Hayek, Powell argues that the increasing socialization of the state—its organizational imbrication with the welfare of all classes of citizens—contributes to the unintended rise of the twentieth-century totalitarian regimes, for socialization additionally entailed the absorption of civil society within a *nationalized* understanding of the state. The kind of political and social associations that had been independent from government control were either suppressed or voluntarily dissolved within the socialized states of Europe at the beginning of the twentieth century. The roots of Nazism thus spread through this collapse between society and state governance.

In contrast to Hayek's argument against social democracy, however, Powell rejects the "inevitability" of the idea that an activist-managerial state leads to totalitarianism. Instead, he says the national, racial, and class-oriented goals of the regimes in Germany, Italy, and France began to fuse not only state and society but also "people and party, individual and collective, civil and political in a total unity."[41] Totalitarianism, in other words, is not the logical culmination of socialism, although totalitarian regimes were made possible by the "welfare" structures of modern socialized state governance. Having presented a fusion of "people and party," the Third Reich stifled forms of civil society that did not conform to its political vision, and only then could Hitler's populism and nationalism seize control of a socialized state edifice. Given the decline of competing forms of civic life, the Nazi regime was able to define the nation's widespread discontent following the socioeconomic hardship created by the Treaty of Versailles (1919). Therefore, according to Powell, it was the erosion of diversity within civic life, and not merely a socialized state edifice, that was the "structural instrument of Nazification in Germany."[42]

Powell's argument recalls certain aspects of one of the most influential accounts of totalitarianism in postwar America: Hannah Arendt's trenchant criticisms of the *Sozialstaat* as an impoverishment of the public realm. Arendt, a German-born Jew who immigrated to the United States in 1941, became one of the leading political theorists of the postwar decades. Her criticisms of the bureaucratic welfare state derive in part from her sweeping account of the advent of modernity, which included the "invasion of the public realm by society."[43] Whereas premodern public spheres centered on collective action and a sharp division from the "private" arena, Arendt argues that the idea of the "social" arises during the modern era as "public" and "private" life become blurred. The explanation for this blurring is largely an economic phenomenon—that is, the advent of capitalism—but it also results from certain consequences of modern technological innovations. For Arendt, the "social" describes an arena of life concerned with negative freedoms and, more importantly, the accumulation of capital wealth and social prestige. Furthermore, the economization of "social" life during the nineteenth century enabled the twentieth-century development of mass society. The result was that, among its diverse effects, the political consequences of the "social" led to the modern welfare state.

Based on this political and intellectual history, Arendt argues that questions of collective welfare, because they are a product of the advent of the "social," can only have bureaucratic solutions.[44] The "rule of administration," as she calls it in her widely read *The Origins of Totalitarianism*, fosters a modern form of tyranny by virtue of its substitution of political deliberation for "rule by decree."[45] In fact, she defines tyranny as a "government that is not held to give account to itself," and the bureaucracy of the modern welfare state presages such a government by constituting political rule "by Nobody."[46] A managerial welfare state, in other words, signals an especially pernicious form of the impoverishment of the public realm because it subordinates shared action and participation to the efficient and bureaucratically anonymous administration of public welfare.[47]

While Powell has more recently argued that civil society provides the underpinnings for the welfare state, Arendt argued during the postwar decades that the "welfare" configuration of our civic life is itself an impoverishment of the public realm. They disagree, in other words, about whether civil society refers to voluntary nongovernmental movements (Powell) or a larger public realm centering on deliberation about what constitutes the good life (Arendt). More importantly, Powell and Arendt's accounts differ about whether a civic sphere separate from the market and the state would oppose or support an activist-managerial government. Indeed, Powell even says that conceptions of civil society have been deployed within "a neoliberal view of the world that has driven the conservative restoration in the West," particularly by replacing an "overweening state" that "has lost its legitimacy because of its remote bureaucratic structure and domination by professional elites."[48]

The long and protean history of the idea of civil society, Arendt's postwar formulation, and the debates in contemporary political theory suggest the following: first, given its multiple usages and histories, civil society is as much a hazard across the liberal tradition as it is a source of great political opportunity; and second, following the Second World War, many theorists and intellectuals attempted to resolve the perceived tension between the "spontaneity" of a vibrant public life and the "intrusions" of organizational liberalism by reference to the philosophical and political resources of civil society.[49] Rather than being invoked to expand on the reform agenda of the prewar era, postwar configurations of civil society were more often deployed to challenge the legitimacy and authority of an activist-managerial state.

While Arendt lamented the absorption of the "social" within the public sphere and the subsequent economization that allowed for the advent of mass consumer society, Friedrich Hayek also contributed to the mid-century resurgence of the civil-society concept, particularly within debates about economic policy.[50] Hayek, who left the London School of Economics to take a professorship at the University of Chicago in 1950, does not invoke the language of "civil society" in his influential opposition to "collectivism." However, his understanding of the economic arena borrows crucially from this discursive tradition.[51] This intellectual debt surfaces when Hayek outlines the social philosophy that justifies his association between economic control and totalitarianism. Hayek contends that the "ultimate ends of the activities of reasonable beings are never economic," for the idea of an "economic motive" behind social behavior only applies to "the pathological case of the miser." He maintains that social behavior is instead driven by "the desire for general opportunity, the desire for power to achieve unspecified ends."[52] Rather than placing economic self-interest at the heart of his philosophy, Hayek insists there is "no 'economic motive' but only economic factors conditioning our striving for other ends."[53] Hayek thus construes the economic arena as the gateway for individuals to achieve goals established through private judgment. In keeping with the classical liberal tradition, Hayek never identifies the specifics of these "other ends," instead only referring the designation of those ends to individual liberty.

The significance of Hayek's rationale for opposing "collectivism" is that he defines political freedom in terms of the capacity for independent private judgments—a view that has its political corollary in Arendt's ideas about political action and the public arena.[54] The economic arena, Hayek says, is not the logic governing social behavior but rather "one of the greatest instruments of freedom ever invented by man."[55] Hayek thus instrumentalizes the economic arena as a venue for achieving liberty, and he consequently construes the market as the manifestation (or, in social democracies, the suppression) of subjective judgments, values, and pleasures. As Hayek presents it in *The Road to Serfdom*, then, the economic is the superstructure built upon a base of either social control or negative liberties.[56] Indeed, one of the foundations of his objections to centralized planning and the socialist use of the state is that these forms of political economy purport to intervene into the "merely economic." Perhaps socialism would not lead to totalitarianism, Hayek argues, if the economic could be cordoned off from the more "fundamental" arenas of life. However, Hayek contends, "Economic values are less important to us than many things precisely because in economic matters we are free to decide what to us is more, and what less, important."[57]

This matters a great deal for how Hayek's brand of liberalism construes state institutions. Economic planning tries to order human existence through principles of rationality and equality, yet Hayek maintains that independence in economic behavior is the principle signifier of the individual's freedom to determine the value not just of objects (e.g., the economic worth of certain goods) but also of existence itself. At the root of Hayek's repudiation of "collectivism" is the idea that it denies and distorts individual value judgments. As he explains:

> The question raised by economic planning is, therefore, not merely whether we shall be able to satisfy what we regard as our more or less

important needs in the way we prefer. It is whether it shall be we who decide what is more, and what is less, important for us, or whether this is to be decided by the planner. Economic planning would not affect merely those of our marginal needs that we have in mind when we speak contemptuously about the merely economic. It would, in effect, mean that we as individuals should no longer be allowed to decide what we regard as marginal.[58]

Hayek therefore justifies his opposition toward state intervention into the economic arena on the grounds that centralized management intrudes upon the *aesthetic* conditions of human life. (He never grapples with analogous threats from the economic planning of large corporations.) Statist economic planning violates the subjective judgments and pleasures comprising constituent elements of "human" and "free" existence. Collectivism, according to Hayek, erodes the subjective grounds for self-possession.[59]

Despite their many points of disagreement, then, Arendt and Hayek both look to the values of spontaneity and self-determined possibility in their critiques of bureaucratic statist management. In other words, Arendt and Hayek justify their political philosophies through related forms of aestheticism, which in turn would prove immensely influential on the varieties of postwar liberal thought.[60] What's more, this tide of anti-managerial political theory—often itself a product of the intellectual exchange between war-haunted Europe and the United States—resonates with the resurgence of forms of aestheticism in postwar literary arena, particularly among writers like Nabokov and Trilling, who insist that individual consciousness loses its immanent value in organizational politics.

The Artist's Studio: Fiction, Reality, and Civil Society

Hayek's, Arendt's, and Nabokov's concerns about the connections between social-democratic institutions and the origins of totalitarianism take their conceptual shape from underlying aesthetic assumptions. The aestheticism underwriting Hayek's economic theory presents the market as a handle for distorting subjective judgments of value. Nabokov, in contrast, presents fiction as an occasion of interiority and pleasure. Despite differences in the *arena* of aestheticism, I've argued that both thinkers valorize subjective judgments as a strategy for challenging the intellectual basis of the US welfare state. Hayek's economic project, as Adam B. Seligman explains, presents civil society as a missing link, lost in the nineteenth century and obscured by current political arrangements. Amid the domination of the *Sozialstaat* in Europe and the "experimentation" of the New Deal in America, Hayek poses independent associational life as a "quest," an ideal that "deconstruct[s] many of the powers of the State and replace[s] them with intermediary institutions based on social voluntarism."[61] Nabokov's aestheticism, on the other hand, presents the cultural arena as an embattled but nonetheless self-referential domain for mid-century writers and readers to find the pleasures of private judgment in the midst of an overly politicized world.[62]

In this section, I develop these connections by showing that Nabokov's staging of the world of fiction calls attention to the self-enclosed nature of the narrative world. Nabokov's view of fiction attempts to circumvent or counteract the politicized use of literature. For Nabokov, fiction functions as a sphere for subjective judgments until writers and readers allow it to devolve into a lower political order.

This depiction of fiction as an arena of separate, apolitical judgments of value first appears in Krug's shift away from philosophical materialism—studying a material world measurable by "integers" and properties, "ruler and scales"—toward an interest in the "finite mind" (*Bend Sinister,* 171). This shift occurs while Krug is putting his son, David, to bed one night. While reflecting on his love for David, Krug becomes convinced of the foundational place of consciousness. He tries to account for the "agony" of loving "so madly a little creature, formed in some mysterious fashion . . . by the fusion of two mysteries, or rather two sets of a trillion of mysteries each" (188). The narrator's description of "two mysteries" refers to Krug and Olga, his late wife, whose "fusion"—their offspring, David—is yet another "trillions of its own mysteries." What makes this "little creature" so meaningful is the value attributed to the boy within the conscious life that Krug's academic labor has thus far left unexamined. Krug's agonizing love for his son calls into question what the narrator earlier describes as a yawning oversight in the philosopher's work: "He had never indulged in the search for the True Substance, the One, the Absolute, the Diamond suspended from the Christmas Tree of the Cosmos" (171).

Krug's dawning revelation about the value of consciousness is later interrupted by Paduk's political agents. Krug responds to their intrusion upon his consciousness with growing indifference, at least until it becomes clear that Paduk's cronies threaten to harm his son David. The agents subdue Krug and, through a bungling bureaucratic edifice, other henchmen accidentally mistake David for an orphan. They send Krug's son to the state's Institute for Abnormal Children, where he is used as a "release-instrument" for inmates in an unworldly and violent experiment (218). Once the regime discovers the error, Krug is taken to the Institute to collect his son. But after Krug arrives, the Institute's Dr. Hammecke absurdly delays delivering the news of David's mutilation by showing the philosopher a film putatively proving that his son has not been harmed. The film shows David tentatively descending stairs to meet a group of "patients," yet the images are hardly consoling: "The whole thing lasted a moment," the narrator recounts, "[David] turned his face up to the nurse, his eyelashes beat, his hair caught a gleam of lambent light; then he looked around, met Krug's eyes, showed no sign of recognition and uncertainly went down the few steps that remained." As the nightmare that his son is about to experience becomes apparent, the prose slips into free indirect discourse: "[David's] face became larger, dimmer, and vanished as it met mine" (223). Dr. Hammecke interrupts the film before the images of David's brutal murder flash across the screen, and Krug's sense of reality is likewise obstructed: "I want to wake up. Where is he? I shall die if I do not wake up" (224).

Krug is finally shown the mutilated body of his son after a series of bureaucratic and pseudo-ceremonial delays. He finds that morticians have tried to reconstruct the corpse of his son: "The murdered child had a crimson and gold turban around its head; its face was skilfully painted and powdered: a mauve blanket, exquisitely smooth, came up to its chin" (224). That the narrator refers to David with the third person pronoun "it" signals the extent to which the brutal "experiment" of the bureaucratic state institution has dehumanized the child. David has become the "painted and powdered" remainder of political life, the individual who is the "accident" or subsidiary of state management. Krug hardly understands the condolences of a "friendly soldier" after viewing his son's corpse—"The sense [of his words] is not at all clear"—and he never regains his connection with narrative reality. His fracturing consciousness perceives that the state has maimed and disfigured not only his son (as if that were not already too much) but also the world of language and subjective experience that he has so recently discovered in his philosophical awakening (225). As a result, the state's interventions into private consciousness become more than intrusions: they incite a form of aphasia.

Bend Sinister answers this bureaucratic tyranny not through opposition but ridicule and negation. After publicly rejecting the state in response to the murder of his son, Krug is predictably imprisoned. He loses consciousness out of exhaustion and is later awoken from a dream by a light that "was somehow the result of a kind of stealthy, abstractly vindictive, groping, tampering movement" (233). This half-dream is as much disorienting for the reader as it is for Krug, for it becomes evident that the narrator himself is responsible for this "tampering." The light that interrupts Krug's sleep becomes the harbinger of a fictive epiphany: "It was at that moment," the narrator says, "just before his reality, his remembered hideous misfortune could pounce upon him—it was then that I felt a pang of pity for Adam and slid towards him along an inclined beam of pale light—causing instantaneous madness, but at least saving him from the senseless agony of his logical fate" (233). Krug's "madness" is the realization that "his reality" is, in fact, a fiction. His world begins to dissolve, and *his author's reality* infringes upon his narrative existence. One immediate result is that when Krug listens to "the usual nocturnal sounds peculiar to great prisons," these are bracketed by "the cautious crackling of a page which had been viciously crumpled and thrown into the wastebasket and was making a pitiful effort to uncrumple itself and live just a little longer" (233–4). The author's rejection of drafts of Krug's world echoes in the insane philosopher's mind.

After his night in prison, Krug the "madman" is presented before Paduk to swear an oath of loyalty to the state (237). Having lost his sanity, the philosopher is as uncooperative as he is insensible. Indeed, in a fugue state, Krug returns to his childhood when he used to tackle and sit on the head of Paduk, whom he called "the Toad." Krug rushes after Paduk, but the narrator brings an end Krug's world during this "mad" attempt on the life of the dictator:

> just a fraction of an instant before another and better bullet hit him, [Krug] shouted again: You, you—and the wall vanished, like a rapidly withdrawn slide, and I stretched myself and got up from among the chaos of written and rewritten pages, to investigate the sudden twang that something had made in striking the wire netting of my window. (240)

In this moment of metafiction, rather than the authorial "I" entering the narrative, *Bend Sinister* itself seems to fade away while the narrator, who describes himself as an "anthropomorphic deity," remains above the artifice (147). The implication is that the literary artist, not Paduk, is the tyrant reigning over the narrative world.

Nabokov's device of dismissing the cast of his fiction is another form of the aestheticism underwriting this period of his career. Nabokov inventively signals as much during an interview with a former student, Alfred Appel. The interviewer asks Nabokov about the device that ends many of his novels, in which "the vectors are removed and the fact of the fiction is underscored." Seemingly evading an answer, Nabokov says, "I think that what I would welcome at the close of a book of mine is a sensation of its world receding in the distance and stopping somewhere there suspended afar like a picture in a picture: *The Artist's Studio* by Van Bock."[63] The significance of Nabokov's response, which Appel has earlier explained are either written or dictated to the interviewer from a prewritten script, is that its evasions constitute an answer.[64] The metafictive break at the end of Nabokov's fiction brings into focus a "picture in a picture," which is an obscure way of saying that the narrative is part of a larger artistic pattern. But which pattern? Nabokov's obscure example—"*The Artist's Studio* by Van Bock"—provides an explanation, for both the artist and artwork are themselves fictions: they are linguistic games referring back to Nabokov himself.[65] "Van Bock" is nearly an anagram (one of the author's favorite language games) for "Nabokov" if only the *c* were enclosed to form another *o*. Nabokov's crafted response to Appel elaborately suggests that the author views his novels as studios of his own consciousness, artistic productions that exhibit his self-gratifying judgments of value. Nabokov explains why "the fact of the fiction is underscored" through an elliptical game that refers to private creative pleasure.

Reading *Bend Sinister* in *Lolita*

Much like *Bend Sinister*'s characters who are reshuffled versions of one another, appearing later wearing different clothes but bearing a marked resemblance to their former incarnations, the aesthetic sensibilities underlying Nabokov's early American period appears in different garb throughout each of his novels. In *Lolita* and *Pale Fire*, Nabokov teases out the hazards of these sensibilities in ways that proved widely influential—sparking debates not only in *The Nation*, *The New Republic*, and *Partisan Review* but also in mass-market magazines.[66] Perhaps most notably, the aestheticism that provides a prophylactic to tyranny and politicized existence in *Bend Sinister* is again affirmed, albeit with important qualifications, in Humbert Humbert, the narrator and nymphet-lover of *Lolita*.

As Humbert himself puts it, *Lolita*'s plot involves "a North American girl-child named Dolores Haze [who] had been deprived of her childhood by a maniac."[67] Yet the cursory reader who sums up Humbert's confession as perverse pedophilia has missed the point, for not unlike Trilling's summons that critics resuscitate liberalism's "first essential imagination," *Lolita* in many ways recalls the possibilities of literary fiction.[68] Humbert is a figure for this recuperative literary project, particularly as his voracious reading tends to transform into acts of writing and creative pleasure. For example, Humbert recounts his "ridiculous failure" to "read and reread a book with the unintentionally biblical title *Know Your Own Daughter*" (174). Through agile and self-referential close readings, he transforms the parental adages of this book into a reservoir of puns and sexual exhortations, repurposing this reading to extort additional pleasure from his relationship to his adopted daughter. Similarly, Humbert reads Charlotte Haze's maudlin confession letter but tries to ameliorate its poor literary quality and "awful French" through his own "matter-of-fact contribution" (68, 69). Humbert, in these cases, subordinates literalism and realism to his creative augmentations, which is less an issue of distorting texts than redeploying the words and images of others to write something that Humbert himself would find pleasure in reading.

Then again, one may be tempted to claim that Humbert recognizes, however dimly, the violence of this self-referential aestheticism. According to this view, the collapse of literary production and readerly consumption would be analogous to his rape of Lolita. After all, while overlooking a group of children playing and noticing Lolita's voice absent from their laughter, Humbert interprets his crimes in terms of having subtracted a measure of innocent beauty from the world. Feeling the weight of this recognition, he exclaims, "I see nothing for the treatment of my misery but the melancholy and very local palliative of articulate art." Humbert finds that his "spiritual solace" cannot redeem the "simple human fact" of the horrors he has inflicted upon Lolita

(283). One way of reading this moment of recognition would be to connect Humbert's scenes of reading with the "melancholy" art of his own articulate narrative. Rather than trying to stimulate belated pleasure from his illicit tryst, the telling that becomes *Lolita* may be a "very local palliative" that reintroduces a measure of the beauty that Humbert himself has divested from the world. In this reading, the contingency ("very local") and impermanence ("palliative") of Humbert's solution suggest he's also aware of the inadequacy of his aesthetic way of life.

Other deficiencies of Humbert's "articulate art" may also seem to signal a fundamental criticism of the tradition of aesthetics. For instance, as Humbert says earlier in the novel, he sees Lolita not as Dolores Haze but as an imaginatively resuscitated figure of his deceased adolescent lover named Annabel Leigh: "It was the same child—the same frail, honey-hued shoulders, the same silky supple bare back, the same chestnut head of hair. A polka-dotted black kerchief tied around her chest hid from my aging ape eyes, but not from the gaze of young memory, the juvenile breasts I had fondled one immortal day" (39). Dolores Haze becomes "Lolita," Humbert's representation, an erotic image resurrected from his adolescence and recreated for his own pleasure. When Humbert looks at his nymphet—which is to say, when he reads her—he does not see the young Haze for who she is but as a phantom-object.

Is it the case, then, that Humbert's aestheticism not only fails to grasp the world but also produces illusory and dehumanizing judgments of value? Even as Humbert seems to take hold only of an enfeebled aesthetic reproduction that he names "Lolita," does he not elide his nymphet's individuality for the sake of literary pleasure? Or, more to the point, isn't Humbert the mirror image of the totalitarianism that Nabokov answers through an aesthetic critique in *Bend Sinister*? Rather than continuing in the same vein as *Bend Sinister*, is not *Lolita* a book about the hazards of Nabokov's earlier remedy to politicized existence?

The trouble with this line of thought is that it reverts to an implicitly moralistic reading, where the stakes of the novel are laid out according to one or another of the modes of violence committed against Lolita. And if Nabokov's novel teases out a fundamental critique of aestheticism even in the terms of symbolic violence, then such a view leaves its advocates within a disturbing cul-de-sac of interpretive positions. For instance, by identifying Nabokov's "critique of Humbert" in terms of the protagonist's "overstepping of the bounds of art in his appropriation of Lolita," Dana Brand argues that a "morally didactic" vision underwrites *Lolita*.[69] Humbert's "nympholeptic images," according to Brand, "degenerate from art into advertising as Humbert comes to believe that he can actually *have* Lolita in the physical world, not merely in his imagination."[70] The *limits* of aestheticism become the novel's moral center,

Brand argues, damning Humbert less for transgressing laws and taboos than for his attempts to find "aesthetic bliss" outside his own consciousness. But the identification of such a "critique" of aestheticism leaves this school of interpretive thought in the disturbing and compromising position of condoning a look-but-don't-touch pedophilia, a morality in which it is somehow not only moral but also laudable to construct an erotic aesthetic image of a child, as long as that aestheticism never crosses the distinction from one's mind to action, from art to the world. The *art* of pedophilia, in this reading, is an expression of the legitimate appreciation of beauty, while the *act* of pedophilia oversteps the bounds of art. Those who gloss *Lolita* in the terms of a "critique" of aestheticism by its proximity to tyranny inevitably rely on the invocation of dubious moral terrain.

In contrast to this aestheticized moralism, Eric Naiman argues that Nabokov places readers in uncertain and anxiety-producing situations in order to train them to read fiction not for its moral usefulness but simply for the puzzle of close reading itself.[71] Naiman's understanding of the compromising or "perverse" positions that result from Nabokov's puzzles recalls the novelist's various descriptions of the "good" reader. In a popular course on European literature that Nabokov taught at Cornell University, the novelist says that "the good reader" uses the "authentic instruments" of "impersonal imagination and artistic delight."[72] As the reader imagines the world of the novel, her work-as-reader becomes its own form of pleasure simply by reconstructing the author's artifice. The "good" or discerning reader, in other words, shares in the author's pleasure by playing the same game, getting lost in the fictional labyrinth. Neglecting the fact that "literature is invention" amounts to an "insult," a denigration of the work of the "magician" whose tricks are meant to please us (5). Thus, if Humbert sometimes fails to check his morality at the door of his writing and reading, it's a lapse that the novel shows readers how to avoid precisely by forcing them to suspend their moral claims. *Lolita*, in other words, imagines a labyrinth in which the perils of Humbert's aestheticism become signposts for the pleasure of reading.

While undoubtedly marking a moment of introspection when compared with the seemingly unqualified aestheticism of *Bend Sinister, Lolita* nonetheless contributes to the postwar resurgence of interest in both philosophical aestheticism and arenas of public life autonomous from moral or organizational imperatives. Nabokov's *Lolita* not only requires readers to suspend social and moral evaluation to avoid sanctioning imaginative pedophilia, but the novel also represents a further entrenchment of the author's earlier aestheticism by insisting on a radical distinction between aesthetic experience and the moral, political, and social demands of the world. Indeed, its seemingly interminable linguistic games and compromising interpretive positions make *Lolita* a book about how to read books: while nodding to the hazards of such a position, the fiction entices its reader into an arena of ecstasy independent from nonartistic demands.

Aestheticism and Life-Affirmation

Nabokov's view of fiction resonates with another permutation of the resurgence of aestheticism in the postwar era—the revival of interest among American intellectuals in Friedrich Nietzsche's philosophy. This revival of interest, in part, gathered around what Nietzsche in *The Gay Science* calls "gaiety," or life-affirmation.[73] Nietzsche argues that the consequence of the "death of God" is that the value of our world resides in the here and now, in the lives we live independently of those forces (God, popular morality, nationalism) that would determine the shape and meaning of life on our behalf (109). Affirming life, for Nietzsche, requires one to repudiate illusions at all costs and instead "love freedom as the freedom of great souls" (94). Nietzsche insists that the only way to take life seriously is through "gaiety," the pleasure we find in existence itself. "A thinker needs no applause and clapping of hands provided he is sure of his own clapping of hands," Nietzsche surmises, for "he cannot do without that" (184).

Among the many curiosities of American intellectual life during the 1950s is the fervent revival of Nietzsche's "gaiety" alongside a radical critique of morality—a critique particularly noteworthy because Italian fascists and German National Socialists had often cited it as a foundation for their political philosophies. As Jennifer Ratner-Rosenhagen explains, Nietzsche's already inconstant standing had declined among American readers during the 1930s: "Given the popular press's image of *Zarathustra* as the Ur-text of European totalitarianism, and the academy's general disregard for him, it was hard to imagine that Nietzsche's philosophy had much of a future in American intellectual life."[74] However, as Ratner-Rosenhagen shows, the "relatively obscure" Princeton University philosopher Walter Kaufmann created an "English-language Nietzsche industry" that ushered "in a momentous shift in intellectual styles and concerns" in postwar America.[75] One year prior to the publication of *Lolita*, Kaufmann published *The Portable Nietzsche* (1954), stylizing the German as "a towering thinker uniquely poised to address many of the pressing intellectual concerns of the cold war era: anxieties about the psychic costs and social dangers of mass society, hostility to collectivist ideologies, and longing for new sources of redemption after the horrors of the recent past."[76] Formerly categorized as symptomatic thinking of political tyranny, the postwar reception of Nietzsche rebranded his work as a critical ally within the literature opposed to totalitarianism.

Kaufmann's *The Portable Nietzsche* had significant trade success and at once situated Nietzsche's writing in relation to the likes of Kant and Freud—an intellectual terrain that Kaufmann had earlier mapped for scholars in a successful academic book *Nietzsche: Philosopher, Psychologist, Antichrist* (1950). But Kaufmann's *The Portable Nietzsche* also portrayed "a fully reasonable and harmonious Nietzsche accessible to the enlightened everyman."[77] In a compilation that would be published in four editions and establish the principal school of thought on Nietzsche's writing during the postwar decades, Ratner-Rosenhagen notes that Kaufmann "used Nietzsche's philosophy to awaken American readers to European existentialism."[78] Indeed, as Tracy Strong puts it, "Kaufmann's Nietzsche was *the* Nietzsche for American and British studies."[79]

Kaufmann's role in reviving interest in Nietzsche's philosophy among a skeptical reading public is noteworthy not only as a feature of the postwar interest in European existentialism—an intellectual history I chart in subsequent chapters—but also because Kaufmann was, as Ratner-Rosenhagen explains, "part of the mass exodus of German-speaking intellectuals, scientists, and artists who fled Nazism from 1933 through the early 1940s."[80] Not unlike Arendt's theory of action, the postwar American interpretation of Nietzsche found an alternative to political tyranny by extoling the virtues of being an independent soul. Nietzsche's rising stock among American readers, the émigré Kaufmann's intellectual work, Arendt's and Trilling's opposition to bureaucratic liberalism, and the aestheticisms formulated by Nabokov and Hayek thus constitute interrelated parts of the cultural and intellectual milieu that turned in concert against organizational and institutional politics. These various strands indicate how the warp and weft of American liberalism was being rewoven with aestheticized thread.

The affinities between these literary and philosophical phenomena had definite political ends, for they imagined carving out space for the self in a world anxious about the advent of centralized managerial authority and the mechanisms of expanding federal bureaucracy.[81] While vivifying the hazards of self-enclosed aestheticism, the Nabokovian figures of Humbert Humbert and Charles Kinbote in *Pale Fire* are, like Nietzsche's "thinker," the producers and consumers of their own "applause." Indeed, as Kinbote's commentary on Shade's poem slips into madness, the inescapability of such a narrative world becomes at once the source of pleasure and an insoluble interpretive problem. The political upshot is that, in *Lolita* and *Pale Fire*, there's a more thorough-going affirmation of the distinction between aesthetic pleasure and social utility. Such an affirmation becomes a first-order remedy for the many dangers of tyranny. Nabokov's fiction, much like Hayek's aesthetic political philosophy and the postwar American Nietzsche, presents anything less than an aesthetic view of existence as violent and even nihilistic—that is, as a denial of individual judgments of value. As features of American intellectual history, these varieties of liberal thought thus reimagined arenas of public life in aestheticized terms, in contrast to earlier associational accounts of civil society.

Nabokov, the New Critics, and the Anxiety of Influence

The New Criticism, founded principally by Allen Tate, Robert Penn Warren, John Crowe Ransom, and Cleanth Brooks, was yet another aspect of the shifting sensibilities in American intellectual life. The New Critics came to occupy some of the most prominent academic positions in the United States and exerted significant influence upon the practice of literary studies during the postwar decades. They contributed to an increasingly apolitical and aestheticized account of the discipline by rejecting the moralism and impressionistic contextual criticism of an earlier era. However, they articulated this disavowal of certain dimensions of social commentary on very different grounds than Nabokov in *Bend Sinister* and *Lolita*.

In his influential book *The New Criticism* (1941), John Crowe Ransom repudiated the idea that literary analysis ought to be beholden to uncovering the moral force of literature, imagining instead the "criticism of the structural properties of poetry."[82] The linchpin of this new mode of literary criticism is the strategy of close reading. Yet, in his disciplinary history of literary studies, Gerald Graff explains that close reading offers more than an emphasis on structural concerns to combat a tritely moralistic view of literature; rather, by emphasizing the difficulty of poetry, the types of literary ambiguity, and the relationship between form and meaning, New Critics believed that close reading was "ideally suited to a new, mass student body that could not be depended on to bring to the university any common cultural background."[83] According to Graff, after the Second World War, New Criticism positioned itself to fill a gap created by the boom of American higher education, for it privileged a direct confrontation between student and text on the grounds of close reading. By disregarding an author's biography or a text's historical political conditions, a reader need focus only on the analysis of the poetic object and thus does not— at least at first—require an extensive reserve of erudition or cultural capital. On one level, then, the New Critics clothed their insistence that close reading affirmed the immanent value of a literary text in the garb of populist democracy: even a blue-collar student attending college on the GI Bill could pay close attention to Wordsworth's or Keats's peculiar choices of imagery.

Yet if the New Critics of the postwar era claimed to affirm the self-enclosed work of art for the sake of democratizing literary criticism, such a configuration of the interpretive task arose in large part from a conflicted political impulse. In his account of the advent of New Criticism, Schryer explains:

> For the first generation of U.S. New Critics, who began their careers as Agrarian ideologues opposed to the industrialization of the South, literature was the only remaining counterweight to the triumph of technical rationality within the welfare state. Their cultivation of close reading was in part an effort to isolate this anti-instrumental dimension of literature, to shelter it from the technocratic pretensions of the new class.[84]

During the 1930s, the New Critics' valorization of close reading affirmed the noninstrumental value of poetic structure not only in opposition to what they perceived as Victorian moralism but also in contrast to the idea of politically useful criticism and the technocratic impulses of the postwar academy. Close reading was of course a *techne*, too, but one that preempted the ideological demands and utilitarianism of an overweening state. The activist-managerial politics of the New Deal had tried to solve the employment problems in the American South through public works programs and by collaborating with unions to industrialize the Southern economy—activities that Ransom and his fellow Southern Agrarians interpreted as forcing the region to adopt an instrumental configuration of the social and cultural arenas for the sake of collective welfare.

Even before Roosevelt's election and implementation of the New Deal, Ransom worried that the "concept of Progress . . . enhances too readily our conceit, and brutalizes our life."[85] This sentiment carried into the postwar era, albeit after undergoing a kind of mutation: that is, the methods of the postwar New Critics looked to prevent technocratic vulgarization through literary attention to difficulty. Thus, while one aspect of the New Criticism seemingly democratized literary studies through close reading, another of its main sensibilities simultaneously construed the interpretive task as a decisively *difficult* one. Cleanth Brooks in his influential *The Well Wrought Urn* (1947) puts this paradox in the terms of a reader's responsibility: "The reader says to the poet: Here I am; it's your job to 'get it across' to me—when he ought to be assuming the burden of proof himself."[86] The close reading of poetry became the self's intellectual labor, a means for affirming an arena of life governed neither by what Ransom terms "moralism" nor "emotionalism."[87] Politics, of course, was an especially pernicious form of both.

Brooks and Ransom enlisted like-minded critics outside the South as honorary representatives of their prescriptions for criticism. In particular, Ransom catalogues the successes and deficits of the English critic I. A. Richards, the ex-patriot modernist T. S. Eliot, and American poet-critics R. P. Blackmur and Yvor Winters. The English literary critic and poet William Empson also enjoyed the New Critics' praise with the revised edition of his study *Seven Types of Ambiguity* ([1930] 1947). As the Southern Agrarians broke and converged with other streams of literary-critical thought, postwar New Criticism not only came to be one of the preeminent forces in the American academy but also underwent transformation. As Schryer explains, a quasi-political opposition to the encroachments of the American welfare state during the 1930s morphed after the war into the institutional image of critics as "formalist aesthetes interested in disseminating the apolitical practice of close reading throughout the academy."[88] Notably, even as New Criticism developed in opposition to a perceived Victorian moralism in literary studies, the close reading of poetic structure also purported to provide a moral service to a wider public. The strategy allowed New Critics to become what Schryer describes as "social trustees," intellectual legislators in the business of cultural education.[89]

Nabokov was no New Critic, but he benefited from their influence on postwar American intellectual culture. As Amy Reading explains regarding Nabokov's tenure teaching at Cornell University, the novelist "cavalierly brushed aside 'modish' literary theory like that practiced down the hall by [M. H.] Abrams, a student of I. A. Richards and a mentor of Harold Bloom."[90] Unlike the New Critics, Nabokov's more radical aestheticism disavowed any interest in the education of GIs. He was insistently an anti-public intellectual. For Nabokov, there are private judgments of the self and a vulgar political world, and never the twain should meet.

However, Nabokov's framing of this anti-public posture suggests common ground he shares with the New Criticism. In the preface to *Bend Sinister*, Nabokov claims the "influence of my epoch on my present book is as negligible as the influence of my books, or at least of this book, on my epoch" (xii–xiii). While Nabokov preserves some possibility that, say, *Lolita* might have influenced his "epoch," the novelist's underlying anxiety about "influence" is also symptomatic: rather than offering sociopolitical commentary, and thus encouraging art to inform the contours of his contemporary moment, Nabokov insists that his work explores only "the beating of Krug's loving heart" (xiv). This view insists on the "negligible" influence of fiction on an epoch of vulgar realities, and vice versa, because any other configuration would force literary and intellectual pleasure to conform to boorish social utility. The greater the "influence," at least in social or institutional terms, measures the distance of a work of art from private judgments of value. The pleasures of reading thus depend upon containment—that is, the separation of literary and institutional forms.

The sensibilities of Nabokov and the New Critics were of a piece with the anxieties of the postwar moment. The national affirmation of New Deal politics during the 1936 general election was, as Brinkley says, representative of decisive support for "a strong and active federal government."[91] While this support was widespread in 1936, not only theorists like Hayek but also the public base of support among American liberals became increasingly reticent about a managerial or welfare state after the war. Given the failed central planning that gave inroads to Mussolini and Hitler, New Deal liberals began "to reconsider their own commitment to an activist managerial state," while congressional conservatives began to challenge and roll back key New Deal programs.[92] In short, postwar liberals increasingly bought the line of argumentation that centralized, managerial politics was associated not with securing economic equality but with the possibility of tyranny. "However serious the structural problems of the capitalist economy," Brinkley concludes, many liberals and intellectuals had begun to believe that "a statist cure might be worse than the disease."[93]

While the New Dealers held sway in the 1930s and, in qualified form, through the planned economy during the Second World War, the strands of American cultural and political history traced in this chapter demonstrate that the crisis of organizational liberalism began prior to the era of Cold War geopolitics. As the transformation of the civil-society concept suggests, and the work of

Nabokov, Arendt, Trilling, Hayek, and the New Critics variously exemplify, postwar liberal sentiment was rife with criticisms of the managerial welfare state. These aesthetic sensibilities developed in often-explicit opposition to bureaucratic solutions. According to this spectrum of liberal thought, those who would impose an organizational pattern on society distort the conditions for human flourishing. As an absurd speech foisted upon Krug says, "the State has created central organs for providing the country with all the most important products which are to be distributed at fixed prices in a playful manner. Sorry—*planful* manner" (149). This parody presents the management of the economic life and social welfare of the nation as yet another absurd misuse of language—a fundamental malapropism in the public's vocabulary regarding judgments of value.

2 }

Existentialism in America

INEQUALITY, POLITICAL ACTION,
AND THE TWILIGHT OF NEW DEAL REFORM

The bookends of Ralph Ellison's *Invisible Man* (1952) depict the nameless narrator at a moment when he has "take[n] up residence underground" (571). As the narrator flees two policemen, who suspect his involvement in a race riot, he accidentally falls into a manhole. In a figurative attempt to seal his fate, the policemen enclose the narrator in the dark underground space by drawing the sewer's metal cover. Being thus segregated from society, the narrator draws larger conclusions about his social and political status: "This is the way it's always been," he explains, "only now I know it" (566). The narrator recognizes himself as an invisible man, set apart from and thus not seen by American society. This forced retreat underground functions as a metaphor for the legal segregation of black Americans in the postwar era, but the narrator also situates his position underground as a metaphorical threshold between alienation and action: "The hibernation is over," he concludes. "I must shake off the old skin and come up for breath. There's a stench in the air, which, from this distance underground, might be the smell either of death or of spring—I hope of spring" (580).

The "stench" that concerns Ellison's invisible man recalls the "bad air" that vexes Nietzsche in *On the Genealogy of Morals* (1887), where the philosopher asks, "What, of all things, am I unable to tolerate? The only thing which I find it impossible to deal with, which makes me choke and languish? Bad air! Bad air!"[1] Nietzsche later explains that this bad air circulates in a "workshop where ideals are fabricated—it seems to me to stink of nothing but lies."[2] For Nietzsche, illusions about moral norms and transcendent values lead to a self-deluded society. In response to the manufactured color line that belts American society, Ellison's invisible man has similarly come to "better understand my relation to [the world] and it to me." Much like Nietzsche's disgust with conventional morality, the invisible man arraigns the unrealized American ideals

49

of equality and freedom—what he terms "The Great Constitutional Dream Book" (280). He has "come a long way from those days when, full of illusion, I lived a public life and attempted to function under the assumption that the world was solid and all the relationships therein" (576). Ellison's narrator discovers that his segregated society, rather than being fixed and coherent, is built upon a mound of illusions.[3]

The invisible man's sharp note of disillusionment marks an important shift in the framing of inequality in the United States. In particular, this chapter looks to Ellison's novel as an especially potent variation on the influence of European existentialism within the American public sphere. The novel clarified public concerns about the hazards of collective and institutional politics, and it modulated those sentiments through existentialist tones. When *Invisible Man* won the National Book Award for fiction in 1953, the public mechanisms of prestige affirmed the novel's existentialist view of "alienation" and its construal of political action in terms of individual authenticity. In part, Ellison arrived at these commitments by reading Jean-Paul Sartre, Albert Camus, Simone de Beauvoir, Søren Kierkegaard, Dostoevsky, and Nietzsche.[4] However, Ellison was not alone in reformulating the problems of the 1950s by drawing on the resources of existential thinkers. Instead, he contributed to a wider intellectual movement that included Richard Wright and Saul Bellow, philosophers such as William Barrett, and painters like Willem de Kooning, Jackson Pollock, and Jasper Johns, to name only a few.[5]

The American adaptation of existential ideas was an active feature of the substantive reorganization of liberal intellectual culture during the late 1940s and 1950s. This rearticulation of liberal ideas through an existential idiom had multiple registers. As Andrew Hoberek argues, the universalizing affinities of Ellison's novel were representative of the "middle-class tendency to project onto all organizations the deindividualizing white-collar workplace."[6] This chapter shows how American existentialism provided an intellectual resource for this tendency to eschew bureaucratically managed structures. Very broad conceptual terrain during the postwar decades—including ideas about authenticity, alienation, and the legitimate forms of political action—were shaped by the rise and mutation of American existentialist sensibilities. American variations on existentialist themes influenced popular Hollywood films and played an important part in the prestige bestowed on many works of literary fiction. Ellison and Bellow, at once beneficiaries and agents of these wider changes, parsed the social and political declensions of existential thought. They reimagined the very idea of America through the lexicon of existential possibility.

The body of cultural and philosophical work analyzed in this chapter provided an imprimatur to growing uncertainty about organizational liberalism after the Second World War. Even as American existentialism became part of the economy of prestige during the 1950s, this movement authorized new forms of liberal thought and feeling. Increasingly, the terms of intellectual legitimacy were written with existential figures. As the formulation of an American existential idiom revised liberal sentiment and inflected the concepts of authenticity, alienation, and angst, this political vocabulary joined Cold War era pressures on progressive politics. These imbricated developments contracted the spectrum of legitimacy within liberal politics. As writers and intellectuals tapped into and developed the vein of existential thought, they characterized organizational authorities and collective political action as sources of alienation and, in turn, they offered existentialist possibilities to match the terms of their assessment.

Ralph Ellison on the Left

Ellison was completing *Invisible Man* as Senator Joseph McCarthy began a witch-hunt for communists. Ellison's unfavorable representation of the communistic organization called the Brotherhood in the novel, while not kowtowing to the politics of the Second Red Scare (1950–1956), still riffs off cultural angst regarding the legitimacy of social-democratic politics among postwar liberals. Ellison's protagonist first encounters a version of progressive organizational politics when he meets a member of the Brotherhood. This organization approaches the narrator after he delivers an impassioned speech against the eviction of an elderly couple in Harlem. "Sister" Provo and her eighty-seven-year-old husband had lived in the apartment for over twenty years. However, having failed to pay rent one month, a leasing agent evicts the couple, which incites a group of Harlem residents to disgust and anger. Before the group turns on the white "paddies" enforcing the eviction, the invisible man intervenes and delivers his second public speech of the novel. He insists that, rather than turning to violence, the group ought to be "law-abiding" and "*Organize*" (276). After learning that the elderly man is a "day laborer," the invisible man asks, "Where has all his labor gone?" (279). The invisible man answers this question with action, leading the group to force their way back into the apartment and return the elderly couple's evicted possessions.

The invisible man's speech invokes categories that resonate with the concerns of the working class, and he even organizes an intervention against socioeconomic injustice. Brother Jack, a member in the leadership of the leftist organization, observes the invisible man's intervention, and he offers him a position in the Brotherhood as its representative in Harlem. At first, the invisible man is hesitant because he is suspicious of how Brother Jack dismisses the importance of the elderly couple's plight on an individual level. Yet, after returning to his dilapidated apartment in Harlem and facing the fact that his rent is soon due, the invisible man accepts Brother Jack's offer. The narrator quickly becomes prominent in the Harlem branch of the Brotherhood, even as he earns an income that far exceeds his earlier economic situation.

   Yet the narrator discovers the racial fissures in this edifice of leftist equality
when he reaches the ceiling for leadership set for the organization's black
members. Brother Wrestrum, a jealous gadfly in the Harlem offices, accuses
the narrator of being a "petty individualist" (401), and the allegation of self-
aggrandizement prompts an internal review requiring the narrator to "slow
down." The racial undertones of the Brotherhood's decision dawns on the narrator after he is reinstated and returns to Harlem, where he finds that his friend
and fellow member of the Brotherhood, Tod Clifton, has disappeared. The
narrator eventually finds Clifton selling "Sambo" dolls on the street. "Sambo"
is a caricature of the obsequious slave, and the doll serves as Clifton's symbol
for how the Brotherhood uses its Harlem members and views the black community more generally. Clifton says about the doll:

> He'll make you laugh, he'll make you sigh, si-igh.
> He'll make you want to dance, and dance—
> Here you are, ladies and gentlemen, Sambo,
> The dancing doll.
> Buy one for your baby. Take him to your girl friend and she'll love
>   you, loove you!
> He'll keep you entertained. He'll make you weep sweet—(431)

In an attempt to sell the dolls, Clifton sexualizes the racial caricature. Sambo
will make the audience "si-igh," incite "loove," and even elicit a pleasurable or
"sweet" sorrow. Playing off the hyper-sexualization of black Americans in the
white imaginary, the entertainment that Sambo provides also represents the
role of the Brotherhood's black members. Clifton explains that Sambo "lives
upon the sunshine of [his audience's] lordly smile" (432). He croons and bows
for "the brotherly two bits of a dollar" (433). Like Sambo, whatever fraternity
Clifton had experienced is only the "two bits" buying his loyalty. The narrator
realizes through this performance that the black members of the Brotherhood
are merely token cases for equality; their actual function is to please the
organization's wealthy supporters, to make their bleeding progressive hearts
"weep sweet." The presence of Harlem representatives in the Brotherhood is
nothing more than a shadow performance, a mere staging of equality.
   Through many such riffs on the "Sambo" caricature, the novel satirizes the
racial programs of progressive organizational politics. In fact, when the narrator learns from Brother Hambro of the organization's decision to withdraw
its support from Harlem, his suspicions about the Brotherhood's commitment to equality are confirmed. Brother Hambro explains that, although the
residents of Harlem have been moved to action, the Brotherhood now believes
"they must be brought along more slowly" (504). Hambro earlier explained
that some members were "expendable," that "some must make greater sacrifices
than others" (501, 503). Seeing the color line belting Hambro's statement, the
invisible man asks, "Are you sure you're not saying that they must be held

back?" (504). The narrator realizes that, at its best, his presence in the leftist organization is a mere nod to equality, as if he were a novelty whose chief purpose were to be obsequious and grateful. At its worst, though, the narrator finds that minorities become fodder for the left's sacrificial fires. As he puts it after Clifton is killed, "their entertainment had been his death" (446).

This damning depiction of the perverse pleasures of progressive politics represents a transitional moment in Ellison's career. Beginning with his migration to New York in 1936, Ellison joined a milieu rife with popular front politics and left-leaning intellectuals. He became acquainted with Richard Wright through the generosity of Langston Hughes. Wright helped Ellison with his first story "Hymie's Bull" and also encouraged his younger friend to pursue a career in writing rather than music. A significant part of this patronage involved tutelage in communist politics, although neither Ellison nor Wright felt beholden to toe the official Communist Party line. According to Arnold Rampersad, Ellison "probably became, at least for a while, a dues-paying Party member. . . . Later, Ralph only hinted at close ties to the Party during [the 1930s]," undoubtedly because membership had become a significant liability as Cold War tensions escalated in the early 1950s.[7]

Ellison's writing during the early period of his career borrowed from the cultural forms and political concerns of democratic-socialist thought.[8] However, Barbara Foley argues that Ellison's publishers tried to hide his early political allegiances when his watershed novel was published.[9] Considering early drafts of *Invisible Man*, Foley argues that Ellison had not abandoned a commitment to progressive politics when he began the novel. For example, in early drafts of *Invisible Man*, the narrator treats the Brotherhood with considerably less hostility. He treats issues of class in ways more consistent with his earlier work. As a result, Foley argues that Ellison's novel is "a conflicted and contradictory text bearing multiple traces of his struggle to repress and then abolish the ghost of his leftist consciousness and conscience."[10] In other words, *Invisible Man* is a palimpsest of the left's waning influence upon the novelist's intellectual life.

According to Rampersad, Ellison first felt cognitive dissonance between his literary aspirations and his commitment to communism around 1941, when his essays begin to cast a "vision of liberal cosmopolitanism" that had otherwise been foreclosed by the party.[11] During the war, Ellison began to distance himself from the radicalism of "black Communists" who idealized the Soviet Union, which had ruled that racial discrimination was illegal. Ellison was disgusted with the political violence of Soviet-style communism, and so the wartime debates regarding the American left's naive posture toward Stalin caused Ellison to become increasingly politically ambivalent. Nonetheless, as late as 1948, Ellison quietly preserved hope that some form of democratic socialism might, as he put it, "survive and become a force again."[12]

By the time *Invisible Man* was published, however, Ellison's political drift had brought him into a more vexed position. Raymond A. Mazurek argues that, with the novel's publication, Ellison "became a major U.S. writer during the early years of the Cold War" and thus felt compelled to suppress many of his early stories and essays.[13] *Invisible Man* negotiates the postwar turn against the social-democratic ideas that had been a constituent part of the spectrum of democratic liberalism by invoking the anxieties of existential philosophy. While *Invisible Man* registers the evident and painful absence of racial equality in the United States, I show in subsequent sections of this chapter that the novel also eschews organizational politics as the locus for democratic reform.[14] The novel presents the self, not the state or collective structures, as the only authentic locus for political action. Anything less becomes another source of alienation.

The Contraction of Liberalism and the Vicissitudes of Postwar Prestige

The narrator's reticence about and eventual repudiation of the Brotherhood, more than a symbol of Ellison's changing private commitments, represents a common trajectory among postwar liberals. As Michael Denning explains, a prominent part of the political scene of the 1930s and 1940s, contrary to the consensus narrative pushed by Cold War era politics, was the "radical social-democratic movement forged around anti-fascism, anti-lynching, and the industrial unionism of the CIO."[15] According to Denning, this leftist coalition was much more expansive than the Communist Party or the American Workers Party: there was a diverse spectrum of leftist politics that was primarily concerned with securing equality and fair working conditions domestically, and opposing fascism abroad in the regimes of Italy, Spain, and Germany. Rather than collapsing leftism into Soviet-style communism, Denning offers a more expansive account of the left by characterizing it in the terms of "popular front" politics. In other words, while postwar Americans tended to think of leftism in terms of the Communist Party, the political liberalism of the 1930s and 1940s was made up of a spectrum of social democrats, New Deal liberals, and even some communists, who gained intellectual and popular traction in their opposition to fascism.[16] Indeed, following Denning, Wendy Wall explains that the "popular front" progressives successfully billed communism as "twentieth-century Americanism" during the early years of the New Deal era.[17] Fascism, rather than Soviet-style communism, was the antithesis to American political and social values during the 1930s.

While the intellectual landscape was more diverse than the consensus culture of the Cold War years retrospectively asserted, the political landscape of the 1930s was also less preoccupied with anti-communist anxieties. In fact, the programs and policies of the New Deal often cooperated with segments of the anti-capitalist left in attempts to achieve common domestic ends, such as the maintenance of unions and strong labor laws. For example, this selective cooperation occurred within the Tennessee Valley Authority (TVA), one of the first projects initiated by President Roosevelt. As Aaron D. Purcell argues, many TVA employees were encouraged to participate in union organizing, a function of the program's wider goal of fostering union activity. This relationship to union activity would later provoke investigations of many TVA employees during the McCarthy era.[18] Indeed, in 1948, Whittaker Chambers, a former member of the Communist Party and an editor at *Time* magazine, testified before Congress that other party members had "infiltrated" several New Deal agencies. However, in contrast to the historical and political rewriting that later occurred during the Cold War era, the relationship between the anti-capitalist left and the projects and policies of FDR's New Deal were not a form of espionage or treason—what free-enterprise conservatives viewed as an undermining of American democracy. This notion of "infiltration" draws on what Marcel Cornis-Pope calls the binary logic of Cold War culture, as if all politics could be understood as "communism" versus "American democracy."[19] Instead, the American liberalism of the 1930s lent itself to greater fluidity as many anti-capitalists simultaneously supported certain US domestic projects alongside an internationalist political program.

The legitimacy of social-democratic thought in this period shaped federal policy in very definite ways. Prominent New Deal legislation, such as the Wagner Act in 1935, fostered a period of ascending labor power. Seizing the opportunities created by this labor-friendly legislation, the Congress of Industrial Organizations (CIO) successfully organized industrial workers across the United States. However, much like the New Deal era itself, the CIO was far from homogenous: it was home to both pragmatic liberals and red-blooded progressives. Still, as the Second World War intensified, the internal differences of the CIO were also aggravated. Beginning in 1940, the rising tide of anti-communist anxieties in the United States began to transform the CIO by requiring its members to denounce loyalty to "isms," including "fascism, nazism, and communism."[20] The conflation of the three political philosophies was a sign of things to come, a harbinger for the eroding legitimacy of socialists who cooperated with—and were accepted within—New Deal projects for the shared goal of "domestic reform."[21]

Although organizations such as the TVA and CIO provided institutional outlets for a more pluralistic liberal democracy during the 1930s, the inclusivity of leftist politics in the New Deal coalition was never uncontested. In 1938, for example, the House Committee on Un-American Activities (later known as HUAC) was formed to investigate the alleged Communist Party ties of both private citizens and public employees. However, President Roosevelt was damagingly censorious of the committee. Martin Dies, Jr., a congressman and Democrat from Texas who began to oppose the New Deal after the Wagner Act (1935), led the committee's investigations. The mounting tension between HUAC and the administration was initially stunted by Roosevelt's popularity and the reported successes of his federal programs. However, the rising conflicts in Europe, along with the conflation of fascism and communism as America's united enemy within popular sentiment by the nation's entry in the war, created footholds for members of Congress in the president's own party to place limitations on the spectrum of legitimacy within American liberal thought.[22] Later, the Taft-Hartley Act of 1947 damaged the legitimacy of union leaders and labor organizations by requiring them to swear under oath that they were not communists. This was like asking someone to swear they hadn't committed a thought crime—the very requirement was a damaging moral indictment. Many CIO leaders refused on principle, but the legislation dealt a serious blow to organized labor and further emboldened the opponents of social-democratic institutions.[23]

The point is that the tide began to turn against a more expansive spectrum of liberal thought in the mid-1940s. Landon R. Y. Storrs demonstrates that anti-New Deal conservatives began to incite and exploit anxieties about Soviet espionage immediately following the war in order to undermine liberals who advocated redistributive and regulatory policies.[24] One fear during this so-called Second Red Scare was that members of the Communist Party were manipulating US policy to the advantage of the Soviet Union. President Truman, less popular than FDR, more anxious about communism, and less resolute about opposing a stronger conservative coalition, instituted a federal loyalty program in 1947 (Executive Order 9835). Not unlike the Taft-Hartley Act, Storrs shows that these institutional anxieties prompted a collapsed distinction between Soviet-style communism and social-democratic factions within American liberalism. This conflation had the sweeping consequence of altering specific policy fields of the postwar liberal agenda, including "labor and civil rights, consumer protection, national health insurance, public assistance, worker education, public works, public housing, Native American rights, and international aid."[25] Truman pushed his own reform agenda, the "Fair Deal," which included national health insurance and civil rights legislation. He also integrated the military by executive order in 1948—something Roosevelt had refused to do, largely in concession to Southern Democrats. Nonetheless, Truman augmented the political pressures against robust activist institutions within the American welfare state. His anxieties prevailed over almost every attempt at expanding the structures to create socioeconomic equality.[26]

In fact, at an institutional level, Truman participated in rolling back many of the New Deal's progressive economic policies through his escalation of the Cold War. In 1948, Truman established anti-communist anxieties as an institutional policy when he introduced the European Recovery Program and developed an interventionist foreign policy aimed at containing communism. Many conservatives seized the underlying concerns of the president's foreign policy and depicted New Deal agencies such as the TVA and WPA as "un-American," which became fodder for the fires of loyalty investigations. The international containment of communism consequently constricted the official Democratic Party mandate for a domestic activist-managerial state. For example, Earl Latham claims that in 1950 the momentum shifted decisively in favor of those who associated New Deal economic planning with the oppression of state socialism. That year began with Alger Hiss's conviction of perjury over his communist past in January and Senator McCarthy asserting in February that the Department of State knowingly employed communists. Other anti-leftist spectacles then began to accumulate, such as the arrest of Julius and Ethel Rosenberg and the HUAC investigations into communist activity in Hawaii, both of which received almost daily media attention.[27] Purcell argues that such fears were put to use during the McCarthy era as a way of undermining New Deal agencies and the economic agenda of the welfare state. "At the end of 1947," Purcell explains, "many former New Dealers found themselves at odds with the national political climate. Gains by Republicans during the elections of the previous year, a tougher foreign policy against Soviet-bloc countries, and efforts to uncover domestic subversives formed the bedrock layers of a cold war culture that would last for decades."[28] Conservative opponents of FDR's early progressive policies—that is, regarding industrial unionism, regulatory intervention, economic planning, social security, and a populist welfare state more broadly—gained significant ground when the legitimacy of organizational reform and its relationship to "Americanism" came into question.

The trajectory of Carlos Bulosan's career from the 1930s until his death in 1956 is, at least in part, indexed to the public currency of social-democratic politics during this period. Bulosan's widely read essay "Freedom from Want" (1943) was published in the *Saturday Evening Post* alongside illustrations by Norman Rockwell. The image associated with the essay initially serves as obvious war-time propaganda. Yet Bulosan's essay complicates this interpretation by documenting the plight of minority workers: "When our crops are burned or plowed under, we are angry and confused. Sometimes we ask if this is the real America."[29] The title of Bulosan's essay specifically invokes FDR's "Four Freedoms," put forward during his 1941 State of the Union address. "The American dream is only hidden away," Bulosan explains to the readers of the *Post*, creating a vivid juxtaposition with Rockwell's illustration of a white middle-class family surrounding a full holiday meal. In contrast to the racially homogenous manifestation of the "American Dream" in Rockwell's image, Bulosan hopes that this dream "will push its way up and grow again."[30]

The discrepancy between Rockwell's image of white middle-class security and Bulosan's meditation on racial inequality deepens, rather than divorces, Bulosan's association of a national imaginary with protections for non-white workers. Instead of repudiating this American "freedom" because of its prevailing and nearly exclusive association with white domesticity, Bulosan invokes the conflict as grounds for reforming the failures of such a national ideal: "We recognize the mainsprings of American democracy in our right to form unions and bargain through them collectively, our opportunity to sell our products at reasonable prices, and the privilege of our children to attend schools where they learn the truth about the world in which they live."[31] Bulosan presents race-conscious social democracy as the highest expression of Americanism. In contrast to this optimistic faith, Denning reads closely related "American" passages in Bulosan's fictionalized autobiography *America Is in the Heart* (1946), suggesting that the author's narrative voice is "a desperate attempt to transcend a United States of violence."[32] Yet this criticism neglects the dialectic at play in Bulosan's work: the contradictions and conflicts in "Freedom from Want" and *America Is in the Heart* complicate easy slogans about Americanism. Bulosan critiques what he also affirms; he questions what he aspires to have realized.

The structural conflict between Bulosan's "Freedom from Want" and Rockwell's image performs this kind of vexed, reformist work, particularly by wedding the vocabulary of New Deal liberalism with popular front politics. Such a gesture was not inconceivable within the spectrum of liberal discourse predating the Cold War era. The *Saturday Evening Post* paid Bulosan nearly one thousand dollars for the essay, which suggests the extent to which a mainstream reading public, at least in 1943, attributed a kind of market currency to the idea that American progressivism was the solution to American inequality. Not long after his essay in the *Post*, Bulosan published a short story, "The End of the War," in the *New Yorker*. However, by 1950 the structures of political sentiment had changed, and Bulosan increasingly had difficulty placing his work in mainstream print media. Indeed, having been blacklisted in the 1950s for his political commitments, Bulosan died in poverty and relative obscurity in 1956.[33]

Invisible Man and the End of History

While what Alan Nadel calls the Cold War era "containment culture" helps account for the diminishing social-democratic elements within the spectrum of postwar liberalism, many intellectuals also advanced a powerful critique of organizational politics at the level of ideas rather than binary ideology.[34] Ellison's novel was an integral part of this milieu. One telling example is when the invisible man rejects (and is rejected by) the black nationalist Ras the Exhorter. As a member of the Brotherhood, the narrator at first justifies this rejection through the organization's official position that Ras's black nationalists are a "gang of racist gangsters" whose first response is to reject white Americans categorically and then resort to violent confrontation (421). After an altercation with Ras, the narrator and Tod Clifton consider whether there might be something to Ras's extremism. "I suppose sometimes a man *has* to plunge outside history," Clifton muses, lest he "kill somebody, go nuts" (377). As part of these musings, Clifton discovers that "history" as an idea is weighted against black Americans.

He finds Ras's approach compelling, in other words, because living "inside" history seems to mean being determined by its racially exploitative patterns. "History" has tended to consign black Americans to the margins, whether it's the "history" of the Brotherhood's analysis of class conflict or the American "history" of republican ideals. Freighting one's actions with such a concept results in madness and frustrated violence.

While the narrator initially rejects Clifton's sympathy with Ras because of the place within "history" that the Brotherhood supposedly provides him, he later revaluates that idea after Clifton's death. A policeman accosts Clifton for not having a permit to sell the Sambo dolls. Clifton puts the policeman "on his ass" for repeatedly pushing him, and in turn he's shot and killed (438). The narrator flees the scene of the murder to the Brotherhood's district office. In an attempt to understand Clifton's death, the narrator tells himself, "The incident was political." The invisible man's understanding of "politics" at this point follows the Brotherhood's definition. He explains, "politically, individuals were without meaning. The shooting was all that was left of him now, Clifton had chosen to plunge out of history and . . . only the plunge was recorded, and that was the only important thing." Clifton's act is isolated; its "politics" are individual. Therefore, the narrator concludes that the "political equivalent" of Clifton's actions are "death" (447). Whatever larger significance Clifton might have had is cancelled out because he acted only as an individual.

Despite these evasions and abstract rationalizations, the invisible man decides to organize a funeral for Clifton and use the event to articulate a "greater" meaning to the murder (448). During the funeral, an "old man" in a "husky baritone" sings "There's Many a Thousand Gone." The spiritual moves the crowd, but the narrator explains,

> It was not the words, for they were all the same old slave-borne words; it was as though he'd changed the emotion beneath the words while yet the old longing, resigned, transcendent emotion still sounded above, now deepened by that something for which the theory of Brotherhood had given me no name. (453)

The ideology of the Brotherhood fails to explain the nameless "something" provoked by the old man's song and the crowd's response. The mythic and folkloric dimensions transcend the programmatic categories of organizational politics. The Brotherhood's analytic criteria fail in the face of an emotion or existential longing "deeper than protest, or religion" (453). The spiritual also begins to unravel the narrator's assumptions about the Brotherhood, for he finds this "transcendent emotion" to be more fundamental than the political. Instead, the narrator discovers that the self's freedom is preeminent: "No more peck o'corn for me," the lyrics proclaim, "No more, no more, / No more peck o'corn for me" (453).

The invisible man's unsettled ideology inflects his eulogy. He laments Clifton in mock-bureaucratic style: "Place of birth: U.S. Some southern town. . . . Address: unknown. Occupation: unemployed. Cause of death (be specific): resisting reality in the form of a .38 caliber revolver in the hands of the arresting officer" (458). The bureaucratic categories of the eulogy—as if the narrator were filling in programmatic slots on a death certificate—symbolize the elision of Clifton's individuality. The "facts," the narrator says, are simple because the laws of the state boil down to a basic reality: a black man may be shot with impunity. Clifton is not an individual with a distinct past; rather, the policemen view him only as "black," that is, as a member of an easily (if not illusorily) imposed category. Clifton's address is now a box that is "far, far too expensive a dwelling," for it corresponds not only to his death but also to his facelessness, his objectification at the hands of an impersonal bureaucracy of violence (458). The narrator's response to Clifton's elided individuality is to turn away from the impersonal categories he mockingly uses, and instead he casts his friend's death in personal terms: "when he fell there was a hole in the heel of his socks" (456). What the narrator conveys is not the economic forces underwriting the white policemen's false consciousness, as Ellison had done in his earlier story "A Party Down at the Square."[35] Rather, the narrator presents an individual tragedy, the loss of the self within a society rife with racially configured and bureaucratically administered alienation.

At the end of the funeral, the narrator looks over the crowd gathered to mourn Clifton. The funeral participants transform in the narrator's eyes from a conglomerate social body—a single organism with undifferentiated parts—and he suddenly finds this generic body differentiated: "I saw not a crowd but the set faces of individual men and women" (459). While the Brotherhood's politics incorporates the self within an impersonal tapestry of ideas and doctrines, Clifton's funeral unravels this ideological fabric. The invisible man's vision of the "flesh and blood" of individuals, rather than the "masses" as an abstract idea, bears the imprint of Clifton's decision to step outside "history" (459). Clifton acts as an individual, his symbolic Sambo performance serving as a rhetorical figure that affirms the self denied by the illusion of racial categories. The funeral finally prompts Ellison's narrator to see the elided black self at the heart of the Brotherhood's political philosophy. What's more, even as Clifton's decision to step outside "history" defamiliarizes the narrator's political certainties, Clifton's choice also becomes a model of action—one that originates from the self and thus speaks on "lower" or foundational frequencies (581). Four decades before Francis Fukuyama declared the "end of history"—that is, the triumph of liberal democracy over communism—Ellison's invisible man felt the ideology of communism die during a Harlem funeral.[36]

The narrator therefore eulogizes the ideas of "class," "political economy," and "structural conditions" as much as his friend Tod Clifton. As the narrator discovers in his underground space, progressive configurations of society in terms of political-organizational categories become worse than the disease they purport to cure. In fact, such organizational categories ("class") have their corollary in the impersonal violence of the police ("he was black and they shot him" (456)). The narrator doesn't abandon the notion of collective problems, but he harbors nagging suspicion about collective political agency as the nucleus for a solution because, as he puts it in a moment of unrecognized irony, organizational politics has an alienating logic: "I'm a cog in a machine. We here in the Brotherhood work as a unit" (396–7). When political agency is written according to such organizational scripts, the narrator finds that the self becomes negligible, nondescript, merely a movable part. In response to this revelation, the narrator finds himself thrown back upon the self that has been alienated from organizational politics and elided by its dehumanizing logic. As a result, the self becomes the final provenance for political action.

Richard Wright Goes to Europe

Ellison was not alone in his suspicions about leftist organizational politics. Chester Himes's *Lonely Crusade* (1947), for example, narrates the failures of a black union organizer during the Second World War. The novel's protagonist, Lee Gordon, organizes other workers at a wartime aircraft factory in Los Angeles, and he soon becomes the darling symbol of the leftist organization that employs him. Yet Gordon is eventually divested of his dignity or "manhood" through party strife and, it becomes apparent, is merely grist for the leftist mill in its wrangling with conservative business groups. These competing forces of alienation prompt Gordon to wonder whether he has a "soul," or if such a grounding of the worth of the self was "what all these people looked for within him and could not find."[37] The "soul" as an idea thus becomes little more than a lever for creating racial distinctions. Much like the invisible man's suggestion that the Brotherhood veils the same order of systemic racism shot through mainstream white society, Himes questions the sincerity of the left's concern for black Americans and chronicles its denigration of the inner life of the self.[38]

In a way initially much like the experience of Lee Gordon in Himes's novel, Richard Wright's work from the 1940s and 1950s represents the discontent among black intellectuals with the racial scripts of organizational progressive politics. Wright joined the Communist Party in 1933 through the John Reed Club. He also found employment in the New Deal Federal Writers' Project and the Federal Theatre Project from 1935–1936, working mostly in publicity offices. During the war, Wright discovered that the Communist Party would not take legal action against the government for its support of Jim Crow laws, and this refusal precipitated his official break from the party in 1942.[39] Wright and his wife, Ellen, who was an important party organizer in Brooklyn, came to believe that "the Party was using the Negro for its own ends," and so they effectively cut ties with it.[40]

Wright elaborates on his souring relationship with the party in his autobiography *Black Boy (American Hunger)* (1993). Wright describes the party's "Negro Communists" as impenetrable silos filled with uncompromising ideology:

> An hour's listening [to their speeches] disclosed the fanatical intolerance of minds sealed against new ideas, new facts, new feelings, new attitudes, new hints at ways to live. They denounced books they had never read, people they had never known, ideas they could never understand, and doctrines whose names they could not pronounce. Communism, instead of making them leap forward with fire in their hearts to become masters of ideas and life, had frozen them at an even lower level of ignorance than had been theirs before they met Communism.[41]

According to Wright, toeing the party line was more than an expectation for black members—it was a blind obsession. Indeed, Wright inverts the critique of organizational authority articulated in other postwar novels, such as Richard Condon's *The Manchurian Candidate* (1959), Madeleine L'Engle's *A Wrinkle in Time* (1962), and Sloan Wilson's *The Man in the Gray Flannel Suit* (1955), which examine the conformity demanded by consolidated, corporatized authority and "mainstream" American mores. Rather than questioning the generic pattern of the middle class, Wright questions the compulsory conformity of the radicalism that positions itself against mainstream culture. Wright's "Negro" with the red armband is as much a symbol of organizational conformity as the businessmen whom Tom Rath scorns in Wilson's novel.

These political debates about communism and democratic socialism were informed by the assorted uses of existential sensibilities among postwar intellectuals. Wright expresses one position within this sliding scale of thought in his essay "I Tried to Be a Communist" (1944). After Wright read magazines given to him at a meeting of the John Reed Club, he "was amazed to find that there did exist in this world an organized search for the truth of the lives of the oppressed and the isolated." In communism, Wright finds a compelling account of "the similarity of the experiences of workers in other lands, by the possibility of uniting scattered but kindred peoples into a whole."[42] Yet Wright then provides two general reasons for his disillusionment with the Communist Party USA: first, because of the ease with which its revolutionary fervor melds into madness and, second, the anti-intellectualism rampant throughout the membership.[43] As a "quiet black Communist" gently explains to him, "We've kept records of the trouble [the party has] had with intellectuals in the past. It's estimated that only 13 per cent of them remain in the party." Wright asks why they leave, and the man responds, "Most of them drop out of their own accord."[44] Wright takes this response to heart. However, he also explains that, while finally "failing" to be a communist, he nonetheless remains committed to a communistic vision of "uniting" groups into a "whole." The difference between this vision of unity and the conformism that sours Wright's view of the party is that his new views are delineated in terms of solidarity. Rather than conformity, which insists, "Be like us," Wright searches for ways of identifying "kinship" among suffering people.[45]

The point is that Wright's distrust of the Communist Party did not translate into a rejection of the politics of solidarity and collective action. In fact, his immigration to France in 1946 enabled Wright to explore other forms of progressive political thought excluded by the increasingly narrow scope of postwar liberalism in the United States. His politics first became colored in the hue of existentialism after striking up a correspondence with Sartre and Simone de Beauvoir in the early 1940s. Sartre's postwar project of reconciling Marxism and existentialism (which I consider in the fourth chapter) appealed to Wright, and in 1948 he began to read deeply in existential philosophy and literature. In that same year he participated with Sartre and Camus in the leadership of the Rassemblement Démocratique Révolutionnaire (RDR). The RDR opposed both Soviet-style communism and the expansionism of US foreign policy, advancing instead the political solidarity imagined in Sartre's later existentialism. Wright even wrote an existential novel, *The Outsider* (1953), which probably to its detriment received its greatest acclaim among French intellectuals. *The Outsider* marks a decisive break with organized communism as Cross Damon, the novel's protagonist, murders several acquaintances, including the communist Gil for his "revolutionary logic" that denies "individual protests" and subjects the life of the self to "the lessons of history."[46] Not unlike *Invisible Man*, then, *The Outsider* decries anti-humanist violations of the self, and it solidified Wright's place among the non-party left in postwar Europe.

While Wright's misgivings about the Communist Party in America deepen in the 1940s and prompt a turn toward other forms of progressive politics in the 1950s, he differs from Ellison in that he does not throw out the organizational baby with the party bathwater. While the broad strokes of their careers are similar—early affiliations with communism, growing discontentment and wartime rejection of the Communist Party, and an intellectual affinity for existentialism—the differences between Wright and Ellison highlight competing responses by those who critiqued the racial inequities of American politics. For example, Wright's early novel *Native Son* (1940) charts the structural social conditions surrounding Bigger Thomas, a black twenty-year-old who grows up in an impoverished area of Chicago. Bigger's environment—its newspapers, magazines, movies, and towering buildings—link human culture with material wealth, even as it prevents black Americans from having structural access to that wealth and consigns Bigger to a life of subhuman poverty. Bigger's environment is so limiting that it prevents him from imagining alternatives. "But what could he do?" he reflects early in the novel. "Each time he asked himself that question his mind hit a blank wall and stopped thinking." Instead, he only looks out his window and sees the "miserable" conditions of workers in "overalls."[47] As Wright explains in the essay "How Bigger Was Born" (1940), his protagonist "is a product of a dislocated society; he is a dispossessed and disinherited man."[48]

The environmental forces that produce Bigger's alienation continue in the tradition of earlier American novels like Stephen Crane's *Maggie: A Girl of the Streets* (1893) and Theodore Dreiser's *Sister Carrie* (1900). Rather than establishing a simplistic, one-way causality in which environments always determine individuals, these novels represent the structural conditions that preclude or hem in self-determination. As Ellison explains in his review of Wright's autobiography, the question of individual humanity "had as little chance of prevailing against the overwhelming weight of [his environment] as Beethoven's Quartets would have of destroying the stench of a Nazi prison."[49] However, Ellison also observes that the combination of forces before which the individual feels powerless is itself an assertion of individuality or, at least, a "groping" for it.[50] In other words, if the environment swallows up the individual in *Native Son* and *Black Boy*, these narratives suggest a form of social protest that aspires to reform that environment, to make structural space for the individuality of the person of color whose humanity those forces deny.

Wright's literary imagination directs his readers' attention to the conditions of capitalist society that shape modern consciousness, and he thus places the burden of reform at an institutional and structural level. Indeed, as part of Wright's hesitant, critical, but finally supportive relationship to the New Deal's relief and public works programs, Susan Edmunds reads *Native Son* as revising the tradition of domestic and sentimental literature that informed the political processes of New Deal liberalism.[51] Wright wanted to correct the false assumptions and racial exclusions of the American welfare state, not to reject it tout court.[52] Aspiring to reform the reformer in *Native Son*, Wright depicts the Thomas family as representative of a two-track welfare system, in which black Americans are subordinated to a lesser order of the security and benevolence doled out by federal power. Edmunds shows that Bigger, as another "problem boy" who works in the home of a white, sentimental couple, embodies the contradictory racial inequalities of American welfare liberalism.

Ellison shares Wright's anxieties about the racial norms embedded within institutional liberalism, particularly in those moments when the invisible man is confronted with the "white" logic of citizenship within the American welfare state. For example, when the invisible man chauffeurs Mr. Norton, an important white donor to the local college for African American students, Ellison's narrator feels a deep commitment to the college's vision of the respectable citizen. Yet the invisible man accidentally exposes Norton to Jim Trueblood, who relays the (possibly fabricated) story of his incestuous relationship with his daughter. As Norton and the narrator return to the college after the unsettling encounter, the invisible man reflects, "I wanted to stop the car and talk with Mr. Norton, to beg his pardon for what he had seen; . . . to assure him that far from being like any of the people we had seen, I *hated* them" (99). The invisible man wants to demonstrate his difference from Trueblood because, among other reasons, he nurtures hopes of one day becoming an assistant to Dr. Bledsoe, the school's president. But more importantly, the young narrator has at this point internalized a vision of democratic virtue promoted by the donor and his benevolent liberalism. He must convince Norton of his respectability; the invisible man feels that he must embody a set of social and, as it turns out, racial norms.

The racial connotations of these norms soon become clear as the narrator describes what is *not* characteristic of his college's expectations. These liberal ideals take on a creedal structure:

> I believed in the principles of the Founder with all my heart and soul, and that I believed in his own goodness and kindness in extending the hand of his benevolence to helping us poor, ignorant people out of the mire and darkness. I would do his bidding and teach others to rise up as he wished them to, teach them to be thrifty, decent, upright citizens, contributing to the welfare of all. (99)

The invisible man doesn't initially perceive the racial norms underlying his confession. He instead suggests that being an "upright citizen" is antithetical to "the mire and darkness" that characterizes "us poor, ignorant people." Given the fact that the narrator includes himself in "us," not just Trueblood or the rowdy customers at the Golden Day, it's clear that he applies these ideas about betterment and welfare to all black Americans. These values are also predicated on black servility ("I would do his bidding"). The invisible man becomes primitive—almost subhuman—apart from the status he could (though never seems to) achieve as a "decent" citizen.

More pointedly, the norms of being "decent" in the Jim Crow South (where the narrator's college is located) were, of course, bound up with segregation. To be a citizen of the Jim Crow South, New Deal or not, meant to be juridically marginalized. This logic of exclusion-by-inclusion ("citizen" yet "separate") is evident in the servile attitude and specious ideas about "darkness" that the narrator's college promulgates. The invisible man later encounters other instances that demonstrate his alienated position within American "welfare" discourse. He is repeatedly cast out from avenues of belonging within what Lizabeth Cohen has called the "consumer's republic" of the postwar era, including disastrous work at a paint plant and discrimination in his attempts to gain white-collar work.[53] Indeed, finally perceiving the exclusionary logic of his society's "welfare" discourse, the invisible man describes the policeman who murders Tod Clifton as a "good citizen": by shooting Clifton, the officer does not violate the law but fulfills it (457).

Ellison's, Himes's, and Wright's suspicions about political organizations expressed the distrust among minority communities toward the New Deal. During the 1936 election, nearly 75 percent of black voters switched to the Democratic ticket to support Roosevelt's reelection bid. At that point, political historians argue that black Americans supported the administration's New Deal because of the economic relief it provided during the throes of the Depression, as well as the support for civil rights among some members of the Coalition from the Northeast. The WPA and the National Youth Administration, for instance, provided economic support to black and white Americans equally. Even Ellison offered qualified praise for one New Deal program, the WPA, which he said had "allowed many Negroes to achieve their identities as artists."[54]

Despite this pragmatic support for certain New Deal programs by people of color, the relationship between racial equality and New Deal economic relief was at best a vexed one. New Deal agencies such as the Agricultural Adjustment Administration (AAA) and the Fair Housing Administration (FHA) systematically weighted their interventions in favor of white Americans. The FHA, for example, supported de facto segregation by refusing to guarantee mortgages to black homeowners, whether in the North or the South, when they applied to live in white neighborhoods. Indeed, many historians are wont to claim that, if it were not for the Southern Democrats, the New Deal would have resolutely passed civil rights legislation long before the 1960s. And there is some legitimacy to this view. However, when viewed in terms of congressional votes, northern Democrats from the 1930s until the 1950s voted more conservatively regarding civil rights legislation than Republicans.[55] The portrait of this voting record suggests that, while there were certainly exceptions in the Democratic Party, the New Dealers were deeply divided regarding racial equality and civil rights—and the Mason-Dixon line by no means cleanly marked these divisions. Exclusionary policies remained a stain on the New Deal's economic reform agenda of the 1930s. Ellison's exposition of the exclusionary logic of "welfare" citizenship was therefore rooted in the undeniable failures of American liberals and, in particular, the slow and often unresponsive New Deal interventions regarding the invisible status of people of color.

But confronting those exclusions is not the same thing as saying the existential framework of *Invisible Man* is the only or inevitable response to the inclusion-exclusion logic of organizational liberalism. There *were* organizational, not existential, alternatives to these exclusions, and they were very real possibilities.[56] Ellison would later register his support for the Kennedy and Johnson administrations, leveraging his cultural position for the Democratic Party in such influential essays as "The Myth of the Flawed White Southerner."[57] However, Ellison's later essays represent a shift from the response to racial inequality that he offers in *Invisible Man*. Because Ellison's narrator is repelled by the violence of Ras the Exhorter, manipulated by the Brotherhood with its elision of the individual, and excluded within the logic of welfare citizenship, he finds himself atomized, cut off from all collectives. All other options being foreclosed to him, the invisible man retreats into the self and its capacities for authenticity. Ellison's narrator is alienated from collectives both social and political, so he consequently enters a state of "hibernation" (580). All other democratic virtues being only another form of alienation, the invisible man finds that this hibernation—this retreat within the life of the self—is the only recourse for his existential predicament.

Existentialism Comes to America

The invisible man's hibernation is a gesture performed on a public stage, but the audience had only recently become familiar with the script. American readers engaged with European existentialism in various and uneven ways as early as 1946. For example, as George Cotkin explains, one of existentialism's forms for arriving in the United States was as a cultural fetish:

> American audiences were introduced to French existentialism in the pages of *Life*, the *New York Times Magazine*, *Time*, *Newsweek*, and fashion magazines such as *Vogue* and *Harper's Bazaar*. These popular discussions stressed Simone de Beauvoir's lifestyle and Jean-Paul Sartre's attachment to the bohemian café scene more than their ideas. A cult of personality developed whereby the general renown of existentialism became intimately connected to the personal life of the philosopher and even to the circumstances of the nation he or she represented.[58]

The mass-market press often presented this "cult of personality" with ironic distance. "Fun is being poked at the pretentiousness of both the French and their American acolytes," Cotkin explains, even as these popular media outlets traded on the pervasive fascination among Americans with French life and thought.[59]

Stanley Donen's comedic film *Funny Face* (1957), starring Audrey Hepburn and Fred Astaire, at once evokes the faddish popularity of existentialism while also exhibiting its tangible influence on American culture. *Funny Face* tells the story of Jo Stockton (Audrey Hepburn), who is a shy clerk at a recondite Greenwich Village bookshop called Embryo Concepts. Stockton is enamored with French thought and, as a dilettante philosopher, "thinks as well as she looks," as Dick Avery (Fred Astaire) puts it.[60] The narrative arc of *Funny Face* charts Stockton's eventual drift from her philosophical preoccupation with anxiety and alienation toward her romance with Avery, an upright fashion photographer. Avery convinces Stockton to visit Paris for a fashion shoot, although the latter is reticent because a French philosopher she admires "doesn't approve of fashion magazines. It's chichi and it's an unrealistic approach to self-impressions, as well as economics." After arriving in Paris, Stockton tours the city and sings with pleasure, "I want to see the den of thinking men, like Jean-Paul Sartre / I must philosophize with all the guys around Monmartre." However, the film tempers Stockton's overtly philosophical ambitions because, as she quips, "My philosophic search, / has left me in the lurch." The French philosopher, it turns out, is a cad. Rather than choosing isolation, though, Stockton dawns a fashionable wedding dress and meets Avery at a small French church, signaling the film's preference for romantic resolution above Stockton's earlier angst.

If *Funny Face* signals such a preference, it also indicates the intelligibility of Sartre and existentialism within the terrain of postwar popular culture. Indeed, Stockton's choice of Avery over "the den of thinking men, like Jean-Paul Sartre" is presented as an existential dilemma. Avery's fashion world is, as his magazine's editor Joan Prescott explains, "a cold lot—artificial and totally lacking in sentiment. So how can you possibly be in love?" Similarly, when the French philosopher that Stockton admires makes a pass at her, she repudiates the "den of thinking men" as a veil for sexual interests rather than "pure" philosophical inquiry. As both the world of fashion and French philosophy are cast in disrepute, *Funny Face* subtly retools existentialist sensibilities about authenticity and free choice, even as it empties those sensibilities of the angst and alienation that underwrite Sartre's philosophical writing. Stockton and Avery are, in other words, faced with a choice between authenticity—the life they freely choose—and artificial forms of bad faith. While *Funny Face* inflects this existential dilemma through a middle-class American domesticity at odds with Sartre's thought, both share complementing positions on an intellectual spectrum regarding the self and its authentic state of being. By the mid-1950s, existentialism had therefore been repurposed in Hollywood as a widely marketable—if not foreign and fraught—cultural signifier.

While one route for the arrival of existentialism came through the popular press and the postwar culture industry, there was also a coterie of intellectuals, writers, and artists based mainly in New York who adapted the thought of Sartre, Camus, and de Beauvoir during the years immediately following the Second World War.[61] This group was so successful in their advocacy that existentialist sensibilities began to flower among intellectuals and writers outside the New York scene by the last two years of the decade. As Cotkin notes, Ellison and Wright were among these initial advocates who insisted on the applicability of existentialism to the exigencies of the postwar moment.[62] During the summer months of 1945, Ellison discovered synopses and then translated works by Sartre, Camus, and de Beauvoir, although he had previously encountered the writers whom the existentialists considered their predecessors: Søren Kierkegaard, Dostoevsky, and Nietzsche. In 1945, Ellison wrote to Wright that the contemporary French existentialists "view the role of the individual in relation to society so sharply that the leftwing boys, with the possible exception of Malraux, seemed to have looked at it through the reverse end of a telescope."[63]

Ellison and Wright weren't alone. Another of existentialism's early advocates was the co-editor of *Partisan Review*, William Barrett, who wrote frequent apologias for the legitimacy of Sartre and his compatriots. (Another principal figure in the *Partisan Review*, Philip Rahv, will be important to the history mapped in chapter 3.) The French philosopher-poet, Jean Wahl, like-wise disseminated the intellectual outline of existentialism in the *New Republic* in 1945.[64] Wahl continued to promote existentialism through dozens of articles and in philosophy courses at the University of Chicago. Existentialism was widely discussed in the early postwar years through a variety of popular media and well-circulated magazines, including *Time* and the *New York Times*.[65] Even the influential theologians Karl Barth and Paul Tillich turned to the writings of Heidegger and Sartre.[66]

The intellectual status of existentialism among academic philosophers was more uneven. Jacques Barzun, for instance, wrote often about Sartre's work, although with modulated enthusiasm and few academic interlocutors.[67] Ann Fulton argues that American academic philosophers were even hesitant to consider, much less embrace, Sartrean existentialism during the 1940s.[68] Part of the reason, Fulton shows, was the slow translation of Sartre's more technical works. Fulton also suggests that influential academics like Sidney Hook disparaged Sartre's work because of his blending of existentialism and Marxism—a period in Sartre's career that was only later translated for American readers.[69] More importantly, though, the rising tide of existentialism in Europe was coterminous with the emerging hegemony of the analytic tradi-tion within American philosophy departments: the two modes of philosophy were thought to be at odds because of their disparate methodologies and concerns.[70] According to American academics, Sartre's work lacked "a solid philosophical structure," an insufficient rigor that undermines whatever nonacademic intellectuals found appealing about his thought.[71] Nonetheless, Fulton shows that by 1952, Sartre's "emphasis on individual freedom, per-sonal responsibility, and authenticity" had garnered some intellectual trac-tion even among many academic philosophers.[72] Therefore, a swath of public figures, Hollywood producers, scholars, writers, and mainstream magazines discussed Sartre's "radical liberty," in which "authenticity was the result of awareness of individual freedom to create values."[73]

These ideas about freedom and authenticity were new wine in liberalism's old wineskins. They imagined the self as the center of gravity for American virtues. Of course, summarizing, contemplating, and debating existentialism doesn't amount to embracing it. Yet, as the critic Stark Young said after the 1946 American premiere of Sartre's play *No Exit*, "It should be seen whether you like it or not."[74] The postwar circulation of existentialism was, in other words, a marker of an emerging felt sensibility, the legitimation of a structure of feeling and thought among other intellectual tastes.

Poverty, the Great Depression, and an Existential America

While the translation of existentialism informed the idiom of postwar American political culture, such a structure of thought and feeling was far from homogenous. The trajectory of Wright's career suggests one form of this heterogeneous emerging sentiment, and Ellison suggests another. The forms represented by Ellison and *Funny Face* elevated an ethics of authenticity within postwar intellectual life. However, those new sensibilities also engendered a cultural feedback loop that, in turn, devalued the currency of the literary style of urban realism on the grounds of its supposedly inadequate treatment of the human condition.

Ann Petry's work is a case in point. Unlike Wright, Petry remained in the United States while sustaining a long-term commitment to the literary left. During the mid-1940s, Petry published her first book, a bestselling novel entitled *The Street* (1946), which intervenes in the tradition of urban realism and employs the analytical categories of progressive politics.[75] *The Street* chronicles the difficulties of a single, black mother, Lutie Johnson, who tries to raise her son in Harlem. Yet poverty, an obsessive neighbor, and Lutie's violent sexualization make their everyday lives nearly unendurable. At the beginning of the novel, Johnson leaves her domestic work for a wealthy family in Connecticut to pursue independent economic security in Harlem. When Lutie contemplates renting an apartment in one tenement, she ironically thinks to herself, "If she were a landlord, she'd rent out the hallways. It would make it so much more entertaining for the tenants."[76] The Harlem housing project provokes her indignation at the tenement's slumlordship. As Heather Hicks argues, the scene also emblematizes the novelist's self-scrutiny by drawing on the tropes of urban realism: "Petry seems to ask whether, in her attempt to dramatize the traumas of racism and segregation, she is actually exploiting those she wishes to champion, turning the intimate dramas of their lives into a public spectacle for her own gain."[77] In this reading, Petry's novel takes realism as a "spectacle" mirroring the socioeconomic difficulties of the tenement project.

Petry's awareness of the hazards of transforming the subjects of imaginative narrative into its exploited objects surfaces in the treatment Lutie Johnson receives from the other occupants of the tenement and 116th Street. Several men view Lutie as a sexualized object, and in fact the tenement super, Jones, persuades her son Bub to agree to steal mail in an effort to get closer to Lutie. Bub agrees because he reasons that the stolen money might help his mother, but he is caught and sent to a children's shelter. Problems compound as a neighbor named Boots also tries to assault Lutie. Amounting to a kind of twisted culmination of her housecleaning work in a wealthy home, Lutie kills Boots in self-defense with a candlestick. It's as if the conditions placed upon her labor elicits a mirroring form of violence. To avoid being arrested for the murder, Lutie flees Harlem to start a new life, leaving behind a son she cannot hope to save and an urban environment that swallows any opportunity for autonomy or freedom.

Petry's novel not only attends to the material conditions of Lutie's poverty but also presents her attempts to work as undermined by social structures that privilege capital production and distort or alienate her labor. As Bill Mullen argues, Lutie herself becomes a fetishized "object of capital" in the imagination of the super Jones and other characters like Junto and Mrs. Hedges. As a sexual object for exchange, *The Street* depicts women such as Lutie mired in class- and race-based alienation to such a degree that their capacity for labor is "mystified" and "erased."[78] This is a very different view of alienation from the existentialist one Ellison presents six years later. Indeed, in contrast to the invisible man's hibernation, Petry's *The Street* suggests that the atomizing effects of modern society provide far fewer existential opportunities than threats to the material conditions of the black lives on its margins. In other words, the difference between Petry's and Ellison's novels is that *The Street* defines alienation in the raced and gendered terms of class consciousness, while Ellison glosses estrangement in the humanistic, universalizing, and interior terms of existentialism.

The urban realism of Petry's bestseller turns on the representational norms of other Progressive era fiction that looks for American vices and virtues among laborers, migrants, and the poor. Indeed, the novel's first readers compared it favorably to Wright's *Native Son*, particularly as the structural conditions tyrannizing the protagonists in both novels seemingly precipitate their acts of violence. Changing literary tastes during the late 1940s would, however, subordinate social and urban realism to other representational modes—a literary-historical shift that I consider in relation to the "decline" of naturalism in chapter 3. But the constriction of postwar political sentiment and their entangled shifts in literary tastes are also apparent in the contrast between Petry's analysis of economic suffering and a prominent novel published seven years later, Saul Bellow's *The Adventures of Augie March* (1953). Bellow's National Book Award–winning novel follows the roving Augie March, a poor Jewish boy who, as one of his lovers puts it, is among "the kind of people other people are always trying to fit into their schemes."[79] Attempts to enlist Augie in idiosyncratic ventures, financial stratagems, and social ladder climbing provide the only real strand of narrative continuity across March's otherwise desultory recollections.

Augie March was Bellow's third novel, but its concatenation of episodic relationships and its more verbally expressive idiom break with the sedated and explicitly philosophical forms of his earlier fiction. Bellow's first novel, *Dangling*

Man (1944), imitates in rote fashion the patterns established by the European philosophical novel. As James Atlas explains, "*Dangling Man* bore the marks of an apprentice work: It was slight—less than two hundred pages—derivative of the existential, European, 'literary' novel that was then in vogue, and nearly plotless."[80] This philosophically programmatic quality is epitomized in the acknowledgment of the novel's everyman protagonist, Joseph, who confesses, "I am unwilling to admit that I do not know how to use my freedom and have to embrace the flunkydom of a job because I have no resources—in a word, no character."[81] Joseph's revelation climaxes at this self-deprecating whimper.

Not unlike Augie, Bellow looked to a series of philosophical chiefs and leaders as a young intellectual, including a pilgrimage to Mexico where the young writer arrived at Leon Trotsky's home on the day of his assassination.[82] However, the "derivative" style of *Dangling Man*, as Atlas explains, came from Bellow's early engagement with existential thought. It is true, as his biographers often note, that Bellow's appraisal of the leading French existentialists became more reluctant after he met Sartre and de Beauvoir in Paris following the war. Bellow's decision to distance himself from the existential fervor of *Dangling Man* derived in part from what he understood to be the French philosophers' armchair pro-communism and contemptuous anti-American rhetoric. William Phillips expressed the reservations among intellectuals like Bellow when he said with heavy irony: "Simone de Beauvoir knew, as any educated Marxist knew, that America was in the death throes of the class struggle and that Russia and the eastern Communist countries represented the forces and hopes of man's liberation."[83] The arrogance of this formulaic view was, according to Bellow, a recipe for alienation and misunderstanding. In response, he began to think existentially without the political banister provided by the existentialist masters. *Augie March* in many ways represents this attempt to annex some domain of existential thought while revising the European commitment to forms of social democracy.

Augie grows up in Chicago as the shock of the Great Depression reverberates throughout the country, but the economic crisis only exacerbates the "destiny molders, and heavy-water brains, Machiavellis and wizard evildoers, big-wheels and imposers-upon" (572). The book's catena of manipulators provides the principal source of narrative continuity, but these "imposers-upon" also represent the threat underwriting Augie's political sensibilities. For example, Augie describes those who wish him to conform to their schemes as "absolutists" (572). Augie's choice of description indicates his persistent association of conformity with tyranny, collective enterprise with the impulse underlying political absolutism. From his brother Simon to the seedy entrepreneur Einhorn, from a job as an organizer for the CIO to his eagle-taming lover Thea, Augie allows himself to be recruited into what he views as second-rate endeavors. Yet he escapes both the mundane and high-political "imposers-upon" in a way not unlike another paradigmatic picaresque hero, Huck Finn, who lights out for uncharted territory because Aunt Sally wants to adopt and "sivilize" him. Unlike Huck, however, Augie gives a more explicitly political cast to the turn away from the "Machiavellis" who wish to acquire power, money, or some other form of satisfaction by integrating him into their schemes.

The political sentiment in *Augie March* informs the novel's framing of the economic disaster of the Depression, yet in ways that may initially appear to be at odds with existential sensibilities. In particular, Augie's treatment of the Depression relies heavily on the notion of "fate," which seems to imply that he and the other characters experience economic disaster on a largely inexplicable, mythic level that, as he explains by reference to Heraclitus, is representative of "a man's character" (1). In *Grapes of Wrath*, Steinbeck also registered the Depression on a mythic scale; however, as I argued in the introduction, Steinbeck's earlier novel imagines a secular community born out of the national economic crisis—a community that, much like Rose of Sharon, provides for the welfare of its nameless poor and needy. Augie's mythic category of "fate," in contrast, builds its stage with the materials of existential crisis, on the one hand, and long-standing American ideas about merit, on the other hand. For example, following his opening reference to Heraclitus and "fate," Augie explains, "in the end there isn't any way to disguise the nature of the knocks by acoustical work on the door or gloving the knuckles" (1). The vernacular clothing of this sentiment dresses up Augie's idea that the "knocks" of fate cannot be assuaged through abstract rationalizations of those calamities ("gloving the knuckles"). Instead, suffering reveals the quality of one's inner life, for even the veneer we present to others ("acoustical work on the door") is an inadequate way to mitigate what fate reveals about the self. Mimi, Augie's neighbor and close friend, puts the point in this way when describing the Depression era losses of Einhorn: "Why should it be any different for Einhorn than for the Poles or sausage-eaters on his street? It would be bad if it were different and helped the old fool to put it over that he was entitled to a better fate than anybody around. But when the things that happen pour over everyone alike, then we can *really* see who is better and who's worse" (325–26). Collective suffering becomes intelligible only on the level of personal character.

This presentation of economic crisis in *Augie March* vivifies the relation between the rise of an American idiom of existentialism and the constriction of political sentiment beginning in the 1940s. After Thea and Augie part ways, he suggests that shared lived conditions most often prompt human beings to present grand but false versions of themselves: "External life being so mighty, the instruments so huge and terrible, the performances so great, the thoughts so great and threatening, you produce a someone who can exist before it. You invent a man who can stand before the terrible appearances" (437). Augie acknowledges that "externals" exert a certain weight upon the life of the self, but he decries the fact that so often these "terrible appearances"—the phenomena of the world that underwrite anxiety and suffering—force the self to "appear better and stronger than anyone else." He claims that the results of self-invention are sweeping and deleterious: "All this time nothing genuine is allowed to appear and nobody knows what's real. And that's disfigured, degenerate, dark mankind—mere humanity" (437). Augie says that external conditions create the stage for inauthenticity, as if the world manipulates or distorts the provenance for "genuine" versions of the real—the inner life of the self—and thus gives rise to "mere humanity." Augie instead looks for a higher plane of being, a more thoroughgoing reality, which facilitates self-invention not tainted by the false appearances of social existence and created pseudo-realities.

Even as Augie looks for a more thoroughgoing reality rooted in the life of the self, he extends that longing into the domain of political sentiment: "And this is what mere humanity always does," he laments. "It's made up of these inventors or artists, millions and millions of them, each in his own way trying to recruit other people to play a supporting role and sustain him in his make-believe. The great chiefs and leaders recruit the greatest number, and that's what their power is" (437). When leaders invent "the world itself," they construe others as means ("a supporting role") rather than as ends in themselves (437). This denigration of others is the dark side of human self-invention, which initially seems to distinguish *Augie March* from the existential sensibilities of *Invisible Man*, as well as from the varieties of aestheticism that I charted in the first chapter. The aestheticism of Nabokov's fiction, for instance, valorizes an image of the self as the artist of its own pleasure and meaning—an image that would ostensibly fall prey to Augie's worry regarding political tyranny.

However, Augie's revelation is not so much a repudiation of these sentiments as it is a qualified affirmation akin to *Lolita*. Both Nabokov and Bellow's novels concede that an aestheticized understanding of the self pairs quite well with tyranny—with "trying to recruit other people to play a supporting role" in one scheme or another. But if self-invention shares an impulse with the mass conformity demanded by totalitarianism, *Augie March* and *Lolita* also take elements of the disease to create a vaccine against it. In particular, Augie answers his lament about the "power" of the "great chiefs and leaders" by reverting to another form of self-invention. His antidote to tyranny is to qualify self-invention through a desultory, nearly atomistic form of freedom. Be the author of the self, but don't stay put while doing it—that's Augie's version of democratic freedom.

Augie articulates this view of democratic virtue by drawing out contrasts with the "power" of tyrannical chiefs and leaders. He says, "I certainly looked like an ideal recruit. But the invented things never became real for me no matter how I urged myself to think they were" (437). Augie says that the inventions of others are contingent, rather than permanent, and thus they do not hold ineluctable power over him. Instead, he explains that his "real fault was that I couldn't stay with my purest feelings" (437). The existential idea of the "world" as a construct leads Augie to conclude that the answer to conformity and tyranny is attention to the life of the self (staying with one's "purest feelings"). To know and pursue one's "chosen thing" is difficult, but Augie says it's a prerequisite for not being subject to the inventions of others (438).

Augie's commitment to a life of impermanence preempts those who wish to make him a "recruit." Indeed, Bellow's use of the literary style of the picaresque—the novel's rambling and episodic form—provides a formal corollary to this account of democratic freedom. Sean McCann argues that *Augie March* contributes to a common postwar literary project to imagine alternatives to the narrative conventions of social realism. More than a cloistered literary project, McCann situates *Augie March* within the literary vanguard's contrast between an emerging "spontaneous form of writing" and "the brute hand of the state."[84] If tyranny in Europe and a consensus culture in the United States demand certain established scripts, Bellow turned to spontaneity and impermanence as countervailing virtues. Therefore, while the narrative mobility afforded by the picaresque offered an antidote to cultural and political conformity, the novel's desultory and decentered episodes are illustrative of an underlying ethic. As Augie acknowledges, "I was eternally looking for a way out," and he avows that just as another's "construction around me was nearly complete I shoved off" (378, 163). These pivots in the narrative away from the schemes of Einhorn, the Renlings, Simon, and others come together to sanction in concert the virtues of impermanent affiliations and transitory freedom—a realization that slowly dawns on Augie across the narrative. Augie's mobility tempers the hazards of self-invention with a liberal commitment to shove off, to leave others to their own inventions.

Augie extends this idea about roving freedom to more explicitly political topics after, for example, an eagle named Caligula harms him. Augie immerses himself in an anthology of political philosophy, "a big book of utopias" (391). Augie's "utopia book" is not merely episodic; it signals an aspiration in *The Adventures of Augie March*. Augie wants to imagine a better state of things through sheer verbal power, which he conveys yet again when he travels among the battlefields of postwar Western Europe at the end of the novel: "Look at me, going everywhere! Why," he muses, "I am a sort of Columbus of those near-at-hand and believe you can come to them in this immediate terra incognita that spreads out in every gaze" (586). Augie's transience draws on the founding moment of the American colonies to sanction his roving life in war-torn Europe: despite his earlier hesitancy regarding types, he becomes "a sort of Columbus," a wanderer and discoverer of new terrain. But his melding of national identity and the vernacular commitment to "go at things as I have taught myself, free-style" authorizes a specific political sensibility (1). As McCann explains, "Bellow positions the vigor of literary imagination against the bureaucratic impositions of social democracy."[85] Augie's invocation of Columbus to explain his final wanderings differ from the organizational habits of a bureaucratic state in the sense that they provide examples of those who assert their being—those who seize existence. As a result, Augie can at once reject programmatic scripts *and* affirm a national identity, as long as the latter is construed in terms of an existential habit of mind, an aspiration to "wrestle the great fear to win a right to exist" (438). As Augie presents it, America becomes the space for existential possibility.

Bellow's existential view of America uses liberal political sentiment to frame social-democratic institutions as hazards to the authentic life of the self. In contrast to the many alienating organizations and associations of their novels, Ellison's and Bellow's work take the authentic life of the self as the provenance for democratic freedom and political action. The very terms for American liberal democracy have thus been transformed. In Carlos Bulosan's earlier vision in "Freedom from Want," he says, "The America we hope to see is not merely a physical but also a spiritual and an intellectual world." But Bulosan's vision tethers a national imaginary to the equality afforded to immigrants and the protections against poverty: "We are the mirror of what America is," Bulosan explains. "If America wants us to be living and free, then we must be living and free. If we fail, then America fails."[86] As opposed to Bulosan's construal of American freedom as support for immigrants, institutions that secure economic equality, and a national commitment to justice, the gloss on freedom in *Augie March* traces a history of the coupling of impermanence and the possibilities of self-invention.[87] "America" and its freedoms become an existential habit of mind, and the notion of authenticity moves into the moral center of democratic virtue.

3 }

The Age of Anxiety

EXISTENTIAL PSYCHOLOGY AND
THE "DECLINE" OF AMERICAN NATURALISM

Theodore Schiebelhut, the independently wealthy painter in Patricia Highsmith's *A Game for the Living*, has difficulty explaining why "all his conscious ideas were those of a pessimist." Theodore insists that his bleak outlook has "no causes that he or anybody else could discover." Conventional psychological explanations—such as his family or sexual history—do not apply in his case. Rather, Theodore at first believes his pessimism is a function of an abstract philosophical commitment to the notion that "the world had no meaning, no end but nothingness, and that man's achievements were all finally perishable—cosmic jokes, like man himself."[1] When Theodore discovers that his lover, Lelia Ballesteros, has been sexually assaulted, murdered, and mutilated, his abstract pessimism is confronted with the violent realities of a senseless world. The murderer is Carlos Hidalgo, an alcoholic friend who becomes infatuated with Lelia. The meaninglessness of the trauma confirms Theodore's pessimism, but he also finds himself driven to make sense of this senselessness according to what his friend Ramón characterizes as an "Existentialist's conscience" (76). Theodore's search for the murderer of his lover is driven less by a demand for moral order than by the vicissitudes and private exigencies of his psyche. Highsmith thus presents detective fiction as a stage for existentialist angst.

Much like Theodore's attempts to navigate an often-hostile world by drawing on the philosophical resources of existentialism, Patricia Highsmith's novels from the 1950s bear the imprint of the flourishing of American existentialist thought during the postwar era. However, in a way that differs from Ellison, Bellow, and Mailer, Highsmith's fiction blends existentialist sensibilities about choice, angst, and authenticity with another prominent postwar development: what Nathan Hale characterizes as psychoanalysis's "golden age of popularization" in the United States.[2] Highsmith's novels from the decade—particularly her widely read *Strangers on a Train* (1950) and *The*

Talented Mr. Ripley (1956)—explore these entwined intellectual threads, which I argue helped redefine the wider political culture of the postwar moment. In particular, this chapter charts the nascent development of the existential psychology movement and, more broadly, the normalization of therapeutic psychology following the Second World War. The growing public purchase of these developments had significant consequences for American public life: in effect, the ego and its vicissitudes—rather than socioeconomic or environmental conditions—became the normative template for understanding society and the self. Highsmith's novels helped shape this intellectual terrain by representing public phenomena such as violence, class envy, and social alienation as existential crises of an embattled private realm.

In her construal of the darker phenomena of human experience, Highsmith distinguishes her work from the literary naturalists who dominated the American cultural scene of the 1930s and early 1940s. In fact, Highsmith frequently adapts and revises certain tropes of the naturalists in order to repudiate a narrative world governed principally by structural, socioeconomic, and environmental conditions. Highsmith's revisionist project reinforces a prevalent assertion of the "decline" of naturalism by postwar intellectuals, who hail instead a new cultural order focused on the interior life of the self. Indeed, the temporary deflation in literary naturalism's cultural authority—a phenomenon I trace through the work of intellectuals such as Philip Rahv and the influential *Partisan Review*—is a marker of the growing public currency of psychological templates for understanding society. I demonstrate that this trend was a central feature of a wider crisis in the intellectual legitimacy of the American welfare state during the 1950s. As the cultural fortunes of naturalism declined, existentialism and a spectrum of therapeutic psychologies flourished, and one consequence of these shifts was that violence and class conflict were increasingly construed as phenomena of the largely autonomous arena of the psyche. These trends in American cultural history helped erode the intellectual grounds for an activist-managerial state, which was predicated on intervening in structural conditions for the welfare of its citizens.

Psychoanalysis, the Professionalization of Therapy, and Their Discontents

The "age of anxiety"—a phrase whose wider circulation begins with W. H. Auden's book-length poem, *The Age of Anxiety* (1947)—is the child of converging historical phenomena and intellectual sensibilities.[3] Beyond the emerging nuclear threats of the postwar era, the anxious *zeitgeist* of the early Cold War is entangled with both the popularization and professionalization of psychological discourse in the United States. Psychology took its first steps toward becoming a formalized discipline in the United States through the work of William James whose two-volume *The Principles of Psychology* (1890) and popular undergraduate courses at Harvard helped institutionalize the field. However, psychology as an object of inquiry existed in less formalized ways long before the late nineteenth century. The roots of American "psychological" fiction reach at least as far back as Edgar Allan Poe's tales from the 1830s and 1840s. (What might be called "psychological" fiction has an even longer history in Europe.) Yet, unlike these earlier varieties of psychological experience, the postwar decades saw an unprecedented expansion in the use of personal trauma and formal mental categories as explanatory mechanisms for everyday experience. Tics, dreams, and banal sensations became markers of unconscious activity on an unprecedented scale. The psychological mapping of ordinary life became part of the common American vocabulary and, as such, normative for public thought and behavior.

One strain of this expansion began when Sigmund Freud visited the United States in 1909. American writers and intellectuals were familiar with Freud not long after the turn of the century, yet his lectures at Clark University were the first time the American media reported on his theories.[4] The year before his visit, Freud's followers met in Salzburg, Austria, to convene the first International Psychoanalytic Congress. Among the small group were a New York–based clinician, Abraham Brill, and Ernest Jones, a neurologist and clinician in London. After the Congress, Brill and Jones began to spread Freud's work throughout the English-speaking world. Jones, in partnership with another early Freudian, the Harvard neurologist and psychologist James Jackson Putnam, eventually founded the American Psychoanalytic Association in 1911. In that same year Brill would also found the New York Psychoanalytic Society.[5] Before these organizations came together, Jones had led efforts to disseminate Freud's work among academics and members of the American medical establishment, playing an important part in the decision of G. Stanley Hall, a psychologist and president of Clark University, to invite Freud to give five lectures in September 1909. Freud called this event "the first official recognition of our endeavors," particularly because he was met with an audience much more open to his theories than he had yet experienced in Europe.[6] The usually staid local press reported accurately, albeit succinctly, Freud's controversial theories about sexuality. The coverage was likely a result of the fact that the event itself was a who's who of intellectuals on the subject.[7] Even a suspicious William James was in attendance.

Freud's visit became the germ for psychological questions later coming to the forefront of the American cultural imagination. However, that spread was initially slow and confined to an intellectual coterie. "In the 1920s and 1930s," John Burnham explains, "psychoanalysis spread among special parts of the population, frequently in forms that Freud and other purists disdained."[8] As a comprehensive psychological theory of everyday life—tics and slips, dreams and private wishes—psychoanalysis was confined to a relatively small group of therapists and authors. Dorothy Ross argues that the members of this group were, first and foremost, advocates of modernism. This dual interest in modernism and Freud makes sense, according to Ross, because modernism itself was "a set of ideas and works of art . . . that revolved around the exploration of subjectivity."[9] Even as Freud was one of the first to chart our interior lives, modernism, at least according to its initial reception in the United States, explored the tortured beauty, ambivalence, and isolation of modern consciousness. But beyond the movement's anxieties, modernists like Mann, Joyce, and Kafka garnered such currency in the postwar moment because, as Irving Howe put it, their sensibilities gravitate toward "the one uniquely modern style of salvation: a salvation by, of, and for the self."[10]

Other advocates of Freud by-way-of-modernism included Lionel Trilling and Herbert Marcuse, Betty Friedan and Daniel Bell, Erik Erikson and Philip Rahv. This motley congregation insisted upon Freud's importance not only to their academic counterparts but also to an educated middle-class public. Furthermore, these advocates had a political motive for their interest in a science and literature of subjectivity because, according to Ross, they had "turned inward, away from their destroyed Marxist hopes of the 1930s to wartime nationalism and a chastened Cold War liberalism."[11] Thus, as modernism became staple fare for critics, public intellectuals, and the classrooms of American universities, the broad strokes of psychoanalysis likewise became entrenched in US intellectual life. While these strokes were variously presented and unevenly received, the impulse to analyze common behavior for its psychological import garnered an unprecedented public currency.

From the germ of Freud's visit to the legitimacy cultured by modernists and intellectuals, American psychoanalysis grew into a mature and widespread intellectual movement during the 1950s and early 1960s. As Burnham explains, it was during this moment "that Freud's ideas exerted the greatest influence on American culture."[12] Some of the key terms of psychoanalysis became commonplace—albeit often disputed—among the middle and upper classes. For example, seizing upon psychoanalysis's new public currency, Frank Wheeler declares in Richard Yates's *Revolutionary Road* (1961):

> This country's probably the psychiatric, psychoanalytical capital of the world. Old Freud himself could never've dreamed up a more devoted bunch of disciples than the population of the United States—isn't that right? Our whole damn culture is geared to it; it's the new religion; it's everybody's intellectual and spiritual sugar-tit.[13]

This hyperbolic condemnation of the consensus surrounding psychoanalysis operates as a way for Frank to shore himself up against his rage at suburban existence. Frank's discontentment with having ended up in suburbia rather than a wider and ostensibly more important world prompts him to turn against this middle-class form of life. Yet his disavowal is deeply ironic in the sense that, even in the private motivations of his war against Freud's theories of the ego, Frank confirms the status of those theories as an explanatory template for his own behavior. When Frank finishes his diatribe, his wife and friends "looked mildly relieved, like pupils at the end of a lecture."[14] Not finding their customary assent to his outbursts, Frank withdraws to the kitchen. It becomes apparent that his anti-mainstream rebellion is a function of his ego, and the sad irony of the episode is that even dissent against the privileged status of psychoanalysis is rooted within an internal, private arena. There is even a psychological explanation, Yates suggests, for the rejection of psychoanalysis.

The road leading to Frank's malaise had been paved during the previous decade, when psychological discourse had acquired such mass appeal that it comprised a central current of American popular culture. In an age when the American television industry enjoyed rapidly expanding and largely consolidated audiences, programming often drew heavily on psychological discourse when featuring violence or socially aberrant behavior.[15] This fact is clearest in one of the most popular shows of the 1950s, *Alfred Hitchcock Presents* (1955–1965). The series was created to ride the coat-tails of Hitchcock's successful films, such as *Rope* (1948) and *Dial M for Murder* (1954), as well as his adaptation of Highsmith's *Strangers on a Train* (1951). Whatever his inheritance from psychoanalysis—the film *Spellbound* (1945) features a character who undergoes treatment by a psychoanalyst, but Freud's precise influence on the famous director is still an open question—Hitchcock's work pushed questions of individual psychology and the irregular and supposedly aberrant dimensions of the human psyche to the forefront of American cultural attention.[16]

Almost every episode of *Alfred Hitchcock Presents* explores some form of violence, framing this trauma through a psychological lens. For example, the first episode of the series, as Hitchcock puts it during his introduction, is a story about "ordinary folk": a middle-class husband, Carl Span, who is an engineer at an aircraft plant, and his wife, Elsa, a former ballerina who has recently suffered from a "small breakdown."[17] Carl, a figure of the working professional, has taken Elsa to a new town for "fresh air" and to recover from her psychological troubles. After settling into a small trailer park, Carl leaves for his first day of work. Not long after he departs, Elsa is attacked by a man in a "gray suit" who, she enigmatically explains, "killed me." Elsa experiences something like a fugue after the trauma—a loss of personality in which her self ("me") is for all practical purposes destroyed. She becomes nonresponsive, her blank face staring aimlessly at the ceiling. A doctor visits Elsa, and he explains to Carl: "I don't think her condition is too serious, physically that is, Mr. Span. Otherwise, well, she's been through a very emotional shock. And coming so soon after the breakdown—well, I can't tell you anything for certain." Questioning Elsa about the episode, the doctor explains, could result in "permanent damage." After Carl moves her to yet another town, Elsa identifies an ordinary-looking man in a gray suit as her attacker. Carl follows the man into a hotel room and murders him with a pipe. Afterward, Elsa repeatedly identifies other men in gray suits as her attacker, and Carl soon realizes that he has killed an innocent person.

This episode of *Alfred Hitchcock Presents* locates Elsa's trauma within middle-class society—a democratization of psychological experience that would become the norm for the series. Carl and Elsa are not members of the intelligentsia or upper class; they are not cloistered from the working or professional world. Rather, the nuances of psychological analysis map onto their middle-class experience. Beyond the actual settings of the episodes, this democratization of individual psychology is also evident in Hitchcock's distinctive filmic technique of using the camera's point of view to create a voyeuristic relationship between the viewer and certain characters. The technique allows the viewer to imagine herself in the episode, as if the consumer viewing the trauma were also its experiential subject. Hitchcock's nearly obsessive close-up of faces similarly places an emphasis on the individual emotional responses of characters. The audience *becomes* Elsa, or *feels* Carl's nauseous recognition that he has murdered an innocent businessman. The viewer is thus invited to employ Elsa's "emotional shock," her psychological trauma, when riding along Main Street at the end of the episode.

Another effect of these filmic techniques is to normalize the fact of psychological "deviance." For example, by putting one's self in Elsa's place, any man wearing a gray business suit becomes the attacker. This attire, as Sloan Wilson's 1955 novel employs it when describing the world of Tom Rath, is the trademark of the organized business community. In Hitchcock's turn on this professional signifier, sociopaths are not confined to the fringes of society; instead, violence is latent within the American Everyman. Hitchcock's series thus construes both the act of murder and Elsa's trauma as darker manifestations of the human condition. Although *Alfred Hitchcock Presents* is occasionally attentive to economic markers—for example, the attacker's professional status, or the fact that Carl and Elsa live in a trailer park—the television series nonetheless invites viewers to understand the trauma as a distinctively psychological phenomenon, a feature of human consciousness as such, rather than as an abstract case of abnormal or elitist psychology.[18]

Hitchcock's series further represents the extent to which psychological experience and the symptoms of internalized trauma had become a widely marketable template within the postwar entertainment industry. Recognizing the mass appeal of Hitchcock's earlier films, the television series was first conceived by an advertising agency and pitched *to* Hitchcock.[19] The agency's intuition paid off, because *Alfred Hitchcock Presents* began as one of the most consistently popular programs during a time when the audience size for television was growing but the options for channels and programming were relatively consolidated.[20] Psychological programs were never as successful as, say, *The $64,000 Question*, which aired on CBS in 1955 and was the top-viewed program on US television.

However, given its longevity and popularity on a primetime slot, Hitchcock's program became a touchstone for subsequent film and television.[21]

Highsmith and the Psychology of Abnormal Behavior

While *Alfred Hitchcock Presents* marks the democratization and mass-market appeal of psychological templates for understanding everyday experience, Highsmith's relationship to these cultural developments signals the heterogeneous threads weaving throughout the fabric of postwar intellectual life. The effects of psychoanalysis were never linear. So, while the tropes of psychoanalysis were becoming household ideas through film and television, Highsmith, like many of her contemporaries, never became an orthodox Freudian. Her fascination with modern psychology began when she was eight years old. In a 1989 interview, Highsmith says that as a child she studied Karl Menninger's *The Human Mind*: "They're case histories of crackpots, sadists, murderers, and other nuts," she explained, "but it's like reading Edgar Allan Poe."[22] This precocious reading inaugurated Highsmith's lifelong interest in the grotesque and psychologically "abnormal."[23]

Highsmith began studying Freud as an eighteen-year-old not long after discovering Karl Marx's writings and enlisting in the Youth Communist League. Highsmith quickly became suspicious of both Marxism and American psychoanalysis, eventually resigning from the League in 1941 after two years of membership. Her suspicions of psychoanalysis, on the other hand, were slow to calcify and never led to the same kind of radical break as with the Communist Party. In 1943, for example, she wrote in her diary, "The highest good is the use of the subconscious mind entirely, almost to the exclusion of the conscious mind, which is patterned after those around us. Within the subconscious lies all one's oil, one's fire, one's flavor, and the measure of divinity allotted to all of us."[24] Although Highsmith would question certain dimensions of her youthful enthusiasms in later works such as *Edith's Diary* (1977), she never broke with Freud's notion of the unconscious, which he insists is autonomous from and prior to the rational mental states and conformist impulses of everyday life.

Still, Highsmith became discontented with psychoanalysis when she underwent therapy in 1948 with the New York psychoanalyst Eva Klein Lipshutz. Highsmith decided to attend this course of therapy to "cure" the disgust she felt during sexual experiences with her fiancé, Marc Brandel. In effect, she wanted to become heterosexual, despite her abiding same-sex desires. American psychoanalysts, to an even greater degree than Freud, tended to pathologize same-sex relationships during the postwar decades. While Americans had become accustomed to visiting a therapist about such putatively abnormal behavior, psychoanalysis for the "non-aberrant" had also become commonplace in urban centers. In *Freud and the Crisis of Our Culture* (1955), Lionel Trilling wrote that psychoanalysis had become "an integral part of our modern intellectual apparatus."[25] Anatole Broyard similarly recounts that there was in New York "an inevitability about psychoanalysis. It was like having to take the subway to get anywhere. Psychoanalysis was in the air, like humidity, or smoke." Broyard offers many reasons for this seemingly pervasive experience, including the idea that the "war had been a bad dream that we wanted to analyze now. . . . There was a feeling that we had forgotten how to live."[26] Highsmith's decision to visit a psychoanalyst was part of the ethic of this moment: private therapy had become integral to the behavior of many postwar Americans.

Yet her therapist's view of lesbianism as a mental illness was never convincing to Highsmith. Lipshutz's diagnosis was, in effect, that Highsmith's same-sex desires derived from her strained relationship with her mother: her sexuality paradoxically proved that she hated women. This formulaic causality failed to convince Highsmith, and she began writing what has become known as her "lesbian novel with a happy ending," *The Price of Salt* (1953), during her sessions with the psychoanalyst.[27] In May 1949 after forty-seven therapy sessions, Highsmith determined that her sexual aversion to men was unchanging and, leaving on a European tour, she never again trusted conventional psychoanalytic therapy.

Highsmith wrote *Strangers on a Train* before these abortive attempts to cure her same-sex desires. She learned a few days before her last session of therapy that Harper & Brothers had agreed to publish the book. Despite the uncertainties that marked her life during the years preceding her first novel's publication, Highsmith found a philosophical anchor for *Strangers on a Train* in European existentialism. Not unlike psychoanalysis, Highsmith was attracted to the nuanced accounts of human angst and the subversion of a rational construal of life that preoccupies this body of philosophy and literature. Highsmith began reading Dostoevsky as a thirteen-year-old, later reading several works by Franz Kafka in 1943 and Albert Camus's *L'Étranger* (1942) in 1946. Highsmith found that Kafka's work traced the lines of her own pessimism regarding the rationality of "God," "government," and "self," while the alienation of Camus's narrator Meursault inspired her to read the other canonical French existentialists—Sartre and de Beauvoir.[28] She read *Crime and Punishment* again in 1947, declaring that Dostoevsky was her "master," as she would also later say about Kierkegaard.[29]

This reading in European existentialism left an indelible impression on her work from the 1950s. For example, *Strangers on a Train* borrows Dostoevsky's technique in *Crime and Punishment* of depicting Raskolnikov's murder as more of a psychological phenomenon than a physical act. Murder and its attendant guilt similarly becomes an *idée fixe* for Highsmith's protagonist. At first, Guy Haines is beleaguered with guilt for the murder of his first wife, Miriam, by the wealthy sociopath Charles Bruno. By chance Guy meets Bruno on a train as they each are traveling to their respective homes. Both men disclose their frustration with others who inhibit their ambitions: Miriam is pregnant with another man's child and wants a divorce in order to marry her lover, Owen Markham, which seemingly injures Guy's professional prestige; similarly, Bruno's father has numerous affairs and also refuses to release his son's share of the inheritance from the mother's wealthy family. In response to these disclosures, Bruno proposes a "perfect murder" in which he and Guy commit the crime on the other's behalf. While Guy is disgusted by the proposition, he also finds Bruno strangely appealing, and the idea of violence becomes a recurring feature of his thoughts.

Mistaking Guy's reticence for the unconscious consent of a virtuous man, Bruno strangles Miriam and later compels Guy to fulfill his end of the agreement. As Bruno's pressure becomes heavy-handed and disturbing, the murder of a stranger becomes the governing center of Guy's psychological life. Based on Bruno's repeated letters detailing how his father might be murdered, Guy develops a clear mental image of the act. Much like Dostoevsky's Raskolnikov, Guy first imagines the murder:

> It would be so simple, as Bruno said, when the house was empty except for his father and the butler, and Guy knew the house more exactly than his home in Metcalf. . . . He must not let his mind go there again. That was exactly what Bruno wanted his mind to do. . . . But having been there once, it was easy for his mind to go there again. In the nights when he could not sleep, he enacted the murder, and it soothed him like a drug.[30]

Much like Raskolnikov's paradoxical disgust and fascination with Svidrigailov, a wealthy profligate, Guy is at once repelled by and finally feels bound to Bruno. In fact, after Bruno drunkenly (but perhaps intentionally) falls off Guy's boat, Guy risks his life by jumping into a tumultuous sea to save him. "Where was his friend," Guy asks himself, "his brother?" (263). The psychological about-face marks Guy's acknowledgment of the murderous other that is an intimate part of his self.

Guy's identification with Bruno is the first instance of a doubling technique that Highsmith would rely upon throughout her career. This technique signals the Gothic sensibilities that underwrite Highsmith's psychological realism: even ostensibly upright and socially responsible human beings not only have the capacity for evil but also a desire for it. In a moment of dire reflection, Guy recognizes the implications of the double lurking in the shadows of his psyche: "But love and hate, he thought now, good and evil, lived side by side in the human heart, and not merely in differing proportions in one man and the next, but all good and all evil" (180). He construes evil as a product of the self, as an internal proclivity distinct from materialist explanations or external influences. Guy perceives that this internal provenance for evil—its borderless relationship to the good and its origins within the "heart," the psyche or soul—explains his contradictory emotional responses to Bruno: "And Bruno, he and

Bruno. Each was what the other had not chosen to be, the cast-off self, what he thought he hated but perhaps in reality loved" (180). Bruno is a "double" of Guy not because they are seemingly trapped within their own subjectivities—and would thus project the self onto another—but because the capacity for violence and evil is, according to the novel, a universal feature of the human condition. Guy admits as much when rationalizing his refusal to discard the revolver after murdering Bruno's father: "it was *his*, a part of himself, the third hand that had done the murder. It was himself at fifteen when he had bought it, himself when he had loved Miriam and had kept it in their room in Chicago, looking at it now and then in his most contented, most inward moments" (178). In fact, it's during these "inward moments" that the value of the weapon becomes most apparent. It is "[t]he best of himself," he explains, the apogee of his psychological life (178).

Guy's insistence that what passes as "evil" is *within* himself positions *Strangers on a Train* as the heir to a tradition of fiction that includes Poe, Charles Brockden Brown, and Horace Walpole. Yet, perhaps more tellingly, these sensibilities about evil also differ from the Judeo-Christian notion of humanity's total depravity. Guy's belief that the human heart is "all good and all evil" is related to but differs from that religious tradition in a way that recalls the existentialist proclamation of the death of God. The Hebrew prophet Jeremiah said that humanity's heart is "deceitful and desperately wicked" (17:9), while one psalmist bemoans the fact that "[n]one is righteous, no, not one; no one understands; no one seeks for God" (Psalm 14:3). Seizing upon such claims in Hebrew scripture, early Christians likewise insisted that all human beings "have turned aside" from divine law (Romans 3:12). According to these claims within the Judeo-Christian tradition, evil takes root inside the soul after humanity fails to meet the dictates of a divine order. Evil, in this sense, is a function of God's laws and humanity's fallible will.

In contrast to this tradition, Highsmith's early work is indebted to Nietzsche's moral philosophy, which questions the concepts of "good and evil" by identifying them as vestiges of a failed religio-philosophical system. According to Nietzsche, our basic moral categories are moored in the Judeo-Christian tradition but have persisted in the modern world after the "death of God," or the collapse of transcendental explanations for human existence and behavior.[31] Highsmith first encountered this view in 1939 when she read Nietzsche's autobiography *Ecce Homo* as an undergraduate at Barnard.[32] Highsmith was fascinated with the subversive quality of Nietzsche's philosophy: "I am not a man," he proclaims, "I am dynamite."[33] The destructive thrust of Nietzsche's ideas resides in his claim that the weak of society perpetuate the lies of "good" and "evil" in order to rein in the strong, despite the "death" of the transcendental and metaphysical explanations that gave rise to those concepts. What passes as "evil," Nietzsche insists, is actually the impulses and proclivities of worldly human life. In contrast to authentic expressions of the will, Christians and humanists alike are nihilists because they deny the importance of *this* life: as they grope for morally higher or spiritual things, they eschew their wills and natural impulses. Yet this denial means that their moral concepts are little more than vapors passing falsely as permanent fixtures of the world.

Impressed by Nietzsche's argument, Highsmith at first embraced this position by rejecting transcendental or metaphysical grounds for good and evil. The so-called amorality that characterizes many of her most intriguing characters—especially Bruno, Tom Ripley, and David Kelsey in *This Sweet Sickness* (1961)—displaces the conventional concern for moral order that underwrites much of crime fiction, searching instead for what Julian Symons, the novelist and former president of the Detection Club, characterizes as "a different and wholly personal code of morality."[34] For Highsmith, evil is only a construct produced by her characters' guilt, while the figure of the criminal is a symbol for the self that asserts its will. Thus, when Guy perceives that the revolver is "[t]he best of himself," the weapon becomes a symbol of what is actually an assertion of Guy's will, even though society has deemed it "evil" (178). Guy's moment of perception about the "evil" within himself is, in other words, a window into the life that he wants, bringing into full view the amorality required to realize those desires. Following Nietzsche's ideas, Highsmith's sensibilities about humanity's penchant for "evil" replace a discourse about crime, truth, and morality with concerns about authentic existence. She presents a narrative world beyond good and evil, identifying instead the authentic willing of the self as the narrative center of gravity.

Highsmith's shift away from moral categories toward these sensibilities about authenticity created confusion and discomfort among many early reviewers of the novel. For example, one critic with the *New York Herald Tribune Book Review* lamented that *Strangers on a Train* "is not always credible, and the characters are not entirely convincing" because it's difficult to see how a respectable architect would fail to inform the police once he's convinced of Bruno's guilt, much less commit the double murder.[35] Indeed, Hitchcock seems to have had similar reservations, for Guy does not actually commit the murder in the film version of *Strangers on a Train*. Yet, rather than viewing the novel as the story of a corrupted "good" man who longs only to live happily with his new fiancé, Anne, Highsmith stages Guy's crime and attendant guilt as a struggle between two selves—one that knows the power and prestige he wants and another plagued by fear, compulsions, and socially constructed prohibitions. This struggle surfaces most clearly in the tension Guy feels between his ambitions as an architect and his former life with Miriam. On the train Guy shares his frustrations about Miriam with Bruno, situating his disdain for her within the context of a commission to design the Palmyra Club in Palm Beach. As Bruno puerilely says about the commission, "You're gonna be famous, huh?" and, in fact, there is significant professional prestige if Guy's design is successful (32).

As Bruno rambles about his own artistic dalliances in the past, Guy reflects about the social capital that his modern design would acquire for him:

> He sipped his drink absently, and thought of the commissions that would come after Palm Beach. Soon, perhaps, an office building in New York. He had an idea for an office building in New York, and he longed to see it come into being. Guy Daniel Hanes. *A name*. No longer the irksome, never quite banished awareness that he had less money than Anne. (32)

While Guy earlier says that he has no interest in "making money" (20), the Palmyra gives him the opportunity to gain social capital and, in turn, to pursue his architectural and artistic interests unencumbered by financial concerns. He would become a *"name,"* a public figure with social clout. Furthermore, the Palmyra commission would obviate Guy's concerns about his inferior socioeconomic position with Anne, whose wealthy family is among the upper classes of New England.

When Guy learns that Miriam wants to accompany him to Palm Beach for "protection" during her pregnancy (her lover is currently married and first needs to get a divorce), he worries that she will "lose him the commission" or, in the least, sully the social capital that it offers him (33). He not only fears that Miriam's extramarital pregnancy might become public knowledge, but he also imagines an equally devastating scenario in which the unsophisticated Miriam meets Brillhart, ruining Guy's image as a member of the cultural elite. Guy thus becomes convinced that Miriam cannot accompany him to Palm Beach. "Yet," Guy suddenly realizes, "it was not the vision of Brillhart's shock beneath his calm, unvarying courtesy . . . but simply his own revulsion that made it impossible. It was just that he couldn't bear having Miriam anywhere near him when he worked on a project like this one" (43). Even if she does not sully his social life, Miriam would poison his imagination or ability to work on such an important project. In almost any scenario, then, Miriam devalues the social capital that Guy gains by the Palmyra commission. Her unrefined manners would impede his slow climb from Metcalf, Texas, into the upper echelons of New York society, and for this reason Bruno's murder of Miriam is nothing less than the manifestation of Guy's actual desires.

Such Nietzschean sensibilities in *Strangers on a Train* are not without their problems, however. What, for example, makes the life that Guy *wills*—his desire to be a *"name"*—any less a social construct than the morality that inhibits the realization of his goal? In terms of Nietzsche's argument, what makes the will-to-power any more "natural" than the meanings and values that human beings produce? Are not the "natural," the "vital," and even *"this* life" concepts with their own contingent histories? This set of tensions often prompts readers to argue that some social-historical critique underwrites Highsmith's novels. Joshua Lukin, for example, argues that Guy's desire to climb the social ladder through his profession is the object of Highsmith's criticism of a constellation of pressures on the postwar professional-managerial class. Through his ostensible commitment to aesthetic purity—to the art of architecture rather than "making money"—Guy thinks of himself as "classless" when, in fact, this professional fantasy is a product of the "psychic pressures" of a booming market for mass consumption and the demands of social mobility.[36] These two streams of "psychic pressure" lead Guy to embrace a pair of paradoxical desires: social mobility and the "classlessness" of an aesthetic life apart from mass consumer culture. Lukin argues that Guy understands himself as something like the dispossessed bourgeoisie, forced into vulgar labor and longing for lost social autonomy. Lukin thus glosses Guy's acquiescence to Bruno as the former's paradoxical desire for social mobility and classlessness—a function, that is, of his professional status.

Yet Highsmith also presents the vicissitudes of Guy's psyche and Bruno's obsession with murder as something more fundamental than outcomes of converging pressures on the professional class. For one, Bruno and the genteel Anne share the same economic status, even if the latter is more adept culturally and socially. Put more broadly and bluntly, the problem is that Highsmith frustrates historicizing interpretations. Rather than capitulating to socioeconomic forces of their respective classes, Highsmith presents Bruno's motivations and Guy's violence as manifestations of a psychological realm. For example, after Miriam's murder, Bruno imagines that he has finally achieved something noteworthy, as if the murder were an accomplishment that bolsters his ego. As Guy puts it, Bruno takes "personal pride in his, Guy's, freedom" (102). After Guy has murdered Bruno's father, Bruno further muses that their freedom enables them to achieve a certain intimacy with one another: "Guy and himself! Who else was like them? Who else was their equal? He longed for Guy to be with him now. He would clasp Guy's hand, and to hell with the rest of the world!" (167). The two murders entangle violence and pleasure: Bruno's strangulation of Miriam is strangely intimate, while Guy murders the elder Bruno as the man lies in his bed.

Bruno fantasizes that these two intimate murders become something like a consummation of his and Guy's relationship. They are wedded to one another through the freedom of a prior lover's death and the murder of an oppressive father. Bruno later even fantasizes about removing Anne as a competitor for Guy's affections: "If he could strangle Anne, too, then Guy and he could really be together" (250). Bruno's Oedipal desire for his mother, which he wears on his gray flannel sleeve while talking with Guy on the train, transfers to the surrogate murderer of his father. The crime thus becomes something like a form of narcissism: Bruno loves the man that has done what he could never do, the self that he wishes he could be. Indeed, Guy has enabled them both to become "supermen," as Bruno drunkenly proclaims, Nietzschean *Übermenschen* who *will* the life they want (261). The explanations for Bruno's murder of Miriam, his subsequent pressure on Guy, and his homoerotic fantasies about a union through violence are each rooted within the realm of the ego and the desire for an authentic expression of the self. The signs of class and socioeconomic distinction that adorn the narrative are subsumed under the auspices of the individual psyche. The arena of psychology serves as the bedrock of the narrative: Highsmith presents her characters' violence, guilt, and class anxieties as performances within a theater of the will and the self.

Existential Psychology and the "Decline" of American Naturalism

Highsmith's work from this period signals her interventions in literary history by alluding to or adapting a novelistic forebear. In *The Talented Mr. Ripley*, for example, Herbert Greenleaf notes that his proposition to Tom Ripley is not unlike the one that Lambert Strether receives in Henry James's *The Ambassadors* (1903). Yet Highsmith's reworking of a literary predecessor in *Strangers on a Train* is more suggestive than the conspicuous foregrounding of her debts in *The Talented Mr. Ripley*. Much like Highsmith's first novel, Theodore Dreiser's *Sister Carrie* (1900) begins on a train with a chance meeting between two seemingly antithetical characters, Carrie Meeber and Charles Drouet. Highsmith's small-town waif desires to be upwardly mobile even as Carrie, like Guy, is initially suspicious of the man on the train who seems to be observing her with peculiar and ambiguous interest. The narrator informs the reader that Drouet is a "masher," or "one whose dress or manners are calculated to elicit the admiration of susceptible young women."[37] Carrie, on the other hand, is a "waif amid forces," an ostensibly innocent young woman who leaves her childhood home to "reconnoitre the mysterious city [of Chicago] and dreaming wild dreams of some vague, far-off supremacy" (2, 3). Carrie, as a "fair example of the middle American class," finds herself far from her original hopes and intentions (2). Indeed, both Highsmith's aspiring architect and Dreiser's middle-class waif seemingly destroy their lives even as they achieve semblances of their desires. For Carrie, her "wild dreams" are seized and manipulated by the city's "large forces which allure with all the soulfulness of expression possible in the most cultured human" (2). Carrie becomes Drouet's mistress after she experiences the difficulties of life in Chicago, including her sister's stifling home, work in a factory, and the hunger of poverty.

As a matter of fact, Carrie's "vague" desires are defined for her as she discovers the allure of urban life (2). For example, after losing her job, Drouet takes Carrie to dinner and orders an expensive sirloin. His charm and liberal spending "captivated Carrie completely" (67). Drouet's interactions with "noted or rich individuals" similarly cast a spell over her (51). His munificence and social standing prepare Carrie to assume "the cosmopolitan standard of virtue," as the narrator puts it, by justifying the decision to become his mistress for the sake of the material opportunity that the relationship affords (2).

"Ah, money, money, money," she muses before agreeing to become Drouet's mistress, "What a thing it was to have. How plenty of it would clear away all these troubles" (74–75). Notably, Carrie has absorbed this fantasy about money through her exposure to upper-middle-class life. When Drouet proposes to "take care" of her, Carrie hears the proposition "passively," as if it were "the welcome breath of an open door" (77). Dreiser's waif is slowly carried away by the currents of Chicago's larger forces.

Having become intimate with this stranger she meets on a train, Carrie allows Drouet to buy her expensive clothes, secure a spacious apartment, and he even enables her to play the heroine in a theatrical performance. In short, Drouet helps define and fulfill Carrie's desires. However, forces beyond this "masher" also influence Carrie. She is "the victim of the city's hypnotic charm," the narrator explains before her older sister, Minnie, has a nightmare of Carrie being swallowed up by dark waters (89). Minnie's dream serves as an occluded sign of the "something" that is "lost" with Carrie—that is, her virginity and, in the narrator's view, her innocence along with it (90). But also Minnie's dream recalls the larger forces swirling around Carrie's life. Environmental imagery pervades the dream, much like the way it recurs throughout the novel, particularly when representing Carrie's "mental state." The implication of this imagery is that Drouet is only one among many forces competing for control over her person. This implication is confirmed again when Carrie begins an affair with George Hurstwood, the manager of an upscale bar. Hurstwood, Carrie tells herself, is "more clever than Drouet in a hundred ways" and also more attentive to her (106). Yet even these shifting desires appear to be products of environmental and socioeconomic conditions. The psychological is little more than an aftereffect: "A blare of sound, a roar of life, a vast array of human hives," the narrator explains, "appeal to the astonished senses in equivocal terms" (2).

Through her vacillating affections, Dreiser presents Carrie as a reed in the wind: her desires are largely unknown to herself and, given the recurring prominence that the narrator attributes to the city, those desires are most often constituted by impersonal "forces." The narrator provides such an explanatory template for Carrie's behavior not long after her decision to become Drouet's mistress. Dreiser's narrator, perhaps in an attempt to create empathy for Carrie's situation, reflects on her "mental state" in relation to "the true answer to what is right." The narrator remarks that common standards for moral judgment are "infantile," because most Americans uncritically recite public conventions (101). Indeed, Carrie's "average little conscience" similarly replicates "the world, her past environment, habit, convention, in a confused way" (103). The narrator's point, however, is not that morality is merely a conventional construct. Rather, even Carrie, whose "mind [is] rudimentary in its power of observation and analysis," finds that her conventional conscience is "never wholly convincing" (2, 104). The unsophisticated Carrie is able to criticize the received standards of social behavior. She is more than a product of her *social* world.

Instead, the narrator suggests that the more forceful determinants exist on a more material register: "There was always an answer [to her conscience], always the December days threatened. She was alone; she was desireful; she was fearful of the whistling wind. The voice of want made answer for her" (104). Carrie's "morality"—her ethic, the underpinnings of her behavior—is driven by the threat of poverty and being cast out into an indifferent world. By framing Carrie's behavior in relation to the cold "December days" and the risk of exposure to natural elements, the narrator connects such supra-human forces and the structural conditions of an urban landscape to the earlier question of "the true answer to what is right" (101). Carrie's "mental state," in other words, is a creature struggling against the material conditions and structural realities that are its creator.

Following its provocative but largely enthusiastic critical reception in the decades following its publication, Dreiser's novel had become a prominent part of the American literary arena by the 1920s.[38] Through the support of H. L. Mencken and other influential intellectuals, as well as the aggregating financial value of the original manuscript, Kevin J. Hayes has shown that *Sister Carrie* attained "canonical" status by the 1930s.[39] This trajectory of canonization maps onto the reception history of naturalism—restricted at first to Frank Norris, Jack London, and Stephen Crane. At the beginning of the twentieth century, naturalist novels were met mostly with skepticism: the first naturalist novels were often dismissed as muckraking fiction that appealed to a mass audience on sensational grounds. Malcolm Cowley explains the naturalists' early reception as a function of the challenge these authors posed to the "genteel" tradition of American letters.[40] Philip Rahv, the New York intellectual and influential founding editor of *Partisan Review*, similarly argues that naturalist fiction was a product of a nineteenth-century world of industry and science. Naturalism, he suggests, protested the conditions of the former through the resources of the latter.[41] Naturalism, Rahv explains, "revolutionized writing by liquidating the last assets of 'romance' in fiction and by purging it once and for all of the idealism of the 'beautiful lie'—of the longstanding inhibitions against dealing with the underside of life."[42] For prominent mid-century critics such as Cowley and Rahv, naturalism was a rebellion against the socioeconomic inequalities of industrial, urbanized existence.

However, many postwar intellectuals noted that by the 1940s the conversation surrounding naturalism had markedly changed. In 1942, Rahv wrote that the "endless book-keeping of existence" that characterized literary naturalism was in "decline." While the naturalist style had come to the front of cultural attention in the 1930s with publications such as John Steinbeck's *The Grapes of Wrath* (1939) and John Dos Passos's *U.S.A.* trilogy (1930, 1932, 1936), Rahv observes that a newer generation of writers "want[ed] to break the novel of its objective habits."[43] Rather than offering sociological or historically impersonal narratives that explore the structural or environmental conditions of human life, Rahv says that new intellectual currents were prompting American writers to become introspective about art, the artist, and the individual. In particular, Rahv claims that the rising intellectual discontent with the naturalist style has its impetus in the political animus toward progressive politics, with its (perceived) view of the individual. In opposition to "the political movement in the literature of the past decade [1930s]," there has been "a revival of religio-esthetic attitudes."[44] Rahv thus formulates an objection against naturalism that would be reiterated among many intellectuals for the next two decades: naturalist novels envision a "closed world," one in which "the environment displaces its inhabitants in the role of the hero."[45] Yet more expansive intellectual movements have deposed that ordering of the narrative world. Among the most important of these forces, Rahv cites "the growth of the psychological sciences and, particularly, of psychoanalysis."[46] These trends prompted American fiction to turn inward, creating a crisis in the interpretation of human experience.[47] The literary devices and intellectual resources of the naturalist style, Rahv concludes, cannot adequately interpret such a newly disassembled world.

By the late 1950s, so many intellectuals were convinced of the decline of the naturalist style that Edward Stone collected a eulogistic anthology, *What Was Naturalism?* (1959).[48] The title's past tense suggests an expired phenomenon, and, indeed, Stone explains that the purpose of the anthology is to introduce "the mind of a buried generation" to young scholars.[49] The "materials" that Stone associated with the movement suggest why he felt that the intellectual era of the naturalists had passed—in particular, selections from Thomas R. Malthus's *An Essay on the Principle of Population* (1798), Marx's *A Contribution to the Critique of Political Economy* (1859) and *Capital* (1867–94), and Herbert Spencer's *The Principles of Sociology* (1874–96). These selections represent the "gist" of "a mind," or the intellectual culture that inspired Hamlin Garland, Crane, London, Norris, and Dreiser.[50] The critical and intellectual shifts of the postwar cultural marketplace mitigated—if not "buried," as Stone suggests— the sociological accounts of society and individuals that had influenced naturalist writers. What's more, American attitudes toward progressive accounts of politics and economics, particularly toward Marxism and its perceived relationship with fascism, led many postwar critics and readers to distrust the narrative worlds that naturalism represented. As an instance of this tendency, Stone's anthology suggests how postwar intellectuals not only associated naturalism with environmental determinism and progressive sociology but also with radical politics more generally. Novels such as Crane's *Maggie: A Girl of the Streets* (1892), Norris's *The Octopus* (1901), and London's story "South of the Slot" (1909) document the squalor created on the margins of urban capitalist society in ways that drew, often quite explicitly, on a sociological and economic explanatory template for the phenomena of violence and the psychological consequences of inequality.

The ostensible decline of the naturalist style was, in reality, a temporary symptom of the intellectual trends of the postwar decades. Mass-market presses such as Penguin would reprint many naturalist texts during the 1980s as American "classics," discovering through the mechanism of canonization that naturalism had a marketable afterlife. Perhaps mirroring this rebranding of naturalism as no longer probing the violent and excessive margins of capitalist society, critics in the 1980s similarly inverted the earlier critical reception, viewing naturalism as "glorif[ying] the culture of consumerism."[51] The avowed decline of naturalism during the 1940s and 1950s, and its critical recoding decades later, testifies to important shifts in American intellectual sensibilities.

As part of the postwar shifts in literary and intellectual tastes, James Gilbert traces the dwindling cultural fortunes of naturalism in relation to a revolution in the editorial policies of *Partisan Review*.[52] In 1934, Rahv and William Phillips founded the magazine to "defend the Soviet Union, to combat fascism and war, and to promote a literature which would express the viewpoint of the working class." The magazine soon folded, however, and its new editorial board in 1937 replaced "proletarian literature" with "intellectual literature."[53] Thus, during the late 1930s the editors abandoned their ambitions of leading a political vanguard—most often through publishing socialist essays and naturalist fiction—and transferred those aspirations to the arena of cultural tastes. By the early 1940s, *Partisan Review* generally refused to publish work that was either naturalist in style or pro-Soviet in its politics.[54] These shifts, Gilbert argues, involved growing anti-communist sensibilities in the 1940s, even as the editors turned "back to the era of the symbolists, the surrealists, and the exiles." The editors' standards for publication established the avant-garde as their gold standard, privileging literary style above concrete political engagement. Consequently, the "naturalism so evident in the early magazine, was banished and replaced by writing that corresponded more to that printed in the *Dial* during the 1920s."[55] As the cultural stock of avant-garde modernism soared, literary naturalism fell out of favor; the tastes of leading postwar editors and critics turned toward writers like Kafka, Joyce, and Eliot.[56]

The avowed decline of naturalism and growing preference for modernist experimentation even became integral to institutional sources of literary prestige and financial support for the arts. Before the postwar era, little magazines such as the *Dial, Kenyon Review, Sewanee Review, Poetry*, and *Accent* had been the primary outlets in the United States for what would later become the intellectual vanguard in the postwar era: avant-garde writing, the emerging New Criticism, and the work of the New York Intellectuals. As Lawrence Schwartz has shown, the postwar commitment to American literary culture by the Rockefeller Foundation is a telling instance of this history of modernism's reception and transformation. After the Second World War, the Rockefeller Foundation began to promote little magazines and, by extension, literary modernism itself.[57] *Kenyon Review* was the principal benefactor of grant funding by the foundation, while *Partisan Review* did not receive funding because of its history of political radicalism.[58] Still, the half-dozen magazines that competed for the foundation's grants each billed themselves as fundamentally committed to the modernist vanguard of literary experimentation. This commitment helped create what Schwartz calls a new "postwar aesthetic" that promoted and gave institutional support to experimental modernism, including the "re-discovery" of work by William Faulkner, Marianne Moore, Ezra Pound, and others. This aesthetic was bound up with institutional investments and changes in the publishing industry, both of which picked "modernist literary culture" and "formalist criticism" as worthy recipients for investment.[59]

The "decline" of naturalist fiction was therefore due not only, as Rahv acknowledges, to the "growth of psychological sciences" but also to wider changes in the political and intellectual landscape of postwar America.[60] Another prominent example of these changes, which I considered in the previous chapter, was the immigration of European existentialism into American cultural life. Many therapists and intellectuals assimilated these phenomena, giving rise to the existential psychology movement. Existential psychology was a forerunner of the humanistic psychology movement of the 1960s, and both theories of therapy had profound effects on popular sensibilities about the self and its route to authenticity.[61] For instance, Rollo May's edited anthology, *Existence* (1958), disseminated existential psychoanalysis to the wider psychiatric profession.[62] May first wed existentialist sensibilities about authenticity with psychological analysis and therapeutic practice in *Man's Search for Himself* (1953), which was a *New York Times* bestseller. This conceptual union was not unique to May, however, for he drew heavily from European psychology, particularly the work of Ludwig Binswanger and Viktor Frankl. May also used the salient terms of existentialism to revise elements from the early humanistic psychology movement exemplified in the writings of Carl R. Rogers and Abraham Maslow.[63] This permutation of professional psychology casts therapeutic work as an avenue for unearthing and expressing an authentic self: psychological analysis becomes the pathway to existential self-realization.

Even as May, Rogers, and Maslow were popularizing psychologized authenticity, other therapists began to employ psychological templates when analyzing social and political events. Most notably, in *Escape from Freedom* (1941), Erich Fromm accounts for the advent of fascism through "the character structure of modern man and the problems of the interaction between psychological and sociological factors."[64] According to Fromm, fascism is a temptation born out of individual psychology: while "modern man" has been freed from the strictures of "pre-individualistic society," modern selves have also become anxious and isolated in their private freedom. The temptation confronting the modern self, Fromm argues, is to abandon the burden of freedom for political dependencies. Fromm thus construes fascism as a form of neurosis—an individual psychological template applied to collective behavior. Fromm's practice of existential psychology frames society and politics after a psychological pattern. This turn is not a retreat from politics—not a turn inward, as Rahv claims—but a reframing of the public sphere after the patterns of interiority.

The mechanisms of Fromm's "psychosocial" analysis would become widely representative of, if not directly influential on, the early literature on totalitarianism, which tended to psychologize the loss of personality among its supporters. Even Rollo May would assert, "People grasp at political authoritarianism in their desperate need for relief from anxiety."[65] Inverting the accounts of violence in both Malthusian sociology and Marxist political economy, the existential psychology movement embedded social and political behaviors within the explanatory resources of a diverse and growing body of psychological knowledge. Such inversions became common among progressive political theorists like Theodore Adorno and high modernist literary figures like Trilling. According to Robert Genter, while "the specter of totalitarianism seemed to reach the shores of America under the auspices of late capitalism," Adorno, Trilling, and the postwar advocates of high modernism "reluctantly revised their original suggestion that a strong ego was an autocratic one and joined with their colleagues in the psychoanalytic profession in trying to fashion an image of democratic personality capable of escaping the psychopathologies of the modern age."[66] Rather than what one of Adorno's commentators called "progressive collective practice," the ego increasingly became the left's principal means of resistance.[67]

The so-called age of anxiety therefore saw the proliferation of a spectrum of psychological templates for understanding the modern self and its relation to society. While existentialism and a heterogeneous body of popular psychotherapies were situating social phenomena within an arena of private authenticity in the 1950s, corporate interests also contributed to this shifting intellectual terrain. As Louis Menand explains, the popularization of psychology "had to do with what might be called the Cold War discourse of anxiety."[68] This discourse about anxiety—or "anxiety about anxiety," as Menand puts it—not only wedded European existentialism and psychoanalytic theory but also depended in large part upon the advent of psychopharmacology and the promotional practices of the pharmaceutical industry.[69] Psychoanalysis had influenced medical discourse about neuroses, and a burgeoning postwar pharmaceutical industry promoted its commercial interests through aggressive advertising campaigns that normalized pharmaceutical drugs. In short, anxiety was not only intellectually chic but also economically profitable. From the trauma of the war, nuclear threats, and even ordinary feelings of existential insignificance, the notion of anxiety became widely understood as a medical disorder treatable by forms of psychological or psychopharmaceutical therapy. The consequences of this "discourse of anxiety" in the early Cold War years, according to Menand, was that "questions of psychology, and mental states generally, [were put] at the center of cultural attention."[70]

The complicated cultural fabric of the postwar moment thus includes the intellectual declaration of the "decline" of naturalism, the normalization of psychoanalysis, and the birth of existential psychology—phenomena that meet not only in Rahv's explanation for changing literary tastes but also in Highsmith's allusion to *Sister Carrie* in the opening of *Strangers on a Train*. While Carrie Meeber's desires are caught within a web of structural conditions and a cold urban environment, Highsmith frames Guy's ambitions and contradictory desires through the vicissitudes of an irrational psychological arena. Indeed, much like the narrator in Dostoevsky's *Notes from Underground*, Highsmith documents the irrational undercurrents of the human psyche as a way of confronting deterministic accounts of human behavior. For example, when Guy and Bruno first meet, Guy is reading a volume of Plato's philosophy. However, his thoughts consistently drift from the book to Bruno: "his mind wandered after half a page. He . . . let his eyes wander to the unlighted cigar that still gyrated conversationally in a bony hand behind one of the seat backs, and to the monogram that trembled on a thin gold chain across the tie of the young man opposite him." The monogram, CAB, attracts Guy's attention more fully than the text of philosophy. No matter how much he concentrates, Guy finds himself reading Bruno rather than Plato: "It was an interesting face, though Guy did not know why" (11). Dreiser's Carrie also tries yet fails to read a novel, but what Florence Dore calls her "guilty reading" is a marker of the sexual norms and class-based cultural capital that preclude her from the "highbrow" world she desires to enter.[71] Plato similarly represents Guy's desire to enter a world of knowledge and order, yet what frustrates Highsmith's protagonist is not the proscriptions of normative behavior but the psychological appeal of the violent and the irrational.

After Guy performs a thorough close reading of Bruno, he feels momentarily satisfied and is able to return to his book. "The words made sense to him and began to lift his anxiety," the narrator explains. Yet the consolation of philosophy is short-lived: "But what good will Plato do you with Miriam, an inner voice asked him" (11). Bruno soon provides a solution that Guy's desire for order, virtue, and reason cannot. Indeed, it's significant that Guy reads a volume by Plato. In Mary McCabe's apt phrase, Plato's dialogues constitute a "dramatization of reason": his philosophy searches for the best ordering for society and an individual's life.[72] Not unlike Guy the architect, Plato weds rational order with a desire for the beautiful. E. R. Dodds summarizes the intellectual consensus of Highsmith's day when he explains that scholars read Plato as a "rationalist" in at least two senses: Plato "believes that reason and not the senses provides . . . the first principles on which scientific knowledge is built," and he maintains that "the life of man and the life of the universe are governed by, or are manifestations of, a rational plan."[73] Guy's interest in Plato, then, serves as a retreat from the distractions of Miriam into planning, wisdom, and the resources of the Western cultural tradition. However, before Bruno mentions his plan, Guy already has doubts about the efficacy of the rational order that Plato represents. An "inner voice"—one among many that will speak to Guy throughout the novel—questions whether such cultured thought is sufficient for the dilemma he faces. Could there be other consolations for Guy's anxieties not bound up with reason and planning? The proposition from Bruno, the man with the "interesting face," gives voice to the irrational impulses that repeatedly appeal to Guy (11).

Later, Guy learns through a note from Brillhart that he has been awarded the Palmyra commission. In despair at the situation with Miriam, Guy tears up the letter and decides to turn down the offer (47). Along with Brillhart's note, Guy also receives a letter from Bruno, who explains that Guy left his volume of Plato's philosophy on the train. Almost as an incidental aside, Bruno says, "I keep thinking about that idea we had for a couple of murders. It could be done, I am sure" (47). When Guy finishes the letter, rather than tearing it up like Brillhart's note, Guy finds that it "pleased him somehow. It was pleasant to think of Bruno's freedom" (48). The juxtaposition between Brillhart's note (an opportunity to draw up a blueprint and build a rational plan) and Bruno's suggestion (an opportunity for violence with vague motivations) poses a choice between a world of order and one of irrational destruction. Guy's pleasure in Bruno's letter suggests yet again that his desire for order is interrupted by the appeal of the irrational. Indeed, Guy's decision to preserve Bruno's note and tear up the letter from Brillhart—much like his refusal to inform the police after Miriam's murder—is explicable only as an unconscious attraction to the "freedom" of Bruno's proposition. Guy's ambitions provide an inlet for an unconscious sea of irrationality to sweep across the ordered landscape of his life. Guy the architect thus becomes the tragic exemplar for the age of anxiety: he is the victim of psychological undercurrents and the hubris induced by rationality.

While Dreiser is undoubtedly attentive to mental states in *Sister Carrie*, the recurrence of the irrational in Highsmith's novel presents a narrative world governed primarily by the disordered and contradictory psychological life of its characters. Highsmith's allusion to Dreiser's novel reframes the conditions of possibility for the mental states of her characters, removing them from the largely deterministic structures that shape the naturalist novel. Dreiser presents Carrie's desires as either a product of structural conditions—the allure of consumerism in an urban environment—or as a weak haven from the whims of larger forces.[74] Highsmith, on other hand, presents her characters' behavior within a different nexus of forces. Bruno describes this nexus while having dinner alone with Anne one evening. During a telling inversion of intimacies, Bruno quotes Guy to Anne: "Every man is his own law court and punishes himself enough. In fact, every man is just about everything to Guy!" (252). Bruno, who seemingly knows Guy's mind more intimately than his wife does, adapts one of Guy's ruminations to explain that "good and evil" are phenomena of an internal arena (251).

Bruno's enigmatic assertion that "every man is just about everything to Guy" also makes an implicit claim about moral judgments: like the conditions of possibility for criminal acts, they are *almost* entirely circumscribed by the individual and the chaotic court of the psyche. Sure, social norms and inhibitions influence human beings, Bruno suggests, but criminality is principally a phenomenon of existential conditions rather than structural or environmental ones. When Guy neglects to inform the police that Bruno has confessed to Miriam's murder in a letter, Guy justifies the decision because of "some sense of personal guilt that he himself could not bear" (95). On the one hand, Guy fears exposure if he were to go to the police. On the other hand, this feeling is irrational because, although Guy is strangely interested in Bruno on the train, he nonetheless rebuffs his proposal. Bruno even admits that Guy has rejected the idea of an exchanged murder, but he strangles Miriam anyway. The point is that Guy's "personal guilt" is, as Russell Harrison says, "an existential guilt, rather than guilt for a specific act."[75] The hesitancies plaguing Guy are a product of his conflicted ego—they derive from the uncertainties about which self he desires to *will*.

Tom Ripley, Kierkegaard's *Sickness*, and the Fate of Structural Reform

The "decline" of naturalism during the 1940s and 1950s was not exclusively in response to the cultural purchase of existentialism and the therapeutic disciplines. For some writers, the deficits of naturalism were not so much its politics or deterministic logic as its marginalization of women of color. Gwendolyn Brooks's *Maud Martha* (1953), for example, recalls the Chicago setting of Wright's *Native Son*.[76] Brooks's novel regularly invokes the tropes of Wright's naturalism, only to juxtapose them with the inner world of its eponymous heroine. One of the novel's early vignettes draws out this contrast by switching from environmental imagery to free indirect discourse: "Up the street, mixed in the wind, blew the children, and turned the corner onto the brownish red brick school court. It was wonderful."[77] The novel introduces Maud Martha's judgments ("It was wonderful") to interrupt the flow of what otherwise appears to be overriding environmental forces. As Megan K. Ahern says, "Brooks carves out a sense of protest that departs from naturalism: either the lachrymal prose of earlier versions of naturalism, such as that of Stephen Crane's *Maggie*, or the raw drama of *Native Son*." The novel, according to Ahern, creates "readerly outrage to fill the gaps left open in the text."[78] Brooks breaks with Wright's literary mode to recover private judgments of value by women of color—judgments that Brooks felt urban realism and naturalism had foreclosed in their sociological configuration of narrative worlds.

Yet the prevailing conditions for the "decline" of naturalism were not rooted in concerns about the experience of marginalized voices. Instead, writers and critics felt the tropes of Progressive era literature subordinated psychological complexity to structural forces. In contrast to what Stone described as the source texts of naturalism, existentialism and the therapeutic disciplines had made the intricacies of the ego newly accessible. This view of the deficits of the naturalist style is raced and classed in ways that Brooks's novel complicates, even though *Maud Martha* follows a similar pattern to the broader postwar marketplace for fiction. As I've argued so far in this chapter, the turn against the tropes of Progressive era literature either reinterpreted the socioeconomic elements of characters' lives through the drama of the ego or subordinated those social phenomena to existentialist sensibilities regarding alienation and authenticity.

One consequence of these existentialist sensibilities is that, in Highsmith's fiction, the amoral presentation of characters and criminal behavior often disorients her readers. This is especially the case with *The Talented Mr. Ripley*. For example, explaining Tom's obsession with Dickie Greenleaf's affluent life-style, Edward A. Shannon says that Highsmith "focuses the reader's attention on the political and economic contexts that define Tom Ripley, who is first and foremost an American bent on ascending the ladder of class and priv-ilege."[79] *The Talented Mr. Ripley* is therefore underwritten by a "critique of American ideas of class."[80] While Tom is keenly attuned to the markers of Dickie's affluence, the deceptive subtleties of Ripley's character frustrate the idea that a "critique" of American narratives of social mobility underwrites the narrative. Instead, Highsmith differentiates *The Talented Mr. Ripley* from earlier American novels, such as James's *The Ambassadors* and Fitzgerald's *The Great Gatsby* (1925), both of which present the ambiguities of class-based self-invention. Highsmith refashions these earlier fictions through sensibilities about free choice and authenticity: the ambiguities of Tom's self-invention are rooted not in his class but his own oddly comic failure to assume or retain his freedom. Tom is an almost Nietzschean individual willing to become the self that he chooses at any cost, yet paradoxically that self abandons its free choice when confronted with the burden of freedom. Tom, in other words, does not want to escape his class or social position so much as his self.

The philosophical contours of Tom's existential crisis become more pro-nounced in relation to Highsmith's intellectual debts from the 1940s and early 1950s. Andrew Wilson suggests that the seed for Ripley was first planted in 1949 when Highsmith read an anthology of Søren Kierkegaard's work. Highsmith describes the Danish philosopher as her "master," and Kierkegaard's investigation of despair in *The Sickness Unto Death* (1849), which Highsmith quoted frequently in her journals, helps explain the paradoxes of Tom's behav-ior.[81] In the anthologized selections from *The Sickness Unto Death* available to Highsmith at the time, Kierkegaard writes about a person who experiences three types of despair: he or she is "in despair at not willing to be oneself; or still lower, in despair at not willing to be a self; or lowest of all, in despair at willing to be another than himself."[82] Those in despair are driven to great lengths by their desire to assume the identity of another. Thus, for Kierkegaard, the self in despair becomes a kind of ouroboros—at once a self-fulfilling and self-destructive creature.

The person in Kierkegaard's lowest form of despair is most relevant to Ripley's character. Kierkegaard describes this person as "infinitely comic" because "this self gets the notion of asking whether it might not let itself become or be made into another than itself."[83] Despairing persons are comic, in other words, because they're so trapped within the immediacy of their crisis that they cannot see the "eternal" quality of the self: they wish to change something that is unchanging. As a result, Kierkegaard identifies a paradox at the heart of this form of despair:

> such a despairer, whose only wish is this most crazy of all transformations, loves to think that this change might be accomplished as easily as changing a coat. For the immediate man does not recognize his self, he recognizes himself only by his dress, he recognizes (and here again appears the infinitely comic trait)—he recognizes that he has a self only by externals.[84]

The despairing self wishes to be other than itself, and thus is caught within the immediacy of that crisis. This "comic" notion leads to disintegration—that is to say, the perception that the self is only "dress," externals that may be exchanged. This inauthentic self-invention, Kierkegaard says, is in reality an especially pernicious form of despair.

The "sickness" of despair within Kierkegaard's framework construes the experiences of envy and social mobility as phenomena of an existential crisis. Whatever social markers characterize the self-that-one-is-not—which is also the self that the despairer desires to become—those markers are peripheral to the crisis of the lowest form of despair. *The Talented Mr. Ripley* follows the pattern of Kierkegaard's thought. When Ripley murders Dickie Greenleaf and temporarily assumes his wealth and identity, his desires for mobility are moored in an existential and psychological crisis of self. When Tom's forgeries of Dickie's signature on three remittances from a trust fund have been discovered, it becomes clear that Tom's self-invention is primarily an avenue of escape from "Tom Ripley" rather than a desire for class status. The Greenleaf trust and Dickie's bank in Naples become suspicious of the forgeries, requesting that he appear in person to continue the remittances of the funds. Tom then realizes that he cannot continue impersonating his murdered friend:

> This was the end of Dickie Greenleaf, he knew. He hated becoming Thomas Ripley again, hated being nobody, hated putting on his old set of habits again, and feeling that people looked down on him and were

bored with him unless he put on an act for them like a clown, feeling incompetent and incapable of doing anything with himself except entertaining people for minutes at a time. He hated going back to himself as he would have hated putting on a shabby suit of clothes, a grease-spotted, unpressed suit of clothes that had not been very good even when it was new. (181)

Dickie Greenleaf's "end" occurred much earlier in the novel when Tom murdered him. Yet, in Tom's view, the "end of Dickie Greenleaf" refers to impossibility of sustaining the performance of an identity. Tom hopes to switch between being Dickie and himself, but, in Kierkegaardian fashion, his desire for self-invention suggests his self-hate and despair rather than his freedom. While becoming the wealthy Dickie allows Tom to become "somebody" rather than "nobody," this distinction has less to do with Dickie's class than Tom's self-appraisal: the persona of "Thomas Ripley" is a "nobody," akin to a "shabby suit of clothes" that one might collect from a closet. Identity becomes nothing more than a feat of sustained impersonation.

Tom's lament at having to return to the "unpressed suit of clothes" of his Ripley identity recalls the moment not long after he first becomes "Dickie Greenleaf" and decides to visit Paris. Enjoying a slow walk through the city's streets, Tom "rather liked the idea of going to bed hungry" but resolves instead to eat at a restaurant in order to gain weight so that his murdered friend's clothes will fit better. To *become* Dickie—"He was Dickie, good-natured, naïve Dickie"—he must fit exactly the new externals of that persona (124). Such minor choices construe the self of another—as well as Tom's identity—as incidental and easily removable as the clothes on his back. To gain the necessary five pounds, Tom goes to a *bar-tabac* and orders "a ham sandwich on long crusty bread and a glass of hot milk, because a man next to him at the counter was drinking hot milk" (124). The causality of Tom's order—*because* another man ordered the milk—suggests that, even in the first moments of his newly chosen identity, Tom abdicates the burden of his decisions by opting for the preferences of others. Similarly, when Tom travels to Arles to discover the spots where van Gogh had stood to paint, his attempts are frustrated by poor weather, which keeps him from bringing a guidebook on the expeditions. As a result, when he searches for the "real" spots where van Gogh stood, Tom is forced "to make a dozen trips back to his hotel to verify the scenes" (124). This adjacent pair of episodes is emblematic of the despair that underwrites Tom's self-invention. In the face of freedom, he repeatedly turns toward external sources of verification: "Is this authentic?" his hesitancies seem to beg.

While social markers figure into Tom's calculus, Highsmith construes the desire for those markers as symptoms of an existential crisis. They're a barometer of his oscillation between freedom and inauthentic self-invention. Highsmith's ironic framing of Tom's freedom recalls the paradox that Kierkegaard diagnoses: having achieved the transformation into a self-that-one-is-not suggests that one's self has, in turn, become merely a set of externals. Much like Kierkegaardian despair at self-invention, Tom is displaced within endless performativity—an eternal loop of becoming a self-that-one-is-not—and thus he suffers a deprivation of personality rather than its "authentic" expression. Tom's version of self-invention becomes a loss of self, as if the only alternative to one persona were another mask.

As another example of this dynamic, Tom must force himself back into "his dreary role as Thomas Ripley" after becoming reconciled to the death of the "Dickie Greenleaf" personality (183). That Tom describes his return to "Thomas Ripley" as a "role" suggests the extent to which his form of self-invention distances him from the authenticity that self-invention ought (at least putatively) to acquire. By wanting to become someone else—"Dickie Greenleaf"—Tom fails to become a self at all. His desire for Dickie's *flâneur* lifestyle is thus not a function of his class consciousness, but instead his persistent dread signals a refusal to assume the burden of a free self. This ironic framing of Tom's "talents" suggests that the evaluative center of *The Talented Mr. Ripley* is not the murder of Dickie Greenleaf or its socioeconomic implications but rather Tom's inauthenticity and the dread he experiences as the fact of freedom confronts him.

The narrative emphasis upon the vicissitudes of Tom's existential psyche is also at odds with the historicizing tendencies that naturalism and even Jamesian psychological realism require for explorations of class and gender. The seemingly compulsive aggregation of biographical data in the naturalist style is, as Jennifer Fleissner suggests, symptomatic of the "historical time" that orients this tradition of fiction.[85] In contrast, as Harrison explains, the omissions in Tom's biography frustrate the "material analysis of character," leaving him historically adrift and undefined.[86] Ripley is a person lacking a personality, and his story proceeds through successive impersonations, not biographical aggregations. Indeed, performativity trumps the hand-to-mouth conditions that Tom leaves behind in the United States, and even his failure to graduate high school (among the few facts we are given) does not prevent him from the cultural capital generally associated with the elite classes: discerning tastes for high art, the ability to read André Malraux in French, a thorough understanding of European history and geography. Rather than being bound to a rung on the ladder of social mobility, he is able to scale its length at will. Thus, while Tom cannot determine the choices before him, Highsmith presents Ripley as the arbiter of his self. As Sartre puts this existentialist sensibility, "Whatever our being may be, it is a choice."[87] Tom's will is capable of determining his self, despite the fact that everywhere his freedom is constrained by "*people*," as he exasperatedly laments (172).

The Psychopathology of American Life

The crises confronting Tom's self, much like the conflicts besetting Guy Haines's psyche, suggest how political and socioeconomic conditions had become insufficient explanatory templates for the complexities of a world more widely aware of the psychological phenomena surging throughout the tics, dreams, and desires of everyday life. Americanized existentialism, the normalization of psychotherapy, the intellectual legitimacy of psychoanalysis, a burgeoning television industry, and shifting literary tastes all contributed to the reworking of American ideas about the self in social space. None of these threads dominated the rich texture of the moment, and certainly no single author or intellectual presided over its warp and weft. Nonetheless, these emerging sentiments in the intellectual culture of the United States challenged the assumptions about structural conditions underpinning both social-democratic politics and the literature of the Progressive era. The circulation of psychological templates for everyday life began to reframe how Americans understood the conditions of possibility not only for their everyday lives but also public phenomena like violence, poverty, and class envy. With the rise of a science of subjectivity and the popularization of psychotherapy, the idea of structural political intervention became subordinate to the terms of an internal existential arena.

One institutional manifestation of this shift toward psychological explanatory templates was the 1965 report by Assistant Secretary of Labor Daniel Moynihan titled "The Negro Family: The Case for National Action" (1965).[88] The Moynihan report attempted to explain the roots of disproportionate levels of poverty among black Americans at mid-century. Conducted by the US Department of Labor, the report concludes that psychologized social conditions—rather than structural ones, such as a paucity of jobs or the segregation of affordable housing from centers of upwardly mobile economic development—explain the levels of poverty in black communities. The Moynihan report attributes blame to a "tangle of pathology," the center of which is the "weak family structure" among the "Negro."[89] Slavery and decades of Jim Crow laws precipitated the deterioration of the nuclear family among black Americans, the Moynihan report says, and the "tangle of pathology" is now self-replicating. The report thus presents socioeconomic circumstances within the terms of normative psychology: the "weak family structure" of black communities becomes a form of pathology, a psychosocial phenomenon that reproduces itself within individual psychological experience, rather than being the fallout from unequal material, racial, and structural arrangements.

The report even invokes the "tangle of pathology" among black Americans to explain the increased need for welfare programs. According to the report, welfare would become irrelevant apart from these social-psychological conditions: "The steady expansion of [the Aid to Dependent Children] welfare program, as of public assistance programs in general, can be taken as a measure of the steady disintegration of the Negro family structure over the past generation in the United States." The expansion of compensatory welfare—that is, one divorced from an activist or regulatory interventionism—is indexed to a psychopathological phenomenon rather than systemic economic disparities.[90] Through its wedding of the psychological with a political explanatory rhetoric, the Moynihan report attests to the institutionalization of psychological accounts for socioeconomic circumstances.

The institutional traction gained by psychological explanatory templates also cut across the partisan divide. During 1952–53 when Thurgood Marshall argued *Brown v. Board of Education* (1954) before the Supreme Court, he cited psychologist Kenneth Clark's research that documented the psychological detriment caused to black children by state-sponsored segregation in public schools. The "Negro child," Clark's research maintained, "accepts as early as six, seven, or eight the negative stereotypes about his own group" simply because of the implicit effects of separate educational facilities.[91] While W. E. B. Du Bois and others had likewise denounced the effects of segregation upon the "psyches of black folk," it was Clark, as James T. Patterson puts it, "who had the ear of the lawyers."[92] Psychological research into social conditions had new currency with legislators and juridical authorities—a cachet that previous invocations of the "psyche" had not possessed. Thus, although some psychologists contested the methodology of Clark's research, it proved persuasive to many district judges in Kansas, South Carolina, and Delaware.[93] Indeed, the Supreme Court justices found this psychological evidence to be a compelling component of the argument against segregation. The *Brown v. Board of Education* decision thus indicates the intellectual history of the psyche's rise as an appropriate arena for understanding public phenomena: it was a watershed moment in which political and judicial authorities first deployed such a framework for institutional ends.[94] The psychological situation of individuals became in the 1950s a central object of inquiry for determining institutional policy.

Beyond being part of reframing social conditions after the image of existential and psychological templates, postwar writers also questioned the legitimacy of social-democratic politics more directly. McCann follows the rise and fall of New Deal liberalism through the "hard-boiled" crime fiction that thrived from the 1930s until the 1960s. According to McCann, authors such as Dashiell Hammett, Raymond Chandler, and Chester Himes revised the classic detective story of Edgar Allan Poe and Arthur Conan Doyle. The twentieth-century evolution of crime fiction "became a symbolic theater where the dilemmas of New Deal liberalism could be staged."[95] As such, the conventional detective story functions as a "parable" of classical liberal political theory, in which evil can be abolished and the integrity of an imagined community restored through the governing order of law and rational self-interest.

As one permutation of this political tradition, the New Deal welfare state had attempted to ensure public well-being through federal regulatory power. The vicissitudes of economic crisis are, according to McCann's gloss on New Deal liberals, an anomaly that can be avoided by ferreting out errors and through reasonable intervention. Yet hard-boiled crime fiction charts the rise and fall of Roosevelt's interventionist liberalism by offering increasingly dissonant images of the public arena. For example, McCann explains that Raymond Chandler's crime novels, such as *The Long Goodbye* (1953), are underwritten by nostalgia for a "fraternally unified culture" that has "fall[en] victim to a society robbed of its cultural integrity and falsely joined by the market, mass media, and bureaucratic government."[96] While the political philosophy of New Deal liberalism depended on the notion of an integrated public that manifested in a consensus culture, Chandler's fiction documents the impossibility of such unity during the postwar moment. Suburbanization, mass consumerism, and a bureaucratic state had, for Chandler, undermined the fraternity that formed the basis for a liberal society by serving as empty surrogates for authentic community.

The sensibilities about individual existential crisis underwriting Highsmith's fiction from the 1950s, in contrast to Chandler's nostalgia, amount to a fervent rejection of an integrated, liberal view of the public arena. Through Highsmith's framing of the isolation and free choice that persistently confronts the individual, the progressive-liberal view of a society based on fraternity and shared responsibility becomes intellectually and experientially dubious. Could society really be an integrated body capable of collective welfare if alienation is such a pervasive diagnosis? And why does an individual's psyche seem to explain the manifestations of that anxiety in more compelling ways than the impersonal accounts of socioeconomic analysis?

Highsmith poses such a dialogue with the social and political thinking that underwrote the welfare state, yet that is not to say that her fiction is analogous to the "paperback noirs" that signal, as McCann argues, a turn toward the individualistic values of the Eisenhower era. The individual in Highsmith's work is fraught, embattled, and obsessed with its own contradictions. However, the very terms of that embattled selfhood affirm and depend on the categories of authenticity and free choice. Rather than promoting something like Mickey Spillane's rugged individualism, then, Highsmith investigates the felt crises of an anxious, ambivalent, and isolated age. When reading her novels within the intellectual debates of the 1950s, Highsmith's fiction offers something like a Pyrrhic victory over the sensibilities of the American social-democratic order: she not only diagnoses the vexed burden of choice that confronts the individual, but she also insists that the darker possibilities of the self cast a long shadow over that burden.

4 }

Southern Comfort

AUTHENTICITY, MALAISE, AND THE SCHOOL OF
THE HOLY GHOST

Binx Bolling, the mock hero of Walker Percy's *The Moviegoer* (1961), maintains that on his thirtieth birthday so far he has "learned only to recognize merde when I see it."[1] Bolling asserts that this skill—"a good nose for merde, for every species of shit that flies"—is his "only talent." This sardonic assertion prompts Bolling to cast a wide net of societal angst, for he professes to live in "the very century of merde" (228). Binx's derision grows out of the anxious, existential soil of his search for authenticity, for the real that is apparently mired in excreta. For example, Binx earlier explains that while traveling for business he often confronts an existential bog when in search of the latest movie. His moviegoing habit is to speak with the ticket attendant or the theater owner because, he says, he otherwise would "be lost, cut loose metaphysically speaking. I should be seeing one copy of a film which might be shown anywhere and at any time" (75). The possibility of becoming a mere iteration of some generic experience prompts Binx to "touch base" (74), to identify the particularities of a situation in the face of a worker at the theater. Binx's attempt to find the particular *beneath* the generic even leads him to make "a mark on my seat arm with my thumbnail" during an "absurd scene" in a John Wayne film. He searches for authenticity—he wants to touch "this particular piece of wood"—under generic conditions that could otherwise occur "anywhere and at any time" (75). It's as if he only has access to nonspecific copies and his efforts to "touch base" with reality occur under mass-produced conditions.

While many critics gloss Binx's angst as problems of religion, suburbia, and the decline of regionalism, his alienation also exemplifies a particular form of the postwar turn against institutions that mediate between individuals and a national community.[2] In particular, Binx's angst provides a window onto two related anxieties in the public discourse of postwar liberalism: the collusion between the welfare state and a consumer economy, on the one hand,

and the rise of what political scientists call an "independence regime" in partisan affiliation, on the other hand. These two phenomena, I argue, further contributed to the eroding cultural legitimacy of social-democratic institutions in the United States. *The Moviegoer* and other postwar Southern fiction help us map this history of political ideas, especially by showing how existential thought questioned the mediating work of national institutions. Percy's conception of the "sovereignty" of the individual knower provides a vantage point for identifying the limitations of this turn in American liberalism.[3] According to this view, alienation is a function of being divorced from "sovereignty" over one's own experience, as if citizens have been deprived of the opportunity to experience unmediated existence. This line of thinking prompts Binx to turn a critical eye toward the state as an alienating external authority—one that's not unlike mass consumer culture. He comes to view the "welfare" of the state as yielding bureaucratic superfluities and generic configurations of the self.

This view of the alienating effects of a secular state's effects on public life was shared by a group of writers who came to be called the "School of the Holy Ghost"—namely, Percy, Thomas Merton, Flannery O'Connor, and Allen Tate. These writers were fascinated with Kierkegaard and Dostoevsky, and they were in part responsible for disseminating—and inflecting the interpretation of—work by Camus, Sartre, and the "Christian existentialist" Gabriel Marcel.[4] During the 1950s, Percy and O'Connor read James Collins's *The Existentialists* (1952), a scholarly work that examines Kierkegaard, Nietzsche, Edmund Husserl, Sartre, and Marcel. Collins's book, much like the work of Percy and O'Connor, tries to reconcile the nihilistic and theistic varieties of this body of thought.[5] The seemingly incompatible philosophies of Christianity and existentialism would inflect Percy's and O'Connor's views of the state's collusion with mass consumer society. By retooling existentialist sensibilities about authenticity alongside anxieties about a bureaucratic state, these two standard-bearers of postwar Southern letters maintained that social-democratic institutions warp and genericize the self for the sake of social welfare. The postwar welfare order would thus foster the "abstraction of the self from itself," as Percy put it, thereby divorcing individuals from authentic existence for the sake of a mere "abstract notion."[6]

O'Connor, *Nausea*, and the Meaning of What-Is

In a 1957 lecture, O'Connor claimed that fiction writers "cannot move or mold reality in the interests of abstract truth." O'Connor explained that writers should learn instead "to be humble in the face of what-is. What-is is all he has to do with; the concrete is his medium."[7] If a writer attempts to conform a narrative to, say, an abstract philosophical program or a set of theological doctrines, then the fictional effort will devolve into a hollow and unnatural creation. This commitment to "what-is" as the origin of fiction may initially seem at odds with both existentialism and the Gothic tradition in which O'Connor writes. For instance, in her short story "Revelation," published in *Everything That Rises Must Converge* (1965), the self-righteous Mrs. Turpin has a vision of a "vast swinging bridge extending upward from the earth through a field of living fire." Mrs. Turpin finds that "white-trash" and "black niggers" lead the procession, along with "battalions of freaks and lunatics." The respectable lovers of order, on the other hand, march behind what she views as this degenerate band of worshippers. The effect of the vision is to invert Mrs. Turpin's sense of righteousness: the dignified members of the procession find with "shocked and altered faces that even their virtues were being burned away."[8] Mrs. Turpin's vision is anything but concrete. Still, the story reveals her respectability and religiosity to be what they *are*—racism and empty pretense. This configuration of "what-is," as O'Connor puts it, assumes the presence of an objective or transcendent standard for evaluating human behavior. O'Connor's view of "what-is" and her prescriptions for writing are therefore tied less to the norms of literary realism than to a philosophy of the real that extends beyond a material world. What-is is not sufficiently defined in physical terms; reality, according to O'Connor, is not hemmed in by matter.

This construal of reality, rather than simply falling prey to what Nietzsche criticizes as the world-abandonment characterizing Christian thought, is consonant with a common existentialist attitude toward the physical world. In Sartre's novel *Nausea* (1938), the narrator Antoine Roquentin contemplates the "frenzied excess" of a black root. The qualities of the root lead Roquentin to reflect on the nature of physical existence: "I scraped my heel against this black claw," he says, "I wanted to peel off some of the bark. For no reason at all, out of defiance, to make the bare pink appear absurd on the tanned leather: to *play* with the absurdity of the world."[9] Roquentin approaches the material with an overriding disdain—a desire to defy it as an essence—and wants instead to expose the physical for what it is: an absurdity, a meaningless plaything. Even the "black" quality of the root loses its meaning to Roquentin: he feels "the word ['black'] deflating, emptied of meaning with extraordinary rapidity."[10] Not only the qualities of the root but Roquentin's language become hollow when he contemplates their reality. He discovers that matter does not have an essence, as if the root or its qualities were somehow representative of a realm *behind* the phenomena of the root. Roquentin wants to repudiate the notion that meaning itself is reducible to physical qualities. It is this idea that leads him to conclude:

> Suspicious: that's what they were, the sounds, the smells, the tastes. When they ran quickly under your nose like startled hares and you didn't pay too much attention, you might believe them to be simple and reassuring, you might believe that there was real blue in the world. . . . But as soon

as you held on to them for an instant, this feeling of comfort and security gave way to a deep uneasiness.[11]

Roquentin's meditation on the absurdity of the world—the notion that existence is fundamentally meaningless—leads him to search for meaning beyond the material, which he insists is at best deserving of our uneasy suspicions. The horizons of the meaning of what-is, for Roquentin, cannot be discovered in mere physicality.

By turning on this existentialist refusal to reduce meaning to an empirical or materialist framework, O'Connor's understanding of what-is imagines fictional worlds rife with confrontations between characters and an uncompromising but often enigmatic reality. The enigma creates daylight between meaning and matter. But the staging of such conflicts prompts a sense of sickness for her characters—an antipathy toward that physicality, or an experience of vertigo within the world. This sensibility is consonant with both Kierkegaard and Sartre. In Sartre's novel, though, Roquentin's experience of the physical world prompts what he often describes as *nausea*: "The Nausea is not inside me," he says obliquely, "I feel it *out there* in the wall, in the suspenders, everywhere around me. It makes itself one with the café, I am the one who is within *it*."[12] Nausea is a psychosomatic manifestation of Roquentin's sense of the world's meaninglessness, and O'Connor's characters likewise inhabit claustrophobic or nauseating spaces. They find their only escape through a confrontation with the real that typically turns out to be damning of their sense of self or their values. Indeed, the stark and often-violent climaxes in O'Connor's fiction, much like Roquentin's nausea, expose the world's absurdity and meaninglessness in order to provide a clearer prospect for intuiting the real.

The unmasking of a character's pretense and fraudulent values owes an acknowledged debt to Sartre in O'Connor's first novel *Wise Blood* (1952). O'Connor described the novel in her letters as "my *opus nauseous*," an allusion to Sartre's work and an indication that understanding the narrative requires one to read Hazel "Haze" Motes and Enoch Emery as inhabitants of a world that drives itself sick with its own meaninglessness.[13] The novel centers on Haze's vehement repudiation of Christianity and a childhood conviction that "he was going to be a preacher."[14] Haze eventually founds the Church Without Christ and preaches the meaninglessness of religion and morality. Much like his grandfather, who was an evangelical firebrand, Haze preaches his atheistic doctrine on the hood of his car and exhorts passersby to look for a "new jesus," which the eighteen-year-old Enoch Emery supplies through a museum novelty: the corpse of a "shrunken man" (56). Enoch steals the corpse from the museum adjacent to the zoo where he works as a guard. He then leaves the "shrunken man" with Haze's lover Sabbath, who holds the corpse and tells her lover, "Call me Momma now" (106). Haze responds by "plucking" the corpse from Sabbath's hands, dashing it against the wall, and throwing the remains out the window. Having seen Sabbath and the corpse as a bastardized recreation of the Madonna, Haze experiences a vertiginous sense of nausea: he "almost los[es] his balance in the door" as he flees the apartment that had been a haven from his childhood convictions (107).[15]

Citizenship, the State, and Sartrean Authenticity

In contrast to the stark and absurd nausea of O'Connor's first novel, Binx Bolling at the beginning of Percy's *The Moviegoer* describes a "very peaceful" domestic existence in the suburb of Gentilly (6). Having settled into a job selling stocks at his uncle's brokerage firm, Binx asserts that he is "a model tenant and a model citizen," and that he takes "pleasure in doing all that is expected of me" (6). Binx explains that an American consumerist economy rewards him for his behavior with a surplus of commodities, exemplified in "an all but silent air conditioner and a very long lasting deodorant" (7). Having found that such a "model" life entails a glut of credentials, Binx observes, "My wallet is full of identity cards, library cards, credit cards." These documents also have various legitimizing functions: "my birth certificate, college diploma, honorable discharge, G.I. insurance, a few stock certificates, and my inherit-ance: a deed to ten acres of a defunct duck club down in St Bernard Parish" (6). This superfluity of papers sanctions his "model" life according to the sur-feit markers of institutions and consumer activities. Not unlike the protagonist in O'Connor's first novel who finds he must spurn both religion and a modern world in his search for the truth, Binx discovers that his "model" life is overrun by commodities and the products of impersonal bureaucracies.

For Binx, the institutional markers of his suburban life—the birth certificate, the college diploma, even the deed to state-sanctioned private property—induce both irony and anxiety: "It is a pleasure to carry out the duties of a citizen," he says, "and to receive in return a receipt or a neat styrene card with one's name on it certifying, so to speak, one's right to exist" (7). Binx's implications about the nature of citizenship are situated within references to his recent military service—"honorable discharge, G.I. insurance" (6)—which the United States has recognized through the mass-produced document of a "styrene card." Binx presents this marker of his service in the Korean War as an object of generic representation: his tenure of service culminates in a bureaucratic document of discharge, as though it were another receipt "certifying" the terms of his rela-tionship with the military. That Percy couches this exchange in terms of the "receipt"—that is, he lumps the discharge papers in with credit cards—links the state's relationship with the soldier to a consumerist logic. It's as if the state provides certain goods in exchange for the soldier's stint in the military. Binx's habit of lumping together the national and the consumerist establishes a pattern in which he depicts his citizenship in mass-produced terms. Later, the association of the national with the mass produced even leads Binx to wonder if his "pleasure" in being a model citizen has been manufactured as well.

Binx soon applies these anxieties to institutional spaces. Describing the buildings in his neighborhood, for example, he says, "I stroll around the school-yard in the last golden light of day and admire the building. Everything is so spick-and-span: the aluminum sashes fitted into the brick wall and gilded in the sunset, the pretty terrazzo floors and the desks molded like wings" (10). The parish school—one of the many institutions that crowd his neighborhood—is well ordered and constructed from mass-produced materials (aluminum, brick, concrete). The building gives Binx the "pleasant sense of the goodness of cre-ation," for he explains that "the brick and the glass and the aluminum [have been] extracted from common dirt" (10). Notably, the "creation" that elicits Binx's pleasure is a derivative, constructed space, one built with manufactured materials that transform organic matter. That is to say, Binx's "pleasant sense" centers not on the natural (dirt) but on its synthetic derivation (concrete ter-razzo). Binx thus intuits the "goodness of creation" only as it is refashioned into a humanly produced construction. He is at least once removed from—if not entirely out of touch with—a nonmanufactured world.

However, Binx is not without misgivings regarding his "ordinary life" and the institutional forces that mediate it. After describing the institution of the Gentilly school, Binx explains, "But things have suddenly changed. This morning, for the first time in years, there occurred to me the possibility of a search" (10). In a subtle turn on his commentary regarding the generic items that "certify" his involvement in the military, Binx recalls that the "search" originates from a traumatic experience in the Korean War:

> I dreamed of the war, no, not quite dreamed but woke with the taste of it in my mouth, the queasy-quince taste of 1951 and the Orient. I re-member the first time the search occurred to me. I came to myself under a chindolea bush. Everything is upside-down for me, as I shall explain later. . . . My shoulder didn't hurt but it was pressed hard against the ground as if somebody sat on me. Six inches from my nose a dung beetle was scratching around under the leaves. As I watched, there awoke in me an immense curiosity. I was onto something. I vowed that if I ever got out of this fix, I would pursue the search. (10–11)

Introducing the trope of the "search" through an exoticized memory contrasts with the earlier generic documents that certify his military service. Whereas a "neat styrene card" might identify Binx as a veteran, his memory of the Korean War is instead specific and experiential: the juxtaposition of the two calls into question the worth of the bureaucratic authorization.

Much like Haze's Sartrean nausea in *Wise Blood*, the contours of Binx's "search" are also significant because they take the form of an awakening to one's self, an awareness that recalls the philosophical centerpiece of Jean-Paul

Sartre's 1946 lecture-cum-essay, "Existentialism Is a Humanism." Sartre claims that the origins of truth reside in "consciousness confronting itself."[16] In Sartre's brand of existentialism, awareness of one's self as a thinking being generates consciousness; yet this awareness makes individual subjectivity into an object. Consciousness is thus at once the foundation for authentic knowledge and, paradoxically, the product of one's awareness of being conscious.

Redolent of Sartre's close association between consciousness and the real, Binx's explanation—"I came to myself"—allows him for the first time to be "onto something" (10, 11). In this juxtaposition between the synthetic "styrene card" and the particular experience in Korea, Binx establishes a connection between consciousness and authentic reality. The contrast between the bureaucratic document of the "honorable discharge" and the experiential confrontation of "coming to one's self" provokes Binx to become suspicious of bureaucratically sanctioned national identity while also rousing his desire for an authentic encounter with the real. Binx's "search" thus configures authenticity in terms of *unmediated consciousness*, of awakening to one's self as distinct from the interpositions of external forces.[17]

It is significant that Binx returns to his "search" later in his life while rummaging through the "little pile on his bureau" of items from his ordinary existence (11). These two moments—the personal experience of war and the everyday artifacts of bourgeois life—are connected in the figure of the dung beetle. Binx, like the beetle, "pokes through" the items on his bureau, as if seeing them for the first time (11). Also, presaging the passage at the end of the novel where Binx's search yields only his "good nose for merde" (228), the particular species of beetle rummaging in front of Binx's nose is of the *dung* variety: it rifles through leaves and other foliage in its expert hunt for "shit." Binx's "search" in Gentilly, then, becomes a form of shit-searching among the surfeit objects of his suburban existence: the quest for the authentic requires Binx to identify excreta.

One exemplary case of Binx's shit-searching occurs later in the novel, after he has purchased a new Dodge sedan and decides to vacation with Marcia, his latest secretary and romantic interest. Binx explains, "When I first slid under the wheel to drive [the sedan], it seemed that everything was in order—here was I, a healthy young man, a veteran with all his papers in order, a U.S. citizen driving a good car" (121). Binx's vacation embodies the ideals of national and economic flourishing: he is both "citizen" and the owner of the crowning product of American manufacturing. Yet his idyll is also unfulfilling: "All these things were true enough, yet on my first trip to the Gulf Coast with Marcia, I discovered to my dismay that my fine new Dodge was a regular incubator of malaise" (121). Binx defines the "malaise" as "the pain of loss. The world is lost to you, the world and the people in it, and there remains only you and the world and you no more able to be in the world than Banquo's ghost" (120). The "malaise," in other words, is the sense of alienation, of being set apart from intimacy with others or an external world. Like Macbeth's murdered friend, the subject who suffers from the malaise has put stock in one version of the real and has been betrayed by it.

The accumulation of manufactured goods—emblematized in the sedan—betrays Binx, preventing him from attaining authenticity on the grounds that even his romance with Marcia occurs within a symbolic complex of mass-produced experience. As Binx says, he and Marcia had "become like the American couple in the Dodge ad" (121), reproducible identities within a mass market of advertisements. Binx's freedom thus amounts only to generic individuality, for he finds that "merde" intercedes between Marcia and himself. Indeed, in Sartrean terms, Binx recognizes that the vacation where "everything was in order" is little more than a sustained evasion, a retreat into "bad faith," or the avoidance of the search for authenticity through boredom and distraction.[18] He encounters Marcia and the Gulf Coast under circumstances produced and approved by mass-marketing campaigns.

Percy returns to this skepticism about programmatic forms of individual happiness in *Love in the Ruins* (1971). Set "at a time near the end of the world," the novel chronicles Dr. Tom More's growing dissatisfaction with his suburban life in the ironically named Paradise, a wealthy community of mostly medical professionals in Louisiana. More, a researcher and therapist, invents the "Qualitative-Quantitative Ontological Lapsometer," which "measures a person's innermost self" through electromagnetic readings of the brain and spine (92). Despite More's diagnostic acuity and the accuracy of his lapsometer, he is a physician ironically unable to understand or heal himself. Alcoholism, alternating fits of elation and depression, and general surliness plague the physician.

More's discontent is not without cause, though, for his adult life has been capsized by the death of his daughter, Samantha, and the subsequent disintegration of his marriage. Samantha's excruciating and disfiguring death, caused by the slow growth of a neuroblastoma, leads Tom to a long-term affair with Early Times whiskey. More's first wife, Doris, becomes lonely and aimless, but rather than turning to Tom's route for comfort she searches for ways to "recover herself" (64). Doris begins to read "spiritual books" that prescribe various paths to happiness and individual fulfillment. The result, More insists, is existentially disastrous:

> Beware of Episcopal women who take up with Ayn Rand and the Buddha and Dr. Rhine formerly of Duke University. A certain type of Episcopal girl has a weakness that comes on them just past youth, just as sure as Italian girls get fat. They fall prey to Gnostic pride, commence buying antiques, and develop a yearning for esoteric doctrine. (64)

The "spiritual books" that Doris reads after her daughter's death are meant to be an antidote to her disenchantment: "That's a loving God you have there," she tells Tom as the neuroblastoma pushes one of Samantha's eyes out of its socket and around her nose bridge (72). Doris's spiritual inquiry attempts to re-enchant a world of suffering through "esoteric" ideas.

Tom is suspicious of Doris's search because she adopts the patterns of thought offered by others in order to legitimate the cultivation of her individuality. When Doris informs Tom that she plans to leave him, for example, she says simply, "I'm going in search of myself," which elicits More's incredulous reaction: "My heart sank," he says. "This was not really her way of talking" (65). "Our marriage is a collapsed morality," she sadly answers Tom's objections, "like a burnt-out star which collapses into itself, gives no light and is heavy heavy heavy." Yet her answers lead Tom to believe that Doris has abandoned her search for a recovered self and has instead retreated into the authority and programmatic individualism of another: "Collapsed morality. Law of life. More stately mansions," Tom laments. "Here are unmistakable echoes of her friend Alistair Fuchs-Forbes," the Englishman with whom she's having an affair (66).

Percy's representation of programmatic forms of individualism suggest such agendas routinize the "true" and "unique" behaviors of the self: "sleep a certain number of hours every night," as Binx recites, "breathe fresh air, eat a certain number of calories, evacuate [one's] bowels regularly and have a stimulating hobby" (*Moviegoer* 86). This recurring skepticism is grounded in an anxiety that impersonal bureaucracies and institutional routines divest the self of what Percy calls "sovereignty." As he writes in the essay "The Loss of the Creature," objects and experiences are "rendered invisible" by theoretical abstractions, such as exhaustive scientific theories or bourgeois cultural expectations. Percy insists that the request to validate whether "this is really it"—to legitimate knowledge, to require certification for some chosen form of individuality—actually obscures the real and the authentic. He argues:

> The dogfish, the tree, the seashell, the American Negro, the dream, are rendered invisible by a shift of reality from concrete thing to theory which Whitehead has called the fallacy of misplaced concreteness. It is the mistaking of an idea, a principle, an abstraction, for the real. As a consequence of the shift, the "specimen" is seen as less real than the theory of the specimen. As Kierkegaard said, once a person is seen as a specimen of a race or a species, at that very moment he ceases to be an individual. Then there are no more individuals but only specimens. (*Message* 58)

It is clearly problematic that the "American Negro" figures here as an object of knowledge alongside the "dogfish." (I return to the racial politics of this problem in the final section of this chapter.) Percy's construal of people as objects of knowledge derives from his concern that our experience is threatened by a set of interpositions that he calls a "symbolic complex." Percy explains that "sanctioned" forms of experience necessarily arbitrate the individual's conscious encounter of a thing, person, or event. He asks:

> Why is it almost impossible to gaze directly at the Grand Canyon under [touristic] circumstances and see it for what it is—as one picks up a strange object from one's back yard and gazes directly at it? It is almost impossible because the Grand Canyon, the thing as it is, has been appropriated by the symbolic complex which has already been formed in the sightseer's mind. Seeing the canyon under approved circumstances is seeing the symbolic complex head on. (47)

The tourist, in this case, encounters not the thing-in-itself but a "prepared experience," a predetermined set of meanings that distances the subject from the landscape that she views (60). The consequence of this sifted consciousness is a gradual concession of agency, incremental "losses of sovereignty" (50).

Percy's philosophy of the self contends that, by experiencing the world only under "approved circumstances," the individual becomes "lost" within the complex of forces that mediate her existence. Such an individual surrenders her "sovereignty" to "a class of privileged knowers," and thereby becomes alienated from her own daily existence. By "sovereignty," then, Percy means the subject's capacity for self-recognition as "a knowing being whose peculiar property it is to see himself as being in a certain situation" (58). The "knower," Percy argues, must reassert her authority over the thing "known" (59).

Percy's argument recapitulates Sartre's claim that the origins of "truth" reside in "consciousness confronting itself" (*Existentialism* 40). Like Sartre, Percy's notion of the "sovereign person" construes authentic knowledge of both the world and one's self as deriving from *self-presence*—the subject exercising control over her subjectivity. Sartre similarly argues that authentic subjectivity lies at the root of reality: anything less than a consciousness aware of itself is a faulty foundation for the real. However, Percy's notion of sovereignty also depends on the *particularity of consciousness*—that is, of seeing one's self as "being in a certain situation." Thus, those forces that obscure the particular— for example, exhaustive accounts of the human body, Ayn Rand's dubious ethical system, or the generic identities produced by a bureaucratic state—prevent one from arriving at authentic knowledge. As a result, Percy maintains that an idiosyncratic authentic subjectivity lies beyond the "certifying" forces of national institutions and mass-produced programs for individuality.

By conflating mass consumerism and the American state, this school of postwar thought levies a fundamental objection against the way that the state structures its relationship to citizens. Citizenship follows a bureaucratic and economized mold. This characterization of citizenship as another form of consumerism is grounded in shifts in the US economy at mid-century. In particular, shaken by a recession during 1937–1938, Roosevelt's administration began to employ Keynesian redistributive fiscal policy. Policy during the active phase of the New Deal had presupposed that the state could responsibly lead an assault on monopoly power and institute "an ordered economic world."[19] In contrast to this aggressive regulation of capitalism and central planning, Keynesianism maintained that an industrial economy is too convoluted for governmental mechanisms to direct, but certain fiscal measures (such as controlling aggregate demand by federal or "deficit" spending) could mitigate the volatility of recessions and depressions in an economic cycle.

Following the wave of Keynesian thought that swept Europe in the 1930s, Roosevelt's administration—particularly Harold Ickes, Harry Hopkins, and Henry Morgenthau—began to strengthen domestic programs of compensatory social insurance, earlier established in the Social Security Act (1935). The administration also eased its heavy-handed relationship to corporate America. The New Deal legislation after the recession thus became "less statist than its earlier counterparts, less concerned with issues of class, less hostile to existing patterns of economic power, committed above all to a new vision of a consumer-driven economy."[20] By the time the United States entered the war, an increasingly common vision among many New Dealers was that the United States should become a "consumers' republic," a conflation of national identity with mass consumption.[21]

This new emphasis on a consumer economy created waves among postwar intellectuals, particularly those interested in what Daniel Bell termed the "theory of mass society."[22] Bracketing the economic viability of this shift, the relevant point within American intellectual history is that it created worry among intellectuals that consumerism would become the prevailing ethos of national culture. Indeed, Erich Fromm, who was the first to use the term "consumer culture," psychologized this "shift" in "emphasis" at a societal level.[23] Deeply influenced by Fromm's work, the sociologist David Riesman similarly argued in his study *The Lonely Crowd* (1950) that consumption, rather than production, pervaded the habits of thought and behavior in postwar America.[24] As Daniel Horowitz says, Riesman's study of postwar suburban affluence "mistrusted centralized power and feared the way mass culture fostered conformity and undermined individualism."[25] The emerging Keynesian consensus regarding consumption became for many critics, writers, and researchers a source not of prosperity but estrangement from the authentic avenues of self-possession.

While fiction by Percy and O'Connor, as well as psychological and sociological public writing by Fromm and Riesman, raised intellectual concerns about consumerism in the United States, changes in public and economic policy left Social Security as the central component of the postwar welfare state. As Daniel T. Rodgers explains, the emphasis on Social Security privatized the political relationship between citizens and the state by patterning it after the "form not of a broad contract between social groups but of myriad private contracts between individuals and the state."[26] The earlier "reform" assemblage of domestic policies and programs construed state politics as the concentration of political will and the institutionalization of an activist agenda, while the postreform welfare state became principally a broker or distributor of services.[27]

The Democratic Party's Keynesian social-economic philosophy had many other consequences. For example, another especially pernicious and misleading result of the conflation of liberal citizenship and a consumer economy was that federal policy increasingly understood the nation as a statistical body of collective consumption, aggregate demand, and income.[28] Questions of "political economy" became almost exclusively concerned during the postwar era with limiting unemployment and evading recessions, which "detached liberalism from its earlier emphasis on reform."[29] Statistical and actuarial models of welfare accumulated the public in an effort to build systems of security.[30] Yet as a result, those models reconstituted the national body after the pattern of the market economy, rather than as unequal social groups in need of protections from the instability of the economy.

The Roosevelt administration's response to the 1937–38 recession therefore planted seeds that would later grow into doubts about liberalism's effects on the nature of citizenship. Many commentators worried that liberalism had, through a consumer economy, merely reconstituted the disease of mass conformity that the nation had tried to cure through a world war. Until the civil rights movement of the 1960s forced the hand of a vacillating and divided Democratic Party, the party's policy centered largely on Keynesian redistributive policies and compensatory mechanisms. This legacy of social welfare as an actuarial science lies behind Binx's conflation of national identity with the surfeit objects of mass consumerism. As Binx presents it, citizenship had become a form of consumption facilitated by a state, which had reconstituted itself as a broker of services. This rebranding of a liberal political economy forecloses the possibilities of social belonging and instead becomes another abstract force that alienates the self from an authentic experience of the world.

Vote for Authenticity

Insofar as Percy and O'Connor criticize national impositions upon the consciousness of individuals, their fiction is suited to what Mark McGurl calls the "World Pluribus of Letters," in which postwar writers imagine literature as "a technology of disaffiliation from empirical nations in favor of something more ideal."[31] McGurl generally applies this description to US minority writers who contest assimilation and commodification by American mainstream culture. These authors find themselves connected to a "global pluralist space." For McGurl, literary disaffiliation from the nation-state establishes a connection between US minority writers and a pluralistic, transnational community.[32] Yet the "disaffiliation" from an organizational intermediary in fiction by O'Connor and Percy does not function as a strategy for finding solidarity with the marginalized around the world; rather, it is a turn away from collective affiliation and toward a preoccupation with self-governing consciousness.

What would be the effects for those domains of American political culture influenced by this ethic of disaffiliation? Percy's scattered political writings and interviews patterns one common response by Democrats in the South who were disaffected with the postwar political order. In short, many Southern Democrats used such an ethic to justify their tepid support for—or even opposition to—the civil rights movement. For example, Percy expressed doubts regarding compensatory relief and federal methods for enacting desegregation, because he believed that these government interventions were poorly executed and caused unforeseen economic and social consequences. Although Percy voiced support for the civil rights movement, he felt his philosophical sensibilities were in conflict with his political commitments. As his friend and priest James Boulware recalls, "My first encounter with [Percy] was around the work for civil rights. . . . I think he was a little hesitant when it got down to being involved in a demonstration. He would do things quietly, but he did not want to get overtly involved in a lot of stuff."[33]

This nominal support for activism, but reticence to participate in it, surfaces in a 1957 essay, where Percy holds up Martin Luther King Jr., as a paragon of "wise and successful" leadership, even as he asserts that the "worst fate that could overtake the struggle against segregation would be its capture by a political orthodoxy of the left."[34] Percy explains that he is opposed to "militant liberalism," which enforces reform rather than encourages it.[35] Percy's response to the civil rights movement—where individual paragons of virtue and decentralized actors seem legitimate, but their institutional organization becomes a hazard—is emblematic of his larger political sensibilities, which frequently center on fears of "growing federal power and federal money."[36] As he often writes in letters and essays, Percy maintains that the "Northern politicians" who "support any and every proposal of federal intervention" are well intentioned but still introduce inadvertent resentment and other ills through their heavy-handed attempts to impose social reform.[37] The implication is that an activist-managerial state is an engine of corruption. Federal interventions are regular incubators of the malaise.

In contrast to "militant liberalism," Percy envisions progressive reform on the "race question" from within society, rather than imposed from the outside by federal authority. He explains that rapid "social changes are taking place which can only have the effect of radically altering the character of the problem, if not solving it."[38] Percy explains two social conditions will alter, if not ameliorate, the "dilemma of the Negro": first, "the ongoing emigration of the Negro from the South," which will disperse the crisis beyond one region of the nation and, second, the South's inevitable accommodation of "its dwindling Negro population as it moves from second- to first-class citizenship, a pattern which has nothing to do with the harsh words and extremist laws, which is imperfect but bids fair to be effective." Percy explains this second inevitability with the more succinct claim: "Racial injustice is bad business."[39] He says, in other words, that federal intervention in the struggles for desegregation is both maladroit and preemptively pointless, for entrepreneurial competition—along with the wise work of individual leaders—is capable of achieving the reform that statist activism aims to institute.

Percy's view of the civil rights movement and federal intervention are symptomatic of the manner in which many liberals developed an ethic of disaffiliation and, as a result, viewed an activist-managerial state at a disaffected remove. Tolson captures this political affect when explaining Percy's liberalism:

> In the early 1950s, as later, Percy was reluctant to label himself politically. Despite his aversion to FDR, he maintained that he always voted for Democrats in presidential elections, but he was never particularly partisan in his political thinking. . . . During the 1950s and 1960s, however, he did seem to find a position on the political continuum—that of a moderate liberal, concerned domestically with civil rights and greater social justice, and internationally with the containment of communism.[40]

Percy's partisan choices had little to do with the Democratic Party's economic policies or what he understood to be its bungling relief and welfare programs. Rather, according to Boulware and Tolson, Percy's liberalism was a consequence of his conversion to a brand of Catholicism that promoted social equality. "Percy made peace with liberals, and liberalism," Tolson explains, "because doing so seemed the only way to work for a political solution to the problem [of civil rights]."[41] This entente with the Democratic Party suggests that Percy was hedging his bets regarding desegregation: while Republicans would oppose reform, the Democrats would only mishandle it.

On the other hand, as his friend Shelby Foote says, President Franklin D. Roosevelt was Percy's lifelong "political bugbear."[42] His abiding conviction was that social-democratic programs and institutions were a political thorn in the side of the Democratic Party. For many Southern political commentators, the Agricultural Adjustment Act of 1933 (AAA) was a notorious case in point. The New Deal, they felt, had disastrous effects on the structure of farming communities. The Act had enabled the federal government to pay subsidies to farmers who reduced their output, thus decreasing the supply of crops and— by virtue of staving off a flooded market—regulating food prices to the benefit of consumers and farmers alike. Such programs simultaneously distributed monetary relief to rural communities while also increasing the value of the goods they provided. Consequently, by 1935 the average income of farmers in the South had almost doubled. At the time, the AAA seemed like a self-evident good to New Dealers.

Yet Percy says otherwise in his 1965 essay "Mississippi: The Fallen Paradise." Percy argues that the "farming parity" of the New Deal agricultural plank misfired, for its outcomes had marginalized some groups at the expense of others, creating unforeseen consequences that would merely reshuffle the social ills that Roosevelt's ad hoc liberalism and centralized economic planning purported to alleviate. He caustically says, "Mississippi desperately needed the New Deal and profited enormously from it. Indeed, the Roosevelt farm program succeeded too well. Planters who were going broke on ten-cent cotton voted for Roosevelt, took federal money, got rich, lived to hate Kennedy and Johnson and vote for Goldwater—while still taking federal money."[43] In Percy's view, the New Deal enabled poor white farmers to construct a populist coalition that later employed its wealth and influence in opposing desegregation and further economic reform. Such results typify the larger inability of a welfare state to achieve its desired ends, for these outcomes undermined the work of the Civil Rights Section of the Justice Department. Percy argues that the imposition of federal authority thus results in a kind of invisible hand of unintended consequences, which undermine the liberal aspiration to foster a social arena of equity through economic planning.

These sentiments are hardly original to Percy, for they were not only common among postwar Democrats in the South, but they were also central to the Republican resurgence underway at the end of Percy's life. Indeed, the two partisan phenomena resided on the same spectrum of political sensibilities. For example, in 1987, Percy chastised his friend Dick Faust for the latter's unquestioning support of President Reagan: "Why do [you] feel obliged to make out Ron Reagan as perfect?" he wrote Faust in a letter. "Nobody has been perfect since Hitler and Stalin. I find it more useful to think of conservatives as ordinary fucked-up humans with perhaps a good idea or two, and of liberals as perhaps even more fucked-up and hardly an idea beyond good intentions."[44] Even if Percy's dichotomy between "good intentions" and "a good idea or two" led him to affiliate with the "even more fucked-up" liberals, he nonetheless felt some sympathy with the Republicans that had come to power in the 1980s. Boulware explains that Percy "admired Reagan's simplification, Reagan's communication of what we all should hold to." Yet even when he accepted a dinner invitation from Reagan in 1987, Percy still distanced himself from affiliating with the president's band of Republican conservatives because of his "serious doubts" about their intentions.[45]

These tensions are striking. Percy was attracted to a "simplification" of federal regulations *and* the social vision of Presidents Johnson and Kennedy; a voluntary desegregation of the South *and* the enforcement of civil rights legislation; the freedom of the individual *and* a set of ideals that resolve by fiat the "shit" surrounding the self. Percy felt attracted, in other words, to competing forms of political thinking: a liberal social arena of "sovereign knowers" and a liberalized economic arena governed by virtuous behavior ("what we all should hold to"). Explaining the paradox of Percy's religious and political commitments, Boulware said simply, "[Walker] kind of wanted that code."[46]

This characterization of the tensions underlying Percy's commitments recalls the persistent but ultimately failed pursuit of a "code" by Lancelot

Andrewes Lamar, the titular narrator of Percy's *Lancelot* (1977). A former "liberal" NAACP lawyer and scion of a distinguished Southern family, Lancelot recounts how he has come to be confined in a mental hospital.[47] The narration is stylized as a series of confessions to a silent second party, a priest-psychologist named Harry, who is also a former college friend of the narrator. Lancelot is confined to a cell in the Institute for Aberrant Behavior because, he slowly allows himself to remember, he went temporarily insane after his mansion, Belle Isle, burned to the ground. The fire killed his wife, Margot, along with three members of a movie crew making a film at the estate. While the therapists at the Institute believe that Lancelot merely finds Belle Isle burning and that he himself is burned trying to rescue his wife, Lancelot later confesses to orchestrating the catastrophe.

Lancelot invokes the idea of a "code" during his failed attempts to have an "innocent" relationship with the patient in the cell adjacent to his own (34). This patient, Anna, is the victim of a violent rape and has refused to eat or speak since the assault. Lancelot draws Anna out of her silence and attempts to communicate with her through a "code," a system of taps upon the shared wall of their adjoining cells. This "code" is simple: each tap corresponds to a letter in the alphabet: "One knock = A, two = B, and so on." He explains that introducing this "code" is not "as easy as you might think," especially to a silent subject who does not initially reciprocate the desire for communication (34).

The symbolic importance of Lancelot's "code" becomes clearer when he later elaborates upon his theory about the "new age." In one permutation of this vision, Lancelot imagines a "young man" standing "in a mountain pass above the Shenandoah Valley. A rifle is slung across his back" (221). The man lives in a world of "great dying cities," collapsing after an unidentified crisis. "He is waiting and watching for something," Lancelot explains. "What? A sign? Who, what is he? WASP Virginian? New England Irish? Louisiana Creole? Jew? Black? Where does he live? It is impossible to say" (221). The "young man" of this apocalyptic age emerges after "Washington, the country, [has gone] down the drain" (220). His attentiveness—"waiting and watching for something"—replaces the passivity of the former age: "The people have lost [the country] to the politicians, bureaucrats, drunk Congressmen, lying Presidents, White House preachers, C.I.A., F.B.I., Mafia, Pentagon, pornographers" (220). The "new man" cannot rely on societal structures, nor do the categories of the former age apply to him. The "impossibility" of these categories derive from the fact that civilization has collapsed—there is no more New England, no more South, no more racial distinctions—and, as such, the apocalypse forces him to become an individual.

Lancelot's fantasy hinges on the return to a state of innocence, which is coded in gendered ways. Unlike his descriptions of Anna, Lancelot specifically notes that the "new age" will allow men to be independent from political institutions. (Women aren't an important part of Lancelot's political schema in either the pre- or post-apocalyptic ages.) The national capitol having fallen, parties like-wise fall away, and only individuals remain. The implication of Lancelot's claim is that partisan politics is a function of the disease infecting the present moment. In fact, in an earlier permutation of Lancelot's apocalyptic dream, he imagines a revolution in which there will be no "speeches, rallies, political parties. There will be no need of such things. One man will act. Another man will act," initiating a sequence of independent action by mavericks and virtuous individuals (157). This new form of existence will allow men to understand one another as "gentlemen used to know each other," rather than as members of a party or movement. No Americans in the present age live according to this code, Lancelot complains, because they refuse to act from "perfect sobriety and freedom" (157). Instead, his peers retreat into absurd sexuality and political dependencies.

Lancelot's notion that the "code" is a "counsel kept" explains why he uses the same term to describe the system of communication that he earlier proposes to Anna. Much like the apocalyptic ideal for the "new gentleman," the earlier simplistic code he develops in his cell is "something held in common," a com-municative order (157). Lancelot hopes, in other words, to establish a shared understanding of the world with Anna from the bottom up, as it were, creating a simplistic language of taps and knocks. He imagines constructing a new lin-guistic plane—an ideal mode of being—because, by implication, the estab-lished order of communication and action has failed.

On the one hand, then, this idea of the "code" is a further permutation of Percy's earlier figure of the "sovereign knower": the new gentleman is the indi-vidual who in full self-possession of himself acts singularly. On the other hand, Lancelot's "code" inflects the ideal of sovereignty through a desire for a shared communicative order, which cultivates understanding among its adherents ("a counsel kept") and even intimacy (e.g., Lancelot's obsessive desire to marry Anna). The idea of the "code" therefore represents a communal permutation of Percy's recurring interest in the sovereignty of the self.

Despite the allure of the "code," Lancelot discovers that this route for re-solving his anxieties about the "present age" are not without its problems. Lancelot explains, for example, that his encounter with catastrophe has taught him that "the only way to avoid imitation is to ask a question and the only way to establish a code is repetition" (34–35). Lancelot's statement exemplifies the paradox that unravels his search for a shared communicative order: the "code" and its constitutive mechanisms of "repetition" are themselves forms of "im-itation," the hazard that demands asking questions in the first place. Not sur-prisingly, this conflict yields uncertainty. As Lancelot puts it when faced with the possibility that Siobhan is not his biological daughter, "One has to know for sure before doing anything" (43). Sober action is the child of conviction, he implies, and so one either has to take the word of another or sort out the truth for one's self.

The standard of absolute certainty chips away at Lancelot's confidence in a shared code. Lancelot comes to suspect that his convictions often form the basis of destruction. Skepticism—the demand for certainty, the questioning of imitation—nurtures Lancelot's anxiety that an individual cannot act singularly while also enjoying intimacy with others. The novel doubles back on its narrator, casting doubts on the few ideals he offers in the midst of an otherwise toxic litany of prejudices. For example, explaining his hopes to "make a new life, an absolutely new beginning," Lancelot muses:

> Begin with a burrow, a small clean well-swept place such as this [cell], with one tiny window on the world and another creature in the next room. That is all you need. In fact, that is all you can stand. Add more creatures, more world, books, talk, TV, news—and we'll all be as crazy as we were before. (108)

Lancelot's "new life" begins with isolation, a space where the self is not crowded by other "creatures" or possessions. The intimacy of Lancelot's "new beginning" occurs at a remove, as if self-possession demands that the individual remain set apart within his or her own enclosed cell. Shared space becomes partitioned space, because any greater intimacy with other "creatures" precipitates "craziness."

While the practice of Catholicism may revolve around communion and codify certain beliefs as orthodoxy, a commitment to existential authenticity unravels those religious threads. O'Connor and Percy's search for a Christian existentialism was thus a doomed project. Even as Lancelot desires a shared code that facilitates mutual understanding among its adherents, his figure of the new gentleman is atomized, cordoned off from others within an oubliette of skepticism, irony, and self-sufficiency. The communal aspirations of Lancelot's code are never established because of his simultaneous, paradoxical desire to retain the "freedom to act on my conviction." Lancelot desires intimacy with Anna, to be recognized as a gentleman, and also to remain within the silo of his sovereignty.

The paradoxes of postwar Christian existentialism, with its emphasis on Marcel's notion of *homo viator*, or "man the wayfarer," made institutional disaffiliation a matter of ethical and existential necessity. Like the other tendencies within liberal intellectual life explored in previous chapters, this variety also turned against the underlying assumptions of the political imperatives established during an earlier era of American liberalism. Indeed, this literary school of thought shared cultural and political sensibilities with a contemporaneous development in American partisan affiliation: the rise of so-called "independent" voters, or those who refused to identify with either the Democratic or Republican Parties. Beginning in the mid-1960s, what Harold Clarke and Motoshi Suzuki call a new "independence regime" developed rapidly in the United States.[48] In 1952 when Gallup and other modern polls began to record what has since been termed "partisan dealignment," 22 percent of voters self-identified as independent. By 1976, dealignment—or not aligning with any registered party—had increased to 37 percent. Helmut Norporth and Jerrold Rusk's itemized analysis of the survey data suggests that the principal source of this rapid dealignment was the entry of a new generation of voters into the electorate.[49] A new political culture had taken hold.

Some political scientists view partisan dealignment as a generational event concentrated between the elections of 1964 and 1976.[50] However, the continuation of this "independence regime" suggests that the nature of party identification has been changing since World War II: disaffiliation has become an ethic within American political culture.[51] The consequences of this political sensibility had tangible effects on the platforms and policies of the nation's main parties. Several political scientists have argued that the attempt to capture the "independent" or dealigned segment of voters has caused the Democratic Party in particular to estrange its progressive affiliates, dilute reformist political beliefs, or back "centrist" public policies.[52] As another feature of the transformation of postwar liberalism, the significant expansion of an "independence regime" led the Democratic Party to adopt increasingly "postreform" positions.

The irony of these shifts in American political culture away from partisan alignment is how little they actually signified about American voting behavior. Studies of voter behavior have typically shown that the "rise" of an "independence regime" is a "myth," for since 1950 approximately 1 in 12 or 1 in 10 voters actually make up an independent segment of the voting populace.[53] That is to say, the vast majority of disaffiliated or dealigned voters consistently align with one party or the other, despite their avowed independence. Since the 1980s, what Marc Hetherington calls the "elite behavior" of elected officials has grown increasingly more polarized, despite the discrepancy in "mass opinion" about disaffiliation.[54] The discrepancy between public policy and American political culture suggests that notions about disaffiliation are more a function of political affect than cogent ideological shifts.

This discrepancy has also deflated the bases and blurred the distinctions between the Republican and Democratic Parties, at least in the later decades of the twentieth century. As Paul Krugman puts it, the "attempt to attract swing voters is a mug's game, because such voters don't exist."[55] Or, more precisely, when they do exist, they do not always vote, and rarely do so based upon informed appeals by political parties. The promise of partisan dealignment is all the more empty because, as Harold Wilensky explains, "the pure independents, 1 in 10 of the electorate, are most ignorant about politics and are least likely to vote."[56] These shifts may therefore be understood, on the one hand, as an avowed but self-deceiving attempt by a growing segment of Americans to preserve political independence and the integrity of the self—to vote with authenticity. On the other hand, these shifts attest to the consequences of a cultural sensibility that privileges the independence and authenticity of the self as

the moral center for political behavior. The "ethic" of an independence regime contributed to the slow death of the institutional progressivism of the
Democratic Party.

Intersubjectivity as Savior?

In addition to the contradictions of Christian existentialism in the United
States, the work of the School of the Holy Ghost is also important for how it
exemplifies the splintering of post-1950 existential thought in both Europe and
the United States. The wedge that caused this splintering was the attempt to
synthesize the ideas of an authentic ego and an "intersubjective milieu."[57] The
concept of intersubjectivity tries to define the nature of the self as a thinking
being in such a way that does not silo individuals within consciousness. The
idea of intersubjectivity among philosophers like Marcel and Sartre, and its
manifestation in Percy's work, vivify a paradox—if not an outright contradic-
tion—at the heart of existentialism's political aspirations.

Sartre's postwar project is the key example of this paradox. His writing after
Being and Nothingness (1943) was animated by vexed attempts to reconcile the
existentialist ideal of consciousness confronting itself with the competing aspiration to establish solidarity among individuals. In his famous 1946 lecture,
"Existentialism Is a Humanism," Sartre tries to answer his Marxist critics, who
charge that his philosophy is tailored to individualistic capitalist societies at "the
very moment in which man fully comprehends his isolation" (18). According
to Sartre's detractors, understanding one's self as an alienated, self-governing
individual in a meaningless world renders the existentialist "incapable of re-
establishing solidarity with those who exist outside of the self, and who are
inaccessible to us through the *cogito*" (18).

Sartre responds to this criticism by clarifying why "our point of departure is,
indeed, the subjectivity of the individual" (40). He insists that his philosophical
starting point "seek[s] to base our doctrine on truth, not on comforting theories
full of hope but without any real foundation" (40). Sartre's reference to "comforting theories full of hope" seems in the context of the essay to refer to dialectical history. In Marx's materialist inversion of Hegel, history is structured
according to the "antagonism of oppressing and oppressed classes."[58] Yet for
Marx and Engels this dialectical struggle also entails a kind of utopian future,
for a class-less and property-less society becomes the inevitable outcome of dialectical materialism. According to this materialist formula, the production of
history resides not in individual consciousness but in the material conditions
of a historical world.

For Sartre, in contrast, the Marxist dialectic is "at the outset, a theory that
suppresses the truth, for outside of this Cartesian *cogito*, all objects are merely
probable, and a doctrine of probabilities not rooted in any truth crumbles into

nothing" (40). The fact that historical-material conditions purport to precede consciousness is, for Sartre, simply unsupportable. Categories such as "history" and "material reality" are comprehensible only as concepts that derive from the certainty of consciousness. Therefore, the individual only "defines himself" after "he encounters himself" (22). Sartre claims that the very concept of history must depend on consciousness confronting itself. By recognizing this view of history as a fundamental truth, human beings discover that they alone are responsible for their actions. Only by "directly seizing" this truth of the self is one able to formulate authentic resistance to forces of oppression (22).

Yet therein lies the rub. After insisting on the privileged place of individual consciousness, Sartre argues that this fundamental positioning of the thinking self does not imprison the individual within subjectivity, as his leftist opponents claim. Rather, Sartre responds that the moment in which "consciousness confronts itself" is actually conditional upon the perception of the existence of others (41). There are ethical ramifications for Sartre's qualification, such as the fact that the existentialist's responsibility for the self does "not mean that he is responsible only for his own individuality, but that he is responsible for all men" (23). Pressing this ethical responsibility into an epistemological claim, Sartre maintains that his philosophy imbricates the self and other, for the individual "who becomes aware of himself directly in the *cogito* also perceives all others" (41). In other words, Sartre argues that consciousness only becomes authentic—that the self is aware of itself—insofar as it recognizes the existence and freedom of other human beings. According to this formulation of existentialism, self-determination occurs within the "intersubjectivity" of the world (42).

After the war, Sartre tried to reconcile his longstanding ideas about authenticity and individual consciousness with Marxist politics. This transition in his work created a notorious interpretive problem for his readers. In 1955, for example, Sartre's longtime friend and cofounder of *Les Temps modernes*, Raymond Aron, criticizes Sartre's postwar turn as an "incompatible" union of Kierkegaard and Marx.[59] Even Thomas R. Flynn, who is more sympathetic to Sartre's project than most postwar American readers, concludes, "It is among the 'revisionists,' if at all, that we must find the criteria for Sartre's Marxism."[60] Flynn argues that the existential perspective that Sartre preserves in later works, *Search for a Method* (1957) and *Dialectical Reason* (1960), distance him from orthodox Marxist thought, even as these later works also revise certain key claims from his earlier existentialism.

The point is that the majority of critics insist that Sartre's refusal to abandon the *cogito* as the centerpiece of his philosophy undermines, or at least weighs down, his postwar project. It is not difficult to agree with this appraisal. Much like Lancelot's attempt to establish a "code" with Anna creates mutually exclusive imperatives—to preserve self-sovereignty and establish a shared communicative order—Sartre's attempt to synthesize the basis of existentialism (the *cogito*) with a philosophical basis for solidarity (the idea of intersubjectivity) enters an impossible cul-de-sac of commitments. Why, for example, is "history" inaccessible apart from consciousness confronting itself but the "other" is requisite for that same confrontation? Percy's fiction, much like Sartre's defense of existentialism, exhibits why notions about the *cogito* and the priority of sovereignty are politically isolating.

Not surprisingly given the familiar anxieties of the early Cold War era, Sartre's later political writings had significantly less intellectual purchase among American existentialists than his claims about freedom, authenticity, and the absurdity of existence. This selective reception of Sartre's work began as soon as his explicit Marxist turn became apparent, and it was spearheaded by New York Intellectuals, such as William Barret, Philip Rahv, and William Phillips. During this phase of American existentialism, as Cotkin explains, many of this group of writers and editors "worked to popularize central texts in existentialism, to evaluate its strengths and weaknesses, and to judge how well it responded to the spirit and needs of the age."[61] But being attuned to the "spirit and needs of the age" also prompted these intellectuals to reject the political agendas of Sartre, Camus, and de Beauvoir, while still refashioning existentialism to respond to that perceived "spirit."

Hannah Arendt, for example, argues in "What Is Existenz Philosophy?" (1946) that modern existentialism has its roots in the German tradition of Kant and Schelling, who establish "the *autonomy* of man."[62] This autonomy fared well in the postwar economy of prestige. The art critic and New York Intellectual Clement Greenberg, for example, offers the following ambivalent description of the French movement's influence upon his compatriots: "Whatever the affectations and philosophical sketchiness of Existentialism, it is aesthetically appropriate to our age."[63] Greenberg's description attests to the felt need for a European touchstone to legitimize anti-Soviet politics and other Cold War anxieties. More importantly, Greenberg presents this grouping of ideas as part of the authorization and circulation of wider social imperatives. Those imperatives created an ultimately self-defeating set of aspirations within the intellectual culture of postwar liberalism.

The New Left and the Aesthetics of Reception

American existentialist thought was a ship that wrecked on a cluster of rocks, and only one was its internal conflicts. Another was the terms under which existentialism was received. The prevailing trend in the reception history of existentialism in the United States was that its initial advocates consistently distanced the movement from any particular political ideology during the 1940s and 1950s. This gesture was somewhat consistent with the proto-existentialism of the nineteenth century—particularly writers like Dostoevsky, Nietzsche, and

Kierkegaard—but it was also an instance of an aestheticism animating the politics of reception following World War II. For intellectuals writing in America about European cultural movements, the valorization of private judgments of value—or the alienating forces that prevent them—became a kind of sieve for filtering the transmission and reception of texts and ideas. This aestheticized reception provided the intellectual backdrop for important elements of public criticism during the 1950s.

Those who wrote about existentialism after the war fashioned a philosophical canon that divested the European movement of its radical political aspirations. Marjorie Grene's *Dreadful Freedom* (1948), for instance, provided one of the first systematic "critiques" or elaborations of existentialism. Grene presents existentialism as "a brilliant statement of the tragic dilemma if not of man, at least of man in our time" because of its "relentless, even extravagant, honesty in the rejection of easy solutions or apparent solutions" to the anxieties of "modern man."[64] Similarly, in 1956, Walter Kaufmann collected the anthology, *Existentialism: From Dostoevsky to Sartre*, which extends existentialism beyond France and also into literary terrain. (In addition to helping define and circulate existentialism in the United States, Kaufmann was also responsible for completing the first English translations of many of Nietzsche's works, as I discussed in the first chapter.) Kaufmann's anthology almost entirely excludes existentialist strains of Marxism and radical politics—an obvious but shrewd editorial decision during the gathering tensions of the Second Red Scare. This selective reception similarly characterizes Hazel Barnes's *The Literature of Possibility* (1959), where she argues that many nineteenth-century American philosophers, including William James, share the European existentialists' "value of consciousness itself."[65]

The first phase of the American reception of existentialism therefore tended to stifle direct discussion of its political radicalism; instead, European existentialism was configured as a philosophical basis for establishing private judgments of value. In the case of Barnes's work, as Cotkin explains, she "attempted to steer existentialism away from its presumed pessimism toward a greater sense of possibility and individual responsibility, even flirting with optimism, themes that might be expected to resonate more deeply with American readers."[66] William Barrett presents this recasting in more directly political terms: in contrast to the "oversimplified picture of man" in Marxism, existentialism "attempts to grasp the image of the whole man, even where this involves bringing to consciousness all that is dark and questionable in his existence. And in just this respect it is a much more authentic expression of our own contemporary experience."[67] This contrast neglects the fact that, at the time of Barrett's writing, Sartre had just attempted to reconcile Marxist and existentialist "pictures of man" in *Search for a Method*.

American critics during the 1940s and 1950s tuned existentialism to the pitch of alienation from the self's capacity for private judgment. They most often presented it as an aesthetic philosophy—one without definite political commitments. This reception history resulted in marginalizing de Beauvoir's and Sartre's accounts of intersubjectivity, in particular: the term receives no sustained discussion in the major American existentialist essays and texts of the 1940s and 1950s, and indeed the French existentialists' various political agendas—particularly their vocal criticisms of American foreign policy—are likewise omitted from these presentations.

In contrast to the movement's early reception history, some American existentialists of the 1960s worked against this aestheticization. The radical New Left invoked Sartre on occasion in the movement's criticisms of American imperialist intervention in Vietnam. For instance, Jerry Rubin, the leader of the so-called Yippie faction of the New Left, referred to Sartre during a 1966 antiwar rally: "Sartre calls the Left in America 'the accursed of the earth' because of the difficulties it faces in this nation." The declaration suggests the faddism of being an outsider. Indeed, based on Sartre's increasingly incendiary rhetoric, Rubin advises, "We must begin the politics of radical alternatives."[68]

As these two contemporaneous adaptations suggest—that is, by the School of the Holy Ghost and the Yippie movement—American existentialism had splintered: following its aestheticized reception in the 1940s and 1950s, American existentialism in the 1960s broke into factions like the Christian existentialism of Percy, O'Connor, and Merton, the political protests of the student movements, and a fraught union with psychoanalysis (as I discussed in chapter 3). More characteristic of the politicized existentialism of the 1960s was a strong preference for Camus over Sartre. The radical student movements of the 1960s looked principally to the work of Camus to anchor its rebellious attitudes and activism against segregation and the Vietnam War.[69] The generation that came of age in the 1960s had, as Tod Gitlin explains, "breathed the intellectual air of existentialism: action might not avail, but one is responsible for choosing." These young leftists found in Camus an opportunity for action, rather than a source for despair, and thus Gitlin says they "leaped to a paradoxical conclusion: that history was alive and open."[70]

Another iteration of this splintering involves the reception of Simone de Beauvoir's writing. De Beauvoir's *The Second Sex* was published in New York in 1953, and it was received with hostility by male intellectuals like Dwight Macdonald and William Phillips.[71] While gaining only modest purchase among mainstream American intellectuals based on anti-feminist sentiments, de Beauvoir primarily influenced progressives of the 1960s by way of Betty Friedan. Sandra Dijkstra suggests that Friedan's landmark feminist study, *The Feminine Mystique* (1963), "translated" de Beauvoir's argument in *The Second Sex* (1949), which claims that women are socialized to accept an artificial "femininity" and, by extension, an oppressive confinement to domestic life.[72] Daniel Horowitz observes that Friedan's reading notes of *The Second Sex* "reveal her great interest in Beauvoir's existentialism."[73] Yet Friedan also partially obscured these debts to de Beauvoir—and to Thorstein Veblen and Friedrich Engels, as well—in order to keep from public view the history of her youthful radicalism: "Her claim that she came to political consciousness out of a disillusionment with her life as a suburban housewife was part of her reinvention of herself as she wrote and promoted *The Feminine Mystique*."[74] Thus, as Friedan's case suggests, even when radical existential thought was deployed in the United States during the 1960s, it often appeared under a veil.

More tellingly, the existential vocabulary of the radical New Left would recast political agency in the image of authenticity, and the presuppositions of this diagnostic frame would enfeeble the form of the treatment. In particular, *The Port Huron Statement* (1965) of the Students for a Democratic Society (SDS) calls for participatory democracy and reform, but it distinguishes itself from the progressive thinking of an earlier era because "the liberal and socialist preachments of the past [are not] adequate to the forms of the present."[75] Instead, the exigencies of the moment—the political affect of the era—radiate from "the press of complexity upon the emptiness of life" and the "loneliness, estrangement, [and] isolation" that separate individuals from one another.[76] Being "estranged" and "empty" had been recast as results of bureaucratic politics.

In response to this sense of alienation, *The Port Huron Statement* declares that the "goal of man and society should be human independence," which is to say "with finding a meaning in life that is personally authentic."[77] Doug Rossinow explains that the New Left radicals believed that "white, college-educated youth could in fact move from alienation to authenticity and help make the new society." They consequently, but ambiguously, "elevated alienation over both exploitation and marginality as the essential sign of inclusion in the revolutionary elect."[78] "Authenticity" and "alienation" were not only diagnostic tools but also intellectual markers of the types of acceptable radical politics. As a result, even participatory democracy and collective political agency orbited around an ethics of authenticity, as if it were an inescapable center of gravity. Yet, much as these existential terms place the SDS on a shared continuum of other postwar liberal thinkers, these diagnostic markers also impoverished that liberal discourse through its ambiguous emphases on "self-cultivation, self-direction, self-understanding, and creativity."[79] Threats to the life of the self—not threats to social-democratic institutions or the already weakened structures of equality—became the front lines of left-of-center political agency.

These sentiments indicate the limitations of the political thought among some of the most radical liberals during the postwar decades.[80] The dissemination and later splintering of existentialism within American intellectual and cultural life was conflictual but deeply established. It inspired political protest and abstract philosophical inquiry; it informed sit-ins in the South and a short-lived interest in Heidegger among American academic philosophers; it even surfaced in presidential media coverage.[81] Following in the vein of American existentialists like Barnes and Barrett, later proponents continued to view existentialism as principally a philosophical avenue for exploring the problems of freedom, the absurd, and individual consciousness, while rejecting those elements of French thought that tend toward institutional political action.

One casualty of this domain of thought within American political culture, I've suggested, is a substantive account of solidarity and community. The protagonist of Percy's *The Last Gentleman* (1966), Will Barrett, is a good example. Barrett, "dislocated to begin with," moves to New York and is overwhelmed by the teeming possibilities around him.[82] Not unlike Highsmith's Tom Ripley, Barrett "hardly knew who he was from one day to the next. There were times when he took roles so successfully that he left off being who he was and became someone else" (20). Barrett eventually meets the Vaughts, a Southern family living in the city so that their son, Jamie, can receive medical treatment. Mr. Vaught invites Barrett to return to the South with them to "show [Jamie] how folks act" (79). Upon his return to life in the South with the Vaught family, Barrett discovers that he "was no less dislocated" (320). His philosophical ruminations and attempts to love one of the Vaught's daughters fizzle out, so Barrett simply continues to be estranged from others. In fact, the lesson he learns is that, as Paul Bowles translates Inez's famous line in Sartre's play *No Exit*, spoken to his fellow victims in hell, "Each one of us is the torturer for the other two."[83] Hell is other people.

The various failed attempts in Percy's career to resolve the isolation of his characters through intimacy with others suggests that his figure of the "sovereign knower" becomes part of the problem, rather than a method for identifying and resolving alienation. Much like Sartre's philosophical negotiations in "Existentialism Is a Humanism," Percy calls attention to the deficiencies of Binx's "search" in *The Moviegoer* by pointing to his blindness to others. This is especially vivid during Binx's interactions with Mercer, the African American butler who has worked for the Bolling family for decades. In a moment of troubling self-irony, Binx admits, "Ordinarily it is hard to see him," he says, for the Bolling family only "retains" Mercer for his services (22). Continuing this instrumental view of the man, Binx says that his "main emotion around Mercer is unease that in threading his way between servility and presumption, his foot might slip" (22). This confession exposes Binx's stratified sense of social order, in which class and race draw the distinguishing lines. Binx is less concerned with "seeing" Mercer—with sifting through the layers of social and racial conventions that impinge upon his consciousness—than with preserving the tenuous ecosystem of his Southern household. It is clear that the novelistic irony points in this direction. The fact that Binx is aware of his difficulties in "seeing" Mercer suggests his ambivalence about both the racial structures of his domestic arrangement and his ironic distance.

Yet Binx "does not know," and across the course of the novel never knows, "what Mercer is" (50). He never finds a route to another human being. The impersonal pronoun "what" suggests the extent to which the racial protocols and class etiquette of their society preclude intimacy and understanding: Mercer is a "what" for Binx, not a "who." And, in many ways, this is a microcosm of the difficulty postwar existentialists faced when they tried to wed authenticity and autonomy with the notion of intersubjectivity: by making consciousness an object to avoid solipsism, they likewise and by extension construed the other as an object of consciousness. The existential pursuit of intersubjectivity construed the other as a "what"—that is, a measure, a means, a route for authentic consciousness.

The ambiguities of Percy's communal aspirations suggest that losing the independence of the self is the cost one incurs by entering social space, by subordinating individual authenticity to collective welfare. As part of the "aesthetically appropriate" rise of existentialism, as Greenberg put it, Percy's exilic position perpetuates the struggle for individual consciousness that emerged as one among many routes for resolving the postwar "malaise." The members of the School of the Holy Ghost maintained that the conflation of social welfare with a commodity culture breeds individual estrangement, but Percy responds to these uncertainties with a waiting, exilic figure. This view construes the "victims of the malaise" as "lost" to themselves by living at a distant remove from the capacity for self-possession. I've argued that this intellectual sentiment was also bound up with the development of an "independence regime" in American political culture and was part and parcel of the dubious justification by Southern liberals for expressing reservations about the civil rights movement. These developments in American political culture were doppelgängers that, through their shared angst, haunted postwar liberalism. Percy's sovereign wayfarer is no third way. This image of the pilgrim has gained the self but lost the social world.

Mergers and Acquisitions

BUSINESS FICTION AND THE THEORY
OF LIBERAL MANAGEMENT

After confessing to his wife that he fathered a child during the war, Tom Rath in Sloan Wilson's *The Man in the Gray Flannel Suit* (1955) stumbles into clarity about the dissatisfaction afflicting his personal ambitions. "I was my own disappointment," he says to his wife Betsy, "I really don't know what I was looking for when I got back from the war, but it seemed as though all I could see was a lot of bright young men in gray flannel suits rushing around New York in a frantic parade to nowhere. They seemed to be pursuing neither ideals nor happiness—they were pursuing a routine."[1] While the title for Wilson's bestseller provided a stock image for 1950s business culture—the gray flannel suit becoming what Jonathan Franzen describes as "a watchword of fifties conformity"—Rath's observation more tellingly documents the absorption of sensibilities about authenticity and behavioral psychology within postwar business culture.[2] What matters to Rath is not so much the longevity of the organization that employs him or even the rationality of the bureaucratic procedures themselves. Rather, his views of business enterprise wed entrepreneurial ambition with self-possession and productivity with authenticity. Rath's revelation illustrates how the vocabulary of what economic historians call "managerial capitalism" had begun to incorporate the idea in humanistic psychology known as "self-actualization."

While attesting to the imprint of the therapeutic disciplines in American public discourse, Wilson's novel invokes a cultural milieu created by several schools of management theory that emerged during the postwar era. Trade books on management—most notably, the bestsellers Martin Mayer's *Madison Avenue, USA* (1958) and William H. Whyte's *The Organization Man* (1956)— lamented the collectivist attitude ostensibly afflicting American corporate culture. While popular presses churned out such anti-conformist warnings, corporate consultants turned to "job enrichment" strategies following the humanistic psychology of Abraham H. Maslow. These theorists often construed income incentives as a function of middle-class resentment or an employee's bad faith—a transgression of the authenticating possibilities of genuine labor. Other consultants similarly advocated greater employee self-direction based on the "management by objectives" theories of Peter F. Drucker, while still others looked to the psychological research of Kurt Lewin to prescribe managerial behavior. The shared gesture across this theoretically diverse body of managerial thought is that corporate culture turned to its employees' personal lives as a domain for increasing productivity. These examples of business fiction and consultancy, I argue, are illustrative of a new philosophy of liberal management.

Postwar theorists of corporate management broke radically with the management theory of an earlier era, most notably the work of Frederick Winslow Taylor, who advocated for "scientific efficiency" and wage incentives. By rejecting Taylorism, this chapter argues that postwar theories of management constituted another front in the intellectual crises challenging organizational liberalism in the United States. In particular, as the managerial concepts of self-actualization, sensitivity training, and objective-based worker autonomy influenced American business culture, their theorists presented personal development and self-motivated fulfillment as preeminent virtues in a democratic society. While theorizing the management of corporate life, these theorists also often reimagined the management of liberal organizational politics. The proper form of management raised a question of the proper form of Americanism, and the theorists considered in this chapter presented self-actualization as the answer.

At the same time as worker autonomy and self-actualization became integral to an American managerial science, novelists like Joseph Heller, J. D. Salinger, Kurt Vonnegut, and Ken Kesey traced the tortuous logic and alienating consequences of bureaucratic life. As part of the rising cultural tide of American existential thought, many intellectuals frequently inveighed against vast, ostensibly rationalized structures, often by borrowing from and inflecting the reception of Franz Kafka's writing. This Americanization of absurdity, in an adjacent way to the tamer shifts in postwar management theory and corporate fictions like Wilson's novel, would challenge the norms of bureaucratic authority while also becoming incorporated into its structural logic. These domains of the literary arena augmented parallel developments in postwar management theory, advancing a new organizational philosophy in the American liberal tradition. This new organizational sentiment denigrated structural parity and wage-based incentives as lower order concerns in a hierarchy of needs; instead, the best managers would be those who enabled their subordinates to develop their authentic selves.

American Managerial Capitalism and
the Birth of Management Theory

In his landmark history of American business, Alfred Chandler argues that professional managers emerged as a distinct elite class during the late nineteenth century. This new managerial class would supplant the structure of family-owned and single-unit industrial production by the start of the Second World War. Chandler explains that a period of unprecedented growth among corporate firms facilitated the advent of the manager, who began to fill a gap between the owners of large "vertically" integrated corporations and the day-to-day operations involved in running their activities.[3] Establishing what is now a consensus view among historians, Chandler argues that "managerial capitalism" had become the dominant economic model in the United States by the 1920s. This new form of capitalism replaced the market mechanisms of industrial production with managerial coordination in guiding "the activities of the economy and allocating its resources."[4] The visible hand of managers supplants the invisible hand that, according to Adam Smith, governs a free market. As a result, the managerial elite became "the most influential group of economic decision makers" because business enterprise had become "the most powerful institution in the American economy."[5] This dramatic transformation of the US economy amounts to what Chandler describes as the "managerial revolution," giving wider historical context to a notion of the changing economic landscape that first gained traction in a 1941 study by James Burnham.[6]

This revolution in the nature of US capitalism led to the formal construction of a new type of knowledge work called management theory. As a result of the rapidly expanding operational demands of large-scale corporate firms, theories of efficient management developed among entrepreneurs, academics, professional associations, and especially engineers, who gave a scientific reasonableness to their consulting work for American factories.[7] The early field of management theory tried to prescribe the most efficient and effective ways of managing an organization. Early management theory found its intellectual and institutional expression in the first business schools at Harvard, Pennsylvania, and Chicago, which offered courses in production, finance, marketing, and general management. This new knowledge work culminated in the first MBAs being awarded in the United States in 1920.[8] Thus, an educational system that, as William Lazonick puts it, "had barely been integrated into the manufacturing sector towards the end of the nineteenth century was supplying it with tens of thousands of graduates by the third decade of [the twentieth] century."[9] The institutions of early twentieth-century higher education were in large part shaped by the mark of the managerial revolution and the organizational demands of large-scale corporate enterprise.

The "scientific" school of management theory is the first and most cohesive example of the formative role of intellectuals and engineers in shaping the norms of pre-1945 managerial practices. In *The Economy of High Wages* (1892), Jacob Schoenhof argues that, in contrast to the assumptions of many industrialists, high wages actually complement decreased production costs as long as those wages are subject to the greater division of labor and processes of mechanization. Schoenhof's theory of management attempted at once to justify mass-produced goods as a socioeconomic boon for laborers while also construing higher remuneration as the most efficient means for stimulating business enterprise. This patina of scientific efficiency would later be polished more popularly by Frederick Winslow Taylor, who argues in *The Principles of Scientific Management* (1911) that the "principal object of management should be to secure the maximum prosperity for the employer, coupled with the maximum prosperity for each employé."[10] The most efficient means of production— and the most profitable for those in charge of the means of production—is to create conducive working conditions and economic incentives for laborers. Taylor maintained that giving workers extensive training, detailed instruction, and then constant supervision would enable them to use machinery and their time more effectively. Greater surveillance thus became a necessary precondition for employee prosperity and managerial efficiency.

Henry Ford's creation of the assembly line allowed for managerial oversight to function in practical application in many of the same ways that Taylor had envisioned. The assembly line required laborers to be given detailed instruction on their tasks, while managers had the responsibility to supervise the quality of production and workers' efficiency. As Jean-François Chanlat explains, Ford's "new production system had a tremendous effect on output. The doubling of workers' salaries to the famous 5 dollars a day aimed to reduce the very high turnover rate. Ford had adopted one of Taylor's principles: 'Men will not do an extraordinary day's work for an ordinary day's pay.'"[11] For both Ford and Taylor, guaranteed high wages were integral to the managerial science of increasing output in firms.

Beginning with the production of the Model T in 1909, the Fordist model of productivity had significant influence not only on the manufacturing sector but also on the notion of wages itself. Day labor for low wages was a form of work organization that, as Marc Doussard says, has more or less been understood as "an artifact from the pre-Fordist age."[12] The boom in manufacturing at the beginning of the twentieth century initiated changes in the wage structure that would eventually allow guaranteed income through ongoing employment to become the standard form of work organization, although those wages were rarely as "extraordinary" on a national level as Taylor had advocated. As Doussard explains, the "viability of Fordist production models in manufacturing industries depended on firms' ability to sustain the virtuous circle of rising wages and rising production by expanding gross output, identifying new end markets, and insulating themselves from competition."[13] In other words, the growth of wages depended on the growth of output itself, so the Fordist model presupposed mass production or, for firms outside the manufacturing industry, buying practices on a mass scale.[14]

While mass production and consumption created a windfall for the owners of the means of production, the efficiency standards of Taylorism and the theories that evolved from Fordist production also helped to revolutionize American corporate practices in terms of guaranteed labor.[15] Even as the managerial revolution of the nineteenth and early twentieth centuries reorganized the elite classes of the United States, Fordist production allowed for the transformation of both blue-collar and middle-class work in terms of a stable correspondence between labor and income. This is important for the history of labor, but it's also significant for the history of ideas because, as Chanlat explains, management theories consistently "bear the imprint" of their contemporaneous "social conflicts."[16] These theories serve as a barometer of corporate culture and practice along with their attendant social pressures.

The scientific management of employee oversight and mass production would seem to be insufficient for the demands of large vertically integrated corporations and the conglomerations of the postwar era. As Neil Fligstein argues, corporate structure and its political expression would shift from the pursuit of monopolized control of a single mode of production to the conglomeration of disparate products and services. Fligstein contends that US antitrust law from the 1890s to the 1930s was responsible for corporations seeking "stability" through conglomeration rather than as monopolies—thus placing the blame for increased corporate power on government regulation.[17] Still, this general history of the transformation of corporate structure helps explain why the industrial-production scale solutions of Taylorism would come to seem inadequate for postwar managers.

According to Fligstein, "between 1947 and 1985, the asset concentration of the largest manufacturing companies increased from 42 percent to 76 percent. Most of this increase occurred through diversified mergers."[18] Louis Hyman similarly notes that U.S. Steel "owned wire, structural, and many other forms of steel manufacturing," but it also produced "golf balls, rental cars, missiles, electronics, and packaged meat."[19] This diffusion weakened federal attempts to regulate concentrations in any given market: "Even the FTC in its 1948 investigation seeking out new conglomerates," Hyman explains, "could only find one in the entire country, despite an enormous rise in mergers during and after World War II."[20] Corporations had learned to negotiate modest antitrust laws by placing less and less emphasis on both "vertical" and "horizontal" mergers. Rather than putting all of their eggs in one basket—manufacturing— the managers of large postwar firms sought control over entirely unrelated aspects of the whole farm. Corporate management thus became less a question of efficiency than the pursuit of diversification, at least until the 1980s.[21] As Fligstein explains, the theoretical term for this new paradigm of corporate structure, the multidivisional form, "became the accepted organizational structure for the large corporation between 1920 and 1970, with the greatest diffusion after World War II."[22] Merging unrelated firms for the sake of growth became the established norm for large postwar corporations.

If the multidivisional form is primarily a postwar phenomenon, the antitrust faction among postwar Democrats hardly seemed capable of impeding this type of concentrated economic power. The Celler-Kefauver Act of 1950, for example, aimed to strengthen the Clayton Antitrust Act of 1914. However, this postwar legislation only gathered judicial traction to block vertical and horizontal mergers. Thus, while antitrust lawsuits reached an all-time high after World War II, the largest firms nonetheless became larger during the 1950s.[23] The trademark of American firms thus became multidivisional complexity. At the time, this complexity allowed for a multifaceted and much less antagonistic relationship between corporations and federal authority. For example, Mark Mizruchi says that the heads of many corporations exhibited "enlightened self-interest" in their vision of American business. In particular, these leaders maintained that working with unions and supporting a social safety net, among other public goods, were in the business community's long-term interests.[24] Mizruchi shows that this amenable attitude prevailed among many leaders of large corporations until the energy crisis of the 1970s.[25]

However, this attitude among many top executives also occurred within the context of a shifting, multilayered reorganization of American corporate life. American firms shifted toward the multidivisional form while theories of management also began to shift up and down the rungs of the corporate ladder. Larger corporations—rather than merging with competitors, related products, or owning their own production processes—diversified their means of output and thus worked around the narrow understanding of antitrust policy that was dominant in Congress during the immediate postwar decades.[26] As a result, postwar managers had to look to new business solutions and theories of productivity to meet the demands of their enlightened chief executives.

The rise of complex multidivisional corporations during the postwar era seemed to demand a commensurate sea change in management theory. For one, as Lazonick argues, the widespread unionization in manufacturing during the mid-1930s required new skills in navigating "shop-floor work organization from craftsmen on the shop floor to line and staff personnel within the managerial hierarchy."[27] But even as the union-friendly environment of the earlier New Deal era demanded management skills in negotiating with trade unions, the postwar era increasingly demanded a confrontation with behavioral psychologists, marketing consultants, and a burgeoning advertising industry to increase both output and sales. As Fligstein and Sukkoo Kim argue, the successful multidivisional corporations depended on sales and marketing strategies. Indeed, marketing divisions often determined production and distribution.[28] On the one hand, then, postwar managers wanted to increase productivity and so turned to new psychological strategies—a series of distinctive shifts *internal* to corporate practice. On the other hand, postwar managerial enterprise became keenly concerned with reading consumer behavior and predicting market value to determine the efficiency of any given product. These changes made managers all the more important to meeting the demands of the postwar economy.

Management Theory against the Gray Flannel Suit

Managers and bureaucrats in the postwar era had to develop "varied approaches to management theory" to fill the knowledge-professional gap, as the business consultant and academic Harold Koontz explained in 1962—a gap that in turn "led to a kind of confused and destructive jungle warfare."[29] Competing professionals and corporate models explained how to "analyze the management process."[30] Executives, engineers, academics, and theoreticians disagreed vehemently about what the new landscape of American business required of its managers. Tracing the most influential schools of postwar management theory, Stephen P. Waring observes that this conflict amounted to "a series of attempts to overcome problems that Taylorism helped create but could not solve."[31] The new generation of practitioners and theorists saw that Taylor's industrial-scale science of efficiency-based management

> helped create conflicts between workers and managers, between departments, between business and the public; it engendered bureaucratic organizations whose specialized operations could not be controlled through time-and-motion study, spawned work that could not be easily managed through separation of planning from doing, and bred workers who resented being treated as factors of production.[32]

While scientific analysis, strenuous oversight, and ostensibly amenable working conditions offered solutions for the efficiency crises of mass production in Taylor's school of thought, postwar theorists argued that this set of solutions alienated workers in all divisions of labor by subordinating the personal to the abstract, sacrificing individual aspiration to corporate goals.

This argument was not foreign to those theoreticians who had associated organizational efficiency with progress and rationality, even if such a conclusion might have appeared to be beside the point. For instance, Max Weber's influential definition of the modern bureaucratic institution centers on technical efficiency and an impersonal organizational structure: "the more the bureaucracy is 'dehumanized,'" he claims, "the more completely it succeeds in eliminating from official business love, hatred, and all purely personal, irrational, and emotional elements which escape calculation."[33] Impersonal organization is the *point* of management; the human "elements" aren't relevant to managed labor. Weber's description of scientific management—as perceptive as it may be regarding some forms of organizational bureaucracy—would apply only intermittently to the managerial jungle warfare of the postwar decades.

The chief postwar theories of management aspired to "humanize" organizational procedures by looking to behavioral psychology, strategies of worker autonomy, and even the rhetoric of the humanistic psychology movement. Many of these theorists insisted that self-governance ought to drive managerial strategy, that pay ought to have less of a role in incentivizing productivity, or, alternatively, that compensation should no longer be fixed to an employment position but instead should be tied to self-motivated performance. These competing theories shared a rejection of Taylorism and looked instead to the rhetoric of "job enrichment" and what certain psychologists described as "self-actualization."[34] The shifts in the theory of management in the decades following the Second World War helped entrench changes in corporate culture that would question the very underpinnings of guaranteed wages and structural parity through its emphasis on individual contentment. The burgeoning postwar profession of consultants often turned to the twentieth-century work of Kurt Lewin, Herbert A. Simon, Carl Rogers, and Abraham H. Maslow. This body of behavioral research construed the workplace as the principal site for negotiating individual contentment, and it thus presented American businesses as the frontlines of American democratic virtue.

Some theorists of what would become known in the postwar era as "human relations" solutions and "job enrichment" strategies expanded on the findings of influential studies at Hawthorne Works in Cicero, Illinois. The "Hawthorne studies" (1924–1932), as Daniel A. Wren and Arthur G. Bedeian explain, were the first to devote resources "to the human side of management, thereby counterbalancing the largely technical engineering emphasis of the scientific-management era."[35] The Hawthorne studies relied in part on "nondirective" interview techniques recommended by the psychologist Elton Mayo, who held a faculty appointment at the Harvard Business School during the 1920s. According to Mayo, companies simply need to establish conversational mechanisms between management and employees—that is, strategies such as interviews where supervisors *listen* to employees' concerns but *do not direct* them to change the performance of their duties.[36] This therapeutic approach also influenced the consultant Joseph N. Scanlon, who recommended cooperation and plant-wide, merit-based rewards for solving labor disputes and productivity problems. Scanlon's collaborative human-relations solutions were designed to wed psychology and the mechanisms of social solidarity, often in ways that would prove supportive of union activity.[37]

During the postwar era, this school of management thought developed what theorists called "human relations" solutions. According to Waring, educators and psychologists began advocating for these solutions in the 1940s, calling for managers "to adopt the values of the therapist and teacher and find ways of satisfying the needs of employees."[38] Following the popularization and professionalization of psychology during the postwar era, as I discussed in chapter 3, the norms of therapy also began to inform the "human" element of managerial calculus.[39] The new Mayoist solutions were widely influential. For instance, Leland Bradford and Ronald Lippitt, two of the earliest psychologists to wed therapy and management theory, promoted deliberative processes as a prophylactic for the tyranny of the institution. Bradford and Lippitt had been influenced by the Rumanian immigrant Jacob L. Moreno and Kurt Lewin, a German Jew who came to the United States to escape Nazism during the 1930s.

The "human relations" school of therapeutic thought prescribed roleplaying as a strategy for managers to become more sympathetic toward employees.[40] Through group activity, employees and managers would come to feel a sense of belonging that, according to this therapeutic strategy, allows individuals to have personal needs met within the wider collective goals of the organization. They were, as Waring quips, "liberal philosophes trying to counsel enlightened despots."[41] The rise of sensitivity training for managers to respond more constructively to employee discontents signals that liberal thinking about corporate life had pivoted from the external standards of workers' environments within the line of production to the internal conditions of worker motivation. In a striking historical inversion, these postwar theorists diagnosed as problems the very solutions that Taylor had formulated to solve the troubles of industrial production. Whereas Taylor's scientific management had prescribed routinized activities, oversight, and a guaranteed wage structure, many postwar consultants insisted that managers be more humane and that workers have a safe, therapeutic space for expressing their discontents.

Yet if Mayo and his "corporatist" heirs used psychology to advocate for collaborative solutions to industrial problems, the shift away from Taylorism became much more pronounced after World War II. During the 1940s and 1950s, consultants commonly adapted the theories of the prominent consultant, Peter F. Drucker, an Austrian immigrant and father of the well-known theory "management by objectives" (MBO).[42] Drucker argues in *The Future of Industrial Man* (1942) and *Concept of the Corporation* (1946) that the workplace has the unique capacity to provide fulfillment to employees while simultaneously benefiting the corporation itself. *Concept of the Corporation* focused on managerial practices at General Motors. Drucker claims to have found in GM a kind of "federalism" that provided white-collar workers with a significant degree of autonomy through participative management techniques.[43] Drucker's study exemplifies the degree to which management theory was as much trying to saddle a sprinting horse as provide a prescriptive vision for smaller corporate practices.

Drucker's strain of postwar management thought is important for American intellectual history because he became increasingly vocal about the political philosophy underwriting his prescriptions for American business. Like many of his contemporaries in corporate consulting, Drucker frequently employed the language of politics to explain his management theory. In *The Practice of Management* (1954), where Drucker first fleshes out the MBO system, he argues that such a managerial style would inspire "internal self-motivation," which in turn would convert "objective needs into personal goals" and provide "genuine freedom, freedom under the law."[44] This economizing of the personal—the transformation of self-possession, its aspirations and expression, into a corporate asset—paves the way for an institutionally sanctioned form of liberty. Entrepreneurial activity expresses democratic virtue. While Drucker left these political sentiments as mere implications in his early work, they later become explicit in his bestselling *Management* (1974), where he claims that management by objectives "is more than a slogan, more than a technique, more than a policy even. It is, so to speak, a constitutional principle."[45] By identifying a "principle" in the American political tradition, Drucker defines constitutional liberty as a guarantee of individual autonomy in enterprise.

Postwar Mayoist solutions similarly reinterpreted collective activity in psychosocial and political terms. According to this school of thought's chief theorist, Kurt Lewin, rugged loners are unfulfilled, unproductive, and either authoritarian or anarchical. Lewin instead suggests corporations practice "democratic leadership." For Lewin and his followers, democratic managers set general objectives and offer advice, but they otherwise allow the group to determine the division of labor and individual modes of production in order to sustain a sense of freedom and autodidactic rewards.[46] Beginning in 1947, the advocates of "democratic leadership" enjoyed the sponsorship of the National Education Association (NEA), establishing the National Training Laboratories and related centers across the nation during the 1950s and 1960s.[47] Riding the coat-tails of these corporate training centers, pop psychologists similarly established self-improvement labs, such as Michael Murphy's Esalen Center and Carl Rogers's Western Behavioral Science Institute. Sensitivity and democratic leadership training thus reimagined corporate life and democratic practice in the terms of psychotherapy. Lewin and his followers helped redefine the workplace as a privileged site for fulfilling the needs of the ego, thereby enacting democratic principles. In turn, human satisfaction became a governing term for theorizing managerial enterprise and democratic flourishing.

In addition to the management theories of Drucker and Lewin, another novel idea called "job enrichment" became influential in the 1950s. This notion received its imprimatur through the work of Abraham H. Maslow.[48] Describing the gray-flanneled discontents of the postwar business boom as a pathology or "sickness," Maslow says that human beings are innately motivated to satisfy a hierarchy of needs: physiological, safety, love, esteem, and what he terms self-actualization. Regarding the last of these needs, Maslow argues that individuals strive to reach an inborn state of being: "A musician must make music, an artist must paint, a poet must write, if he is to be ultimately happy. What a man *can* be, he must be . . . to become more and more what one is, to become everything that one is capable of becoming."[49] The desire for self-actualization—for the musician to make music, to *become* what one *is*—is the deepest of human needs and the most difficult to attain. It is therefore also the most powerful source of motivation. To work toward self-actualization, or to enable others to do so, is the centerpiece of Maslow's "holistic" motivation system.[50]

Maslow's theoretical system broke with the Freudian model of basing psychological patterns upon cases of neuroses, developing instead a "humanistic psychology," or what would also become known as the "Third Force" in psychology in addition to psychoanalysis and B. F. Skinner's behaviorism. In contrast to the mechanistic relationships that Maslow associated with other psychological schools of thought, humanistic psychology accounts for "the majority of well-adjusted individuals leading productive lives" and construes the motives for human action according to radically individual needs.[51] But more than a slap on the wrists of Freud and Skinner, Maslow's philosophy of the human being also departed in significant ways from prior organizational thought. Maslow's "self-actualizing man," as Waring explains,

> differed from Taylor's economic man or Mayo's social man. Taylor had assumed that people worked only to earn a living, and because they wanted to expend as little effort as possible, their work had to be closely monitored and rewarded for performance. Mayo, by contrast, had presumed that nurturant managers could provide a social wage for which workers would exert themselves. Yet both Taylorism and Mayoism shared the assumption that people did not like work. But Maslow's self-actualizing man could like working, could see it as more than merely a means to money or fellowship, and could value work in itself as an act of self-expression.[52]

The management theorists influenced by Maslow claimed to uncover a yawning gap in previous attempts to organize American business culture: earlier theorists suppressed or neglected the needs of individual psychological wellbeing and self-determination. Maslow's theories, coupled with closely related work by Carl Rogers, Bruno Bettelheim, Erich Fromm, Gordon Allport, and others, reconfigured managerial thought during the 1950s until well into the 1970s as the site for the self's fullest realization.[53] As Maslow puts it in *Eupsychian Management* (1965), self-actualizing people view work as "part of the self part of the individual's definition of himself."[54] Work is "psychogogic (making well people grow toward self-actualization)."[55]

Corporate Fictions and Their Costs

This new emphasis on personal motivation and humanistic satisfaction led many consultants to denigrate using the wage structure either as a mechanism of incentives or for securing productivity. For instance, writing in the *Harvard Business Review* in 1968, Frederick Herzberg advises managers, "Forget praise. Forget punishment. Forget cash. You need to make their jobs more interesting."[56] This caustic formula was underwritten by a series of psychological studies, which gave rise to Herzberg's underlying theory of human motivation (closely related to Maslow's hierarchy). Herzberg rejects fringe benefits and growing wages as motivators. Instead, Herzberg asks, "What is the cost in human problems that eventually cause more expense to the organization— for instance, turnover, absenteeism, errors, violation of safety rules, strikes, restriction of output, higher wages, and greater fringe benefits?"[57] Herzberg describes wages as "hygiene," or as meeting "basic biological needs," and notes that such incentives by their nature inevitably become too costly. The overhead quite simply fails to justify such benefits.[58] To construct management theory around wages and benefits diminishes corporate cost efficiency and fails to address "that unique human characteristic, the ability to achieve and, through achievement, to experience psychological growth."[59] Rather than supporting or legitimizing the postwar boom of high wages, managers are encouraged to cultivate the inner life of their employees.

If postwar managers should not foist gray-flanneled conformity on their employees, they should instead enable workers to become who they *are* on a more authentic level. These sentiments find literary clarification in Wilson's bestseller. At the beginning of the novel, the dilapidated state of the Rath's home signifies the family's many discontents. The suburban house, as Catherine Jurca puts it, represents Tom and Betsy "as aspiring but failed 'Do-It-Your selfers' who lack financial as well as creative resources."[60] "A thousand petty shabbinesses bore witness to the negligence of the Raths," the novel's narrator explains. In addition to the "ragged lawn and weed-filled garden," the "vengeful" interior and "huge crack" in the living room wall speak to their fractured life (5). Tom's job with the Schanenhauser Foundation likewise mirrors this shabbiness, seemingly growing out of the same garden of dissatisfaction. He says the pay is low, the work is not challenging, and after vacillating on the issue he eventually decides to search for new employment. He learns of a possible job in marketing at the United Broadcasting Corporation (UBC) and applies, almost out of desperation. When Rath learns that he has been invited for an interview, Betsy writes a note to her husband insisting, "The money doesn't matter." Yet Tom says to himself, "The hell with that. . . . . We might as well admit that what we want is a big house and a new car and trips to Florida in the winter, and plenty of life insurance" (10).

This opening discontent establishes a line of thought that becomes gradually suspect throughout the narrative. At first, though, Tom's "uniform of the day" and aspiration to escape suburban existence set up tropes of programmatic conformity (10). Jurca connects Wilson's transvaluation of Rath's values with a "preponderance of popular novels that borrow from and mimic sociology," particularly such psychological research as C. Wright Mills's *White Collar: The American Middle Classes* (1951) and Riesman's *The Lonely Crowd*.[61] Tom's experience embodies such analyses of middle-class dislocation, and its comedic arc resolves by denying the very "massification" at the heart of the postwar economic boom. Rath's rejection of the suburban doldrums and their discontents provides fuel, according to Jurca, for "an engine of mobility that frees [the white middle class] from the constraints" of the suburbs and the corporation.[62]

While *The Man in the Gray Flannel Suit* signals white disaffiliation from the conditions of its own "middle-classness," the novel nonetheless provides scope for Rath to find solace and authenticity in the workplace. Rather than a disavowal of corporate America, Wilson's novel is an entente with it. The two principle occasions for this settlement are Wilson's ironizing of Tom's financial discontents, on the one hand, and the possibilities for authenticity that Tom surprisingly discovers at UBC, on the other. Tom's longing for higher wages and greater economic status are an internalization of what finally becomes another type of conformity, this time to hollow material aspirations. Tom worries privately, for instance, "Money, I need money. . . . If they don't build a new public school, I should be able to afford a private school. I should get everything but money out of my head and really do a job for Hopkins. I ought to be at work now" (256). The novel ironizes Tom's desire for money and the sacrifices it requires in his personal life. In fact, that irony is a corollary to the novel's depiction of anxieties about income as merely a base form of resentment, a sign of conformist envy and personal dissatisfaction.

This depiction of the worry over wages as a symptom of bad faith becomes clearer after a wartime acquaintance, Caesar Gardella, explains that Rath's former lover, Maria, and their child live in poverty. After learning that she's in dire straits, Tom wonders "what Maria will do if Caesar tells her where I am, and that I look rich" (200). Tom's worries strike a self-disparaging note that are part of a refrain throughout the novel—that he only *looks* rich—implying that such appearances are belied by his actual limitations and the several threats to his financial situation.

The realities of Tom's wages are not, however, as dire as his anxieties suggest. According to the US Bureau of Labor Statistics' CPI Inflation Calculator, in 1953 a salary of $7,000 (Tom's salary at the Schanenhauser Foundation) is equivalent to $62,065 in 2014. A $9,000 salary, which Tom negotiates from Bill Ogden at UBC, amounts to nearly $80,000 (Wilson 63). Even an $8,000 yearly salary—Ogden's initial offer—has the same buying power as $70,932.13 in the year 2014.[63] These figures are particularly telling when set within the contemporary wage structure. The US Department of Commerce and the Bureau of the Census estimated in 1954 that the median family income was approximately $4,200, which is less than half of Tom's initial salary at UBC.[64] Therefore, his income from both the Schanenhauser Foundation and UBC, when coupled with his $9,000 in savings and the inheritance of a large estate and mansion, places Rath in the upper-middle class.

The Raths' actual economic status—Tom's income and family wealth— shows Betsy's lament that they are "smart and broke" to be both ironic and naïve (118). Tom and Betsy's financial anxieties elide actual poverty and precarity. (Even in the novel, Rath's deliberations about salary are closely juxtaposed with Maria's plight.) These unfounded anxieties also raise an interpretive problem: Why would the novel frame Betsy and Tom's life through such economic discrepancies? Surely postwar readers would have recognized the relative financial security of Rath's situation.[65] Would they not have been immediately suspicious of Tom and Betsy's angst? Indeed, either the Raths' financial woes are an ironized symptom of self-delusion and psychological dissatisfaction, or Wilson himself was woefully ignorant of the postwar wage structure.

Given the treatment of discourse about money throughout the novel, the former seems to be much more likely. For example, when the UBC president, Ralph Hopkins, attempts to persuade his reckless daughter to reform her life, if only because of the wealth and responsibility she will one day inherit, the executive explains that if "everything I have were liquidated today, there would be more than five million dollars" (230). He acknowledges that "this talk of money" seems "vulgar" but that his daughter's choices occasion "a time for plain talking" (230). Hopkins's exception to raising the issue of personal finances proves the rule: such anxieties and concerns belong to the baser registers of our nature.

Betsy's antipathy toward her suburban neighbors likewise suggests how the discourse about wages is associated with a vulgar and inferior mode of living. Lucy Hitchcock, a friend and neighbor, invites Betsy to a party where she finds "concentrated everything she disliked" about middle-class suburbia. "The intensity of her displeasure surprised her," the narrator recounts, "and long after she had gone to bed, she lay awake trying to analyze it" (120). Betsy here becomes both analyst and patient, evaluating the psychological distaste provoked by her social circle. What Betsy especially dislikes about the neighborhood is the fact that the "finances of almost every household were an open book. Budgets were frankly discussed, and the public celebration of increases in salary was common" (120–1). The neighborhood breeds economic comparisons and social envy. She quips, "On Greentree Avenue, contentment was an object of contempt" (121). Self-abasement is the suburban norm. Indeed, Tom's final rejection of the "parade to nowhere," of "pursuing a routine," associates the discourse about wage increases with an alienating conformity (300). To put stock in income is, in the world of the novel, to be common-minded and empty-souled.

If the discourse about wages is a sign of base envy and psychological pettiness, the novel offers the pursuits of authenticity and self-possession within corporate work as its virtuous alternatives. Rath discovers this possibility through the surprising inversion of the conformity and lifelessness he expects from United Broadcasting during his initial interview. Tom applies for an opening in UBC's public relations department, but during the interview with a middle manager Tom finds himself tempted toward inauthenticity because of his assumptions about the corporate world. Gordon Walker, the manager responsible for the screening, asks Tom his reasons for applying: "'It's a good company . . .' Tom began hesitantly, and suddenly impatient at the need for hypocrisy." When asked about his financial expectations, Tom falsely replies, "The salary isn't the primary consideration with me," a response glossed by the third-person narration as Rath "trying desperately to come up with stock answers to stock questions" (13). Through his denigration of the importance of salary, Tom assumes that the "stock" requirements of a vast and impersonal institution demand employees to speak in a similarly nonspecific and hackneyed voice.

Yet Tom soon finds his assumptions about corporate life to be unfounded when Walker asks him to write an autobiography in "precisely an hour," a task that sends Tom into a state of panicked confusion and creative impotency (14). After several false starts and digressions, which serve the narrative purpose of providing Tom's backstory, the beleaguered would-be manager hastily writes out the facts of his history—birth, education, rank in the military, employment history—and then concludes, "I will be glad to answer any questions which seem relevant, but after considerable thought, I have decided that I do not wish to attempt an autobiography as part of an application for a job" (17). Tom insists that the story of his life is not "relevant" for employment—a declaration that seemingly divorces the personal from the corporate, the realm of the self and its expression from the calculus of business practice.

Yet only seemingly. Tom's decision to *write* a few cursory facts about his life and then refuse to be self-promoting is prompted by his anticipation of Betsy asking about the interview. This domestic calculus for deciding "to try" is itself preceded by Tom's "good-luck charm," a watch he purchased at an Army post exchange and that he then wore throughout the war. Tom explains that the watch "was more reassuring to look at than the big impersonal clock on the wall, though both said it was almost twelve-thirty" (17). The mundane contours of the episode set up a contrast between the massive corporation's "impersonal" marker of time and an icon of Rath's personal history with its own private value. These two ways of marking time take on symbolic importance within the moment of Rath's (admittedly melodramatic) crisis during the interview: Will he conform to the "big impersonal" mode of structuring existence, or will he treat life with personal fidelity? Will he hypocritically publicize himself, or will he be the author of his own sincerity? The interview is not so much an evaluation of his professional credentials as a test of his private character, if not for UBC, then for Tom himself.

Rath's refusal to conform provides a kind of moral center to the novel. As Evan Brier argues, the episode gives a "literary cast" to the tensions confronting

Rath, as if a writer's authenticity were beset by mass society.[66] This decision to write against the grain of corporate compulsion is framed within the novel's biography of Rath, such that the refusal to write with inauthenticity provides the occasion for seemingly authentic literary production. Even as Tom refuses to write a programmatic autobiography, Wilson uses such an occasion to fashion the various experiences of Rath's life that do not easily assimilate into a corporate narrative: "The most significant fact about me," Rath muses, "is that I've become a cheap cynic," or, "The most significant fact about me is that as a young man in college, I played the mandolin incessantly" (16). This narrative device complicates the formulaic idea of "the most significant fact" about any individual. It denies what Walker demands and Rath assumes to be necessary for corporate success: a succinct and catchy (and therefore ultimately marketable) tagline.

The significance of this interview is that Tom's moment of writerly authenticity does not undermine his candidacy. Rather, his attention to the humane contours of existence appears to be compatible with the position at the mass communications corporation, for Walker offers him the job without mention of the written refusal to comply fully with the organization's procedures (28–29). This peculiarity establishes a pattern in which, as Brier says, "the organization rewards [Rath] for his polite refusal to conform and is, moreover, the site of and the enabler of his honesty."[67] United Broadcasting thus appears to be an organization interested in employees and their genuine commitment to work, not their willingness to play a corporate game of guess-the-boss's expectations. Sincerity and humanity take pride of place above bald avarice and ambition.

Rath's assimilation within the managerial ranks of UBC validates the idea that authenticity and personal fulfillment are at least potentially compatible with the route to corporate success. Rath's refusal to write in an inauthentic and self-promoting way further suggests that corporations need not require workers to don the gray flannel suit of conformity. However, even as Rath's sense of postwar displacement unexpectedly leads him to discover a route for authenticity in corporate work, that discovery not incidentally requires him—along with Wilson's readers—to look with increasing suspicion on his anxieties about income. The authenticity of the working self and the discourse regarding wages are, according to these sensibilities, antithetical. The latter is little more than a symptom of Rath's psychological self-pity—his unfounded envy that distracts from the more pressing search for existential meaning, which the corporation helps him overcome. Forget wages. Rath needs the pursuit of significance.

Democracy, Heidegger, and the Burden of Higher Management

If Wilson's bestseller imagines a cultural settlement between the ethics of authenticity and the demands of managerial capitalism, many other novelists would respond with a more deep-seated animus toward the tyranny of institutional structures. The fiction of the 1950s that refused to settle with bureaucracy tended to revert to a loose pluralist foundation for the saving grace of individual freedom. McCann has argued, for instance, that J. D. Salinger's *Catcher in the Rye* (1951) thematizes a "commitment to shapelessness" not only as a matter of novelistic form but also as the expression of an anti-bureaucratic social philosophy. Reading the novel as part of the anti-welfare sentiments of 1950s liberalism, McCann traces spontaneity as the alternative to coercion in the "emergent design of literary narration" in Salinger's fiction. The novel elevates spontaneity through Holden's adolescent brio and also the wider renaissance of the picaresque form that *Catcher* helped inspire. This narrative mode, according to McCann, valorized spontaneity and fluidity to such a degree that made them seem "like a reassuring stay against confusion."[68] Rather than lapsing into the forms of coercion that harass Holden—including the "phonies" at prep school—Salinger's fiction, much like Bellow's *The Adventures of Augie March*, holds up impermanence and contingent affiliations as preeminent democratic virtues. These instances of an emerging "spontaneous form of writing" stand in opposition to "the brute hand of the state" preoccupying much of the "literary renaissance of the fifties."[69] For this body of fiction, much like the liberal political theory of its day, "satisfaction comes from the way a reassuring collective agreement can seem to arise naturally from the apparent randomness created by individual choice."[70]

However, even satisfaction has its discontents. This grim paradox lies at the heart of Saul Bellow's other fiction from the 1950s, namely *Seize the Day* (1956) and *Henderson the Rain King* (1959). These novels consider an existentialist form of self-actualization, except in these cases the protagonists have at least one foot in the corporate world. For instance, as an aged and less sane answer to Augie's fugitive transience (which I discussed at the end of chapter 2), Bellow's millionaire executive in the 1959 novel, a man named Henderson, flees to the heart of Africa because of a general longing sometimes expressed as a summons to his psyche, "*I want, I want, I want.*" This demand refuses "to name names," which is to say that the beckoning voice neglects to identify either the object of longing or its remedy.[71] While for Augie such indefiniteness allows for democratic virtues, with Henderson it invites despair, self-sabotage, and externalized harm. Being an existential fugitive helps Augie avoid tyranny, but that same state of being is its own form of bondage—a Sisyphean burden—for the affluent Henderson.

This paradox becomes clear during Henderson's encounter with the benevolent Arnewi, a remote tribe whose leader provides initial language for the impulse that drives the American millionaire. "Grun-tu-molani," the tribal queen diagnoses his psyche's drive, a phrase translated as "Man want to live." The "primitive" language at once signals a more fundamental desire and Bellow's exoticized representation of the remote African tribe. The queen's description elicits an enthusiastic declaration from Bellow's wanderer: "Yes, yes, yes! Molani. Me molani," Henderson exclaims, "Not only I molani for myself, but for everybody. I could not bear how sad things have become in the world and so I set out because of this molani" (85). Henderson wants to affirm life, to get at the marrow beneath its surfaces, and he understands such hunger as somehow both exemplary of humanity and also socially redemptive. He later declares, "But every man feels from his soul that he has got to carry his life to a certain depth" (105). He believes, in other words, that by living—or by finding out what it means to live—he might find something substantial for an otherwise gaunt and lifeless world. Henderson understands his personal quest as a social good.

After ruining the Arnewi's only source of water by discharging a bomb in the community's cistern to remedy a frog infestation, Henderson finds that his hunger for some fundamental meaning causes more literal conditions of hunger and geographical displacement. These glimpses of the collective effects of his existential striving are nonetheless absorbed within Henderson's affliction and indeterminate philosophy of life. As he explains to his son, Edward, who asks, "What do you fight for, Dad?" Henderson insists that he fights "for the truth. Yes, that's it, the truth. Against falsehood. But most of the fighting is against myself" (124). In an ironic evasion of the myriad of ways he has neglected his son through his "fighting," Henderson construes his quest as a personal struggle. He blindly subordinates the ethical to the metaphysical, the interpersonal to the existential. While he exclaims, "For Christ's sake, we should commune with people," Henderson flees his family for an African expedition in hopes of realizing that wider communal vision (125).

So, do the fraught costs of Henderson's quest mean that Bellow throws the cat among the existentialist pigeons? In reality, *Henderson the Rain King* reiterates authenticity's many paradoxes, which were familiar to the continental tradition of philosophy. Henderson, who does not always name his literary and philosophical interlocutors, borrows from the vocabulary of Martin Heidegger when he further explains his role as a "traveler" or "wanderer." According to Henderson, the difference between himself and the rare few, like the king of the Wariri tribe, Dahfu, is that the latter are content with "*Being*." "Others were taken up with *becoming*," Henderson explains. "And if I had really been capable of the alert consciousness which it required I would have confessed that Becoming was beginning to come out of my ears. Enough! Enough! Time to have Become. Time to Be! Burst the spirit's sleep. Wake up, America!" (160). Henderson's declaration offers a national and self-actualizing turn on Heidegger's notion of *Dasein*, or Being. He suggests that the distinction between "Being people" and "Becoming people" is that the former are content with their nature, while the latter lapse continually into self-justifications. In fact, Henderson believes somnolence is generally characteristic of the United States. The state of becoming is a state of sleeping life away. Forget the national aspiration of striving and becoming, Henderson here exhorts, just *be,* America.

Yet that notion of finding a final equilibrium of being is neither Heidegger's nor Bellow's. According to Heidegger, the question of the "meaning of being" must begin by taking into account the "situated" or worldly conditions of human thought and existence. This situated-ness—one's being is being-in-the-world, as he puts it in a famous construction—means that humans cannot create the terms of their existence ex nihilo. However, the situated nature of being sets up a paradox. In Heidegger's cryptic phrasing, the "I" is "an entity whose what is precisely to be and nothing but to be."[72] Heidegger means that the "what" or existential reality about being human is simply to be, rather than instantiating some Platonic form of identity or the being of another. Appeals to a wider system or grounds for the meaning of that "entity" would amount to an obfuscation or distortion of the "I." The "I" is the artist of its own being.

Yet Henderson often admires those who seemingly violate this Heideggerian idea. For example, the king Dahfu keeps a captive lion named Atti in order to siphon off some of its strength through a vaguely defined mystical transaction. If "to be" is the "what" of the "I," to continue in Heidegger's phrasing, would not Dahfu's mysticism violate Heidegger's principle? Wouldn't this transaction deny the "to be" of the "I" for the sake of an extrinsic conformity? Henderson nods in this direction, even if he keeps those reservations to himself, because he respects Dahfu and finds that the king's intensity of living gives off an "extra shadow of brilliance" (298). In contrast, Henderson believes that his pursuit of being will be much more modest: "I would never make a lion, I knew that; but I might pick up a small gain here and there in the attempt" (298). Henderson, in fact, persists in claiming that he is "[b]ound by a thousand constraints," even as he refuses to shirk the burden of attempting (152). If the human creature is "the artist of suggestions," Henderson finds that the canvas is neither a tabula rasa nor a self-contained experiment (237).

Henderson's recognition of these constraints suggests his engagement with Dahfu's way of life does not tritely affirm the "bourgeois idea of the autonomy of the individual mind," which the millionaire was taught to scorn as a schoolchild (288). Henderson's condition instead inspires him to confront the contingencies of his being, as much as his aspiration to be, which is not unlike the negotiations central to what Heidegger terms being-in-the-world. While Heidegger says that self-definition is necessary for freedom and choice, he explains that such capacities for choice are inevitably constrained by some "possibility of Dasein that has been there."[73] Being is not by fiat; self-definition paradoxically borrows its figures. The "I" will "choose my hero," as Heidegger puts it with rare colloquial clarity.[74]

In this way, then, there are closely located central burrows of thought in the philosophical warrens of both Heidegger and Bellow. "Observe that Atti is all lion," Dahfu tells Henderson. "Does not take issue with the inherent. Is one hundred per cent within the given" (263). As a "hero" or possibility of *being* whose suggestions Henderson might adapt for his own purposes, Atti the lion provides Henderson with a means to confront consciousness and thus reality itself. Exemplars of *being* trace routes for the self-actualization of others. As Dahfu contends, Atti "will make consciousness to shine. She will burnish you. She will force the present moment upon you" (260). Indeed, when Dahfu and Henderson later confront another lion in the wild, Henderson exclaims that the lion's roar occurred "at the very doors of consciousness" (306). Bellow's explorations therefore swim in an existential stream through this complex view of self-actualization. Henderson remains on the cusp of consciousness, knocking on the door of reality, but even if his liminal state is perpetual, he finds that his exposure to Atti and Dahfu enable him to mitigate the vices of avoidance.

Not incidentally, Bellow's treatment of self-actualization in *Seize the Day* is the mirror image of the virtue of transience that *Augie March* advances. As one example, Dr. Tamkin advises the novel's frustrated entrepreneur-protagonist, Tommy, "you can't march in a straight line to the victory. . . . . You fluctuate toward it. From Euclid to Newton there was straight lines. The modern age analyzes the wavers."[75] In Bellow's fiction from the 1950s, what is virtuous about the "wavers" is that they strive against organizational tyranny, institutional authorities, and social constraints to ferret out the good and the real in a warren of competing ideas. And as both Tommy and Henderson discover, the exemplary position of the wanderer is not without more literal hazards: for instance, the king of the Wariri is strangled to death upon reaching a certain age. When Henderson is appointed the rain king—an honorific that makes him the successor upon the death of an heirless Wariri king—he learns that, to enter the world and discover the real, he must accumulate threats and burdens. The fraught quest to live "one hundred per cent within the given," as Dahfu puts it, may demand a confrontation with death (263). To be in charge of oneself—to be the manager over the production of the self—becomes all the more virtuous, noble, and democratic because of that heavy onus.

The Literature of Bureaucracy and the American Kafka

I have argued that the corporate vocabulary regarding income was inflected during the 1950s and 1960s through the terms of behavioral psychology, self-actualization, an emergent science of private satisfaction and motivation, and the norms of therapeutic discourse. The market for fiction, too, shared these sensibilities. This incorporation of the ethics of authenticity to remedy the crises of managerial capitalism helped give new language to how many Americans understood bureaucratic authority. How that ethic surfaced in the novels of the period is tenuously affirmative of organized corporate life at the most, while more often the cultural vanguard imagined sweeping condemnations of bureaucratic structures. This spectrum of literary reactions to rationalized bureaucracy therefore resides on the same spectrum of thought as its contemporaries in management theory. Perhaps, as Wilson's novel imagines, some exceptional corporations may be amenable to the pursuit of a genuine and ideal form of life. Or, as Bellow's fiction chronicles, perhaps the preeminent virtue for a sick and saddened 1950s America is not greater loyalty to institutions but for individuals to assume the fraught burden of the self. In either case, the rationalized structures of organizational authority are the antithesis of self-actualization. A concern with wages becomes only another symptom of the enfeebling and alienating ethic of an organizational society.

Yet if figures of the book-trade establishment and the literary vanguard contributed to the circulation of self-actualizing sentiment, another important variation on this theme involves the counterculture of the postwar decades. While the antiwar movements of the late 1960s would later absorb much of the postwar counterculture, an earlier moment in the genealogy of American political thought had its roots in the countercultural anxiety regarding, among other things, the seemingly lifeless demands of bureaucracy.

In *On the Road* (1957), for instance, Jack Kerouac cites the affiliations of one patron saint of the 1950s counterculture, a wanderer named Bull, who imagines an America "wild and bawling and free, with abundance and any kind of freedom for everyone. His chief hate was Washington bureaucracy; second to that, liberals; then cops."[76] Kerouac and the other Beats complemented their disdain for a bureaucratic state with an unqualified view of freedom—that is to say, a philosophy in which, as Alan Watts puts it, Kerouac's "beat Zen" conflates "'anything goes' at the existential level with 'anything goes' on the artistic and social levels."[77] While Kerouac was interested in a desultory narrative form, that set of literary values implies, as Bull suggests, that freedom is only free if individuals are not constrained across the full scope of human experience. In short, freedom cannot be institutionalized. For the Beats of the 1940s and 1950s, even liberal settlements with the political order amounted to a bastardized form of freedom and a veiled version of authoritarian control.

This antiestablishment sentiment allowed the early Beat writers and poets, as Maria Bloshteyn notes, "to go from marginal underground classics of the 1950s to the official voice of dissent and cultural opposition of the 1960s."[78] Yet the Beats' rejection of "Washington bureaucracy" and their subsequent position as a resource for the antiwar movement was first and foremost part of what Leerom Medovi describes as the diffusion of the "concept of identity" across many arenas of postwar life:

> Social science had diffused widely across multiple sectors of postwar culture. Social science had adopted the term wholesale. Consumer youth culture, in these intervening years, had learned to mass-produce images of the bad boy with enormous financial and cultural success. Rock 'n' roll had taken over radio, Hollywood teenpics were making enormous profits

for an otherwise declining movie industry, and figures such as Brando, Dean, and Presley had rapidly become dominant icons of the American teenager as rebel.[79]

Rather than being a sui generis avatar of radicalism, then, the Beats riffed on a widely reproduced fascination with rebellious identity.

The rebel, however, was a figure on a sliding scale, and the Beats weighted their cultural work based on several literary and philosophical debts—namely, to Dostoevsky, the French existentialists and surrealists, the essays of Emerson, and the poetry of Walt Whitman.[80] While reflecting on the debts of his generation and their counterculture heirs during the 1960s, the Beat novelist and poet John Clellon Holmes explains that existentialism

> exerts a powerful influence on both generations, and probably constitutes the only philosophic point of view that is broadly typical of this time. But whereas it was existentialism's conception of the nature of man that spoke so clearly to *us*, it is existentialism's engagement in the community of men that most appeals to *them*.[81]

For Holmes, the American counterculture of the 1960s used existential philosophy as a form of civil rights activism. This body of European literature and philosophy provided the earlier Beats with "the only way of remaining a human being."[82] For the counterculture of the 1940s and 1950s, existential thought was a haven from an intrusive political bureaucracy, an intellectual refuge that allowed them to simply *be*. More than being the "only way" of achieving authenticity, however, the history of ideas provided in the preceding chapters shows that existential sentiment was a widely reproducible and attractive route for postwar intellectuals and writers.

In contrast to Holmes's insistence that the American existentialist scale slides away from the personal and toward the communitarian during the 1960s, it is clear that many authors who were part of the counterculture in the United States continued to look for forms of unqualified freedom and individual mobility as routes of escape from bureaucratic life—one that may be unfettered even from the demands of a public community. For example, despite his numerous communal trips recounted in Tom Wolfe's *The Electric Kool-Aid Acid Test* (1968), Ken Kesey continued the counterculture's opposition to bureaucratic authority by way of the unpredictability and irrationality of an atomized self. Kesey's cult classic *One Flew Over the Cuckoo's Nest* (1962) stages this dilemma through an inhumane and unreasonable institutional landscape—the ward of a mental hospital—that is populated by "cartoon figures" and excessive, surrealist events.[83] Kesey presents this conflict through the narration of Chief Bromden, a Native American who pretends to be "deaf and dumb," which, not unlike the ancient Tiresias, also functions as a signifier of the moral clarity of his vision (4).

Bromden recounts the conflict between Big Nurse Ratched and Randle Patrick McMurphy, but he more generally frames this struggle as representative of the tyrannical control of an organization called "the Combine." The Combine, according to Bromden, is "a huge organization that aims to adjust the Outside as well as [Nurse Ratched] has the Inside." Both the Big Nurse and the Combine wield "a sure power that extends in all directions on hairlike wires too small for anybody's eye but mine" (25). Given Bromden's framing, his narrative is not so much a conflict between, say, patients and the authority of psychologists than it is a fable about organizational power. As Robert Faggen says, "Psychiatrists are peripheral in *One Flew Over the Cuckoo's Nest*. The ward depicts the nightmare of middle management, and Bromden transforms Nurse Ratched into a minion of the Combine who makes sure it runs efficiently and on time."[84] Kesey's novel, more than being a parodic condemnation of the discipline of institutional psychology, describes the human costs of managing a vast institutional bureaucracy.

The language of science, efficiency, and machinery pervades the Big Nurse's dehumanizing management of the ward. Bromden's first description of Nurse Ratched typifies this relation:

> She's carrying her woven wicker bag like the ones the Umpqua tribe sells out along the hot August highway, a bag shape of a tool box with a hemp handle. . . . It's a loose weave and I can see inside it; there's no compact or lipstick or woman stuff, she's got that bag full of a thousand parts she aims to use in her duties today—wheels and gears, cogs polished to a hard glitter, tiny pills that gleam like porcelain, needles, forceps, watchmakers' pliers, rolls of copper wire. (4)

Nurse Ratched transforms a human artifact made from organic material into a repository of manufactured items and technical necessities. She subordinates the natural to the mechanical, and Bromden also depicts the Big Nurse as genderless—her purse is devoid of "woman stuff"—an indication of her generic, lifeless person, at least according to Bromden's deeply and often violently gendered view of the world.

While Bromden frames his narrative as a fable of intrusive bureaucratic management, his account situates the loss of the human as the inevitable hazard of scientific efficiency. Kesey's novel was not alone among postwar fiction in this antipathy toward bureaucracy and institutionality. For instance, in *Player Piano* (1952) Kurt Vonnegut imagines a dystopian society of almost complete automation designed by an elite group of mechanical engineers, thus extending to an absurd degree the mode of efficient production and management established by Frederick W. Taylor and other likeminded engineers. Vonnegut's protagonist, Paul Proteus, is the lead engineer and factory manager of the Illium Works, which provides for the needs of a vast segregated part of the city of Illium, known as the Homestead. Unlike the coterie of managers who oversee the machines providing electricity, food, and all other manufactured goods, the residents of the Homestead are aimless and alienated—a state of mind that we learn is the result of an absence of meaningful work. The citizens' lives are effectively lived for them by society's vast "works" or machines.

Early in the novel, readers learn that Proteus has become discontent with his managerial responsibilities of maintaining an efficient automated system, in part because his own tasks are becoming automated. In an encounter with a member of the Homestead, James Lasher, who leads a secret anarchist group known as the Ghost Shirt Society, Paul and another alienated manager, Ed Finnerty, discuss the discontents of the system. "Sooner or later someone's going to catch the imagination of these people with some new magic," Lasher ominously predicts. "At the bottom of it will be a promise of regaining the feeling of participation, the feeling of being needed on earth—hell, *dignity*."[85] In Vonnegut's dystopia—much like Camazotz in L'Engle's *A Wrinkle in Time* (1962) and the fascist governments in Philip K. Dick's *The Man in the High Castle* (1962)—the logic of scientific management divests human beings of a sense of self-worth by routinizing labor and thus foreclosing meaningful work. The engineers' and managers' vision of an automated, fully rationalized society is an engine of alienation.

Cuckoo's Nest echoes such antipathy toward the ethic of scientific efficiency, but it extends that criticism beyond Vonnegut's novel by incorporating such strategies as group therapy into the same alienating logic as the Combine's system of minute control. As Bromden explains, the Big Nurse aspires to "a world of precision efficiency and tidiness like a pocket watch with a glass back" (26). In order to achieve this fusion of mechanical efficiency ("like a pocket watch . . . ") and oversight of a system without privacy ("with a glass back"), Nurse Ratched has adapted the liberalizing tendencies of therapists who practice group confessions, thus allowing for a veneer of equality to cover the program. Doctor Spivey, who runs the Therapeutic Community, is a "frightened, desperate, ineffectual little rabbit, totally incapable of running this ward without our Miss Ratched's help" (56). He runs the group therapy according to the "goal" of creating "a democratic ward, run completely by the patients and their votes, working toward making worth-while citizens to turn back Outside onto the street" (44).

Redolent of Lewin's management theory of "democratic leadership" and his followers' justifications for group therapy sessions and sensitivity training— strategies that they argued were correlates of democracy—Spivey's theory of the Therapeutic Community similarly aims to reintroduce the patients to the norms of an "Outside" social space. Through collective deliberation, therapists like Spivey believe that patients will absorb the normative virtues of a democratic society. However, this "democratic" discussion of the complaints and neuroses of others causes the patients to "burn with shame like they have just woke up to the fact they been played for suckers again" (50). After each session the group recalls how therapy only alienates them: "For forty-five minutes they been chopping a man into pieces, almost as if they enjoyed it, shooting questions at him" (50). The relationship between corporatist therapy and democracy in Kesey's novel is fundamentally destructive: it breaks down the self and further subjects the individual, along with the other members of the group, to the authority of the Combine. Indeed, Murphy compares the Therapeutic Community to "a Red Chinese prison camp" (59). Rather than reintroducing patients to democratic experience, the management of the ward through group therapy works as tyranny's snare.

Bromden lumps ostensibly humane solutions like group therapy into the Combine's mechanisms for totalizing mechanical control, and consequently the novel's only remedy for that systematic alienation is the individual's escape from the system. After McMurphy attacks Nurse Ratched for precipitating the suicide of another patient, she orders his lobotomy to prevent further dissent. Afterward, Bromden smothers his friend to keep him from remaining a "Chronic," an incapacitated permanent patient in the ward. Bromden then picks up a large control panel—an instrument of mechanical organizational power—and throws it through a window of the hospital. The contrast between the panel's "chrome fixtures and glass gauges so cold" with the natural moonlight of the Outside inverts Nurse Ratched's earlier transformation of the wicker basket, for Bromden has now exploited a mechanical instrument to return to humanity's "natural" habitat (280). What's more, in contrast to the democratic virtues of the Therapeutic Community that Ratched coopts for the Combine's purposes, Bromden's final escape from the ward suggests that the atomized subjects of organizational authority only retain a sense of self through exiting the system—through rejecting efficiency and tidy engineering for a humane and privately determined world. An atomized remedy is required for the totalizing, estranged crisis caused by bureaucratic management.

Bromden's diagnosis of the nightmarish managerial world of the Combine recalls the narrative worlds of another important European literary figure whom many postwar novelists looked to as an intellectual resource—Franz Kafka. While the evolving counterculture in the postwar United States bears the imprint of existentialism, psychotherapy, and the resurgence of aestheticism, a reinvigorated interest in Kafka's work would also animate the counterculture during the 1950s and 1960s. Kafka's novels and short stories were not new to American readers: Knopf had been the first US publisher to circulate a novel by Kafka when it released *The Castle* in 1930. Later, when *The Trial* was published in the United States in 1937, there were eleven reviews, including one by William Philips.[86] In 1940, both Kafka's unfinished novel *Amerika* and *A Franz Kafka Miscellany* were published, the latter suggesting the growing interest in Kafka's work.[87] However, while W. H. Auden wrote briefly about Kafka in 1941, interest in Kafka's work took a backseat to the war driving the thoughts of the nation, for only a handful of critical writings and popular references appear from 1941 until 1944.[88]

Then, only a few months after D-Day, as victory had proven costly but possible, and as critics and intellectuals had the ear of readers interested in reconsidering a civilization that had nearly destroyed itself through statist power, Kafka's intellectual status in the US began to regain momentum. This happened when Hannah Arendt wrote about Kafka and his work in *Partisan Review*.[89] Arendt established what became one of the central modes of interpreting Kafka. She argues that the Czech-Jew had diagnosed an acutely modern problem: the individual's convoluted and tortuous struggle against state and corporate bureaucracies.

Arendt followed her *Partisan Review* essay with two others, "The Jew as Pariah: A Hidden Tradition" (1945) and "Franz Kafka, Appreciated Anew" (1946). Arendt's reintroduction of Kafka to postwar readers had the effect of at once situating his work within the history of the bureaucratic *Sozialstaat* while also sketching an optimistic arc to his oeuvre. In "Franz Kafka, Appreciated Anew," Arendt says,

> Kafka envisioned a possible world that human beings would construct in which the actions of man depend on nothing but himself and his sponta- neity, and in which human society is governed by laws prescribed by man himself rather than by mysterious forces, whether they be interpreted as emanating from above or from below. And in such a world—one to be immediately constructed and no longer simply dreamed of—Kafka by no means intended to be an exceptional case, but rather a fellow citizen, a "member of the community."[90]

This gloss on Kafka pits the individual against a vast juridical bureaucracy. Arendt's political philosophy, as I discussed in the first chapter, contributed to the common anxiety among postwar intellectuals that the structures of the European welfare state had enabled the rise of totalitarianism. The juridical and bureaucratic edifice of this statist threat, as Arendt here claims by refer- ence to Kafka's work, enjoys an ultimately arbitrary authority, unlike the polit- ical community spontaneously created by "man himself." Arendt thus opposes spontaneity—and what she elsewhere calls *natality*, or the capacity to begin, to start something unexpected and new—to the alienating demands and proce- dural scripts of modern institutions.[91]

Arendt's view of Kafka proved to be fodder for her own philosophical vision of citizenship in a post-bureaucratic, post-*Sozialstaat* political community. However, her view of Kafka derives in part from a reasonable but mistaken deduction based on how Kafka had been published. Reading the melancholic death of Josef K. in *The Trial*, for instance, it is difficult to see how modern cit- izens can expect anything but violence, estrangement, and death from the world they inhabit. Yet Arendt finds in Kafka's work the possibility of a world where human beings have seized the burden of meaning-making and spontaneous existential possibility:

> In order, at least in theory, to become a fellow citizen of such a world freed from all bloody apparitions and murderous magic—as [Kafka] tentatively tried to describe it at the end, the happy ending, of *America* [*sic*]—he necessarily had to anticipate the destruction of the present world. His novels are just this anticipated destruction, and through its ruins he carries the image of man as a model of good will who can truly move mountains and construct worlds, who can bear the destruction of all misconstructions and the rubble of all ruins because the gods have given him an indestructible heart, if only his will is good.[92]

Arendt maintains that the devastating vision of works like *The Trial* have a cathartic effect, purging us of our illusions about modern institutions so that we may instead recreate the world through our natal capacities—an interpretation that hinges on the seemingly utopian ending of *Amerika*. Only by coming to grips with the horrors and absurdity of statist politics can our wills become free so as to "move mountains and construct worlds."

However, positioning the "destruction" of Kafka's work within a trajectory that culminates in a "happy ending" relies on a false chronology introduced by Kafka's first editors. His friend and literary executor, Max Brod, had seemingly billed the early novel *Amerika* as Kafka's last, which led the first generation of readers—including Arendt's influential essays in 1944 and 1945—to find a sense of hope for escape from the total authority of bureaucracy, building in each work and culminating in the "Nature Theatre of Oklahoma" chapter of *Amerika*. This reception tamed the early American criticism on Kafka, if only by enclosing it within a comedic arc or redemptive outlook.[93] Arendt's claim that Kafka imagined a society "governed by laws prescribed by man himself rather than by mysterious forces" is predicated on the comedic contours of this chronology. Kafka, it would seem, was far less sanguine.[94] The irony that a corporate and institutional misrepresentation had mitigated the severity of his vision would not have been lost on Kafka.

While Arendt looked to Kafka as an imaginative resource for the destruction of bureaucratic life and thus for the creation of space for human spontaneity, Kafka's influence on American fiction was felt more directly in the late 1950s and 1960s. For instance, Joseph Heller and his friend Frederick Karl, who met as composition instructors at Penn State, cited Kafka as an intense shared interest. Along with Nabokov and Céline, Kafka "had kindled [Heller's] interest in styles and techniques other than realism."[95] But even more than style, Heller culled the idea to narrativize "the sense of being trapped in a system that could not withstand scrutiny, and the attempt to survive with a certain brand of verbal humor."[96] That Heller read Nabokov, Céline, and Kafka while writing the novel that would become *Catch-22* (1961) helps elucidate the intellectual texture of the novel's political sensibilities and its more general animosity toward the relation between the self and organizational oversight. However, much like Arendt's optimistic gloss on the absurdist vision of the Czech novelist, the Kafkaesque American fiction of the period tends to ameliorate depictions of ludicrous, intrusive bureaucracy through various forms of comedic escape.

The ever-rising ceiling of requisite flights for bombardiers in *Catch-22* epitomizes the vacuity and tyranny of military bureaucracy, not to mention the absurdity of the war itself. Heller's central character, John Yossarian, is among the bombardiers who fly dozens of missions, some more dangerous but few more militarily strategic than others. This oddly fluid bureaucratic management of the regiment prompts Yossarian to assert calmly, "They're trying to kill me" (16). He repeats this assertion throughout the narrative and applies it not only to the enemies of the United States but also to the military's majors and corporals. But even more than the threat to life that bureaucracy poses, Yossarian finds that the nature of bureaucratic authority is to establish mutually dependent or self-enclosed conditions that ensnare soldiers and non-military citizens alike. Hence the famed Catch-22. After requesting that a friend, Orr, be grounded because of his psychological instability, Yossarian discovers, "If he flew [more missions] he was crazy and didn't have to; but if he didn't want to he was sane and had to" (46). In effect, the organizational catch is that only the unstable and insane can exit the program, but to want to exit the program is to be sane because it demonstrates a reasonable concern for one's life. There is therefore no institutionally sanctioned exit from the program. Catch-22 is the law of an organization that denies the very rights it ensures.

While Heller would later trace the quotidian aftereffects of military bureaucracy upon a veteran and businessman in *Something Happened* (1974), *Catch-22* only confines its suspicions to the wartime government. This cultural antipathy was linked, in part, to the historical augmentation of the bureaucratic state from 1940 to 1945. Not unlike the expansion of powers that occurred during the First World War, Roosevelt's administration enacted the mass mobilization of the economy to win the war through centralized planning. In practice, this coordinated bureaucratic effort became increasingly chaotic. As Hugh Rockoff demonstrates, the united mobilization of the American economy during World War II was far from an undifferentiated event. Domestic business interests attempted to assert their private freedoms amidst the economic planning of the wartime years.[97] Many liberals, on the other hand, felt that Roosevelt was ceding too much power to the military and, by extension, to the private industries he had tried to regulate in 1933–1938. The result was "bureaucratic chaos" caused by the administration's "confused, stumbling process" to develop a wartime plan for industrial production.[98]

While some Americans viewed mass mobilization as necessary to oppose the nation's enemies, the mechanisms of central planning were anything but integrated. Roosevelt had expanded federal bureaucracy during the 1930s and then set it at odds with itself in the 1940s. Thus, much of corporate America and industry contested the interventions of federal authority, while the administration's advisors disagreed among themselves about the right forms of central planning and the appropriate scale of federal regulation. On top of this bureaucratic chaos came the postwar querying of an American industrial military—one that even President Eisenhower, during his farewell address on January 17, 1961, warned would likely ensnare the democratic process within its interests.[99] Given these multifaceted objections and revisions to the now-militarized bureaucratic state of World War II, Heller's suspicion of freedoms ensured by a bureaucratic democracy is less an expression of antiwar sentiment as it is an identification of the problems of organizational liberalism at war with itself.

Yossarian's solution to the torturous logic of modern state bureaucracy is in-geniously simple: refuse to accede to the demands of the system. He refuses to fly more missions, which prompts Colonel Korn to say accusingly to Yossarian, "The men were perfectly content to fly as many missions as we asked as long as they thought they had no alternative. Now you've given them hope, and they're unhappy" (421). Korn's solution is to send the bombardier home on the con-dition that he will become a "public-relations" patsy for the military and the Pentagon (427). Yossarian must gloss over his earlier dissent and stand in public support of the importance and beneficence of the military hierarchy. "A whole new world of luxury awaits you once you become our pal," Korn promises (427). Yossarian initially agrees to the duplicity—"Thanks, pal," he says to Korn—but later reneges on the offer and decides to desert the company (429). He tells Major Danby, "Don't talk to me about fighting to save my country. I've been fighting all along to save my country. Now I'm going to fight a little to save myself. The country's not in danger any more, but I am" (446). The "deal" with Korn, Yossarian explains, is "a way to lose myself" (447). What is at stake in the relation between a contradictory bureaucracy and the individual, as Yossarian frames it, is personal integrity.

Heller's great achievement in *Catch-22* is that, unlike an overweening bu-reaucracy, which believes it can confine its subjects to limited options of action or constricted modes of thought, the novel includes scope for another response to institutionalized absurdity in addition to Yossarian's flight. While Yossarian's commitment to recover his self was almost immediately taken as the overriding symbolic act of the novel by its first readers—indeed, such a response is signi-fied by the iconic fleeing figure printed on the cover of most versions—Heller also offers the chaplain's choice to remain within the institution. In a somewhat overeager declaration, the chaplain says, "I'll stay here and persevere. . . . I'll nag and badger Colonel Cathcart and Colonel Korn every time I see them," he enthusiastically tells Yossarian, "I'm not afraid" (451). Even if the novel's final image is Yossarian "taking off" to save the integrity of his self, Heller also provides scope for challenging bureaucratic authority by remaining within its strictures and serving as a gadfly, an annoyance and moral harrier who perseveres within the institution.

The potentially overriding image of a fleeing Yossarian affirms the common postwar revision of Kafka, in which the novel affirms the hope of resolution through the possibility that the self can exit modern bureaucracy. Such an image redeploys the impermanence and contingency of Salinger's and Bellow's earlier fiction. It privileges Yossarian's authenticity—his rejection of the "deal" with Colonel Korn being the final crucible—above all other considerations. On the other hand, the chaplain's commitment to "persevere" and provoke, unlike its predecessors in this vein of fiction, also seems conceivable. Even if the other hand is weaker in the novel, Heller nonetheless makes it imaginable.

Self-Actualization and the Philosophy of Liberal Management

This chapter has analyzed a range of texts that reimagine organizational authority and liberal approaches to management. Fiction by Wilson, Bellow, Kesey, Heller, Salinger, L'Engle, and Vonnegut variously affirm self-actualization as the prevailing ethos in a moment otherwise characterized by impersonal corporate structures and centralized managerial authority. Bellow's fiction also elevates self-actualization as a heavy but nonetheless socially significant burden. Not unlike Hopkins's leadership in Wilson's novel, the burden of managing one's own authenticity enjoys a patina of democratic virtue in this body of postwar fiction.[100] The management theory of this era, too, signals a turn away from wage-based and rationalized, bureaucratic solutions. I've argued these various strands of thought are further dimensions of the postwar fracturing of liberal sentiment and represent granular expressions of broader furrows in American intellectual history.[101] This history of ideas enables us to examine the place of self-actualization in postwar public discourse and, in particular, in what I describe below as an emerging federal approach to labor and managing the national economy.

In 1972, the US Department of Health, Education, and Welfare (HEW) released a report entitled *Work in America*. The report surveys the problems of the American economy in the late 1960s and early 1970s—namely, the issues of "absenteeism, turnover rates, wildcat strikes, sabotage, poor quality products, and a reluctance by workers to commit themselves to their work tasks," and, as a result, diminished productivity.[102] The *Work in America* report frames these ills as a function of "alienation and disenchantment" rife among workers.[103] The HEW task force reiterates the diagnosis by both management theorists and cultural commentators in the preceding decades: bureaucratic rationality had planted the seeds of its own discontents. Not unlike President Carter's in-famous "malaise" speech at the end of the decade, the *Work in America* report claims that "discontent" has increased in the US workforce since World War

II.[104] College graduates expect "an interesting job" more than "a job that pays well."[105] The report claims that the most urgent problem facing the American workforce is that "[d]ull, repetitive, seemingly meaningless tasks, offering little challenge or autonomy, are causing discontent among workers at all occupational levels."[106] Drawing on the management theory of the preceding decades to make its recommendations, the *Work in America* report positions its diagnosis and solutions in opposition to what men in gray-flannel suits signified: the recursive impersonal processes and conformity of bureaucratic life.

In response to its diagnosis of the "alienation" throughout the working hierarchy, the federal task force maintains that the workplace "can be transformed into a singularly powerful source of psychological and physical rewards," particularly "when workers participate in the work decisions affecting their lives, and when their responsibility for their work is buttressed by participation in profits."[107] The journalist Irving Kristol initially characterized the report as "faded neo-Marxism" in the *Wall Street Journal*.[108] However, the report's case studies in "the humanization of work" suggest that its fruit had not fallen all that far from the capitalist tree. For example, referring to the "problems of frequent shut downs, costly recycling and low morale" plaguing a pet food plant in Topeka, Kansas, *Work in America* praises the "humanizing" technique of organizing employees "into relatively autonomous work groups with each group responsible for a production process. Pay is based on the number of jobs an employee can do rather than on what he does at a particular time." The "human results" of this management technique, which was measured by a later survey of the plant's employees, found that "job attitudes . . . indicated 'positive assessments' by both team members and leaders. There was evidence suggesting the increased democracy in the plant led to more civic activity."

This philosophy of liberal management associates a pay-for-performance ethos with democracy. It replaces citizenship and worker protections with a theory of "human capital" under the guise of incorporating the psychological state of workers and managers within its calculus of efficiency and productivity.[109] If democracy and a more satisfactory work experience were the "human" payoffs of autonomy, the "economic results" of this shift in managerial practice were equally beneficial: "The plant is operated by 70 workers, rather than the 110 originally estimated by industrial engineers. Also, there were 'improved yields, minimized waste and avoidance of shut downs.'"[110] Rather than breaking with Taylor's earlier theory of scientific management, this case study transforms management into a meritocracy inspired by a psychology of motivation. The task force behind *Work in America* replaces oversight with autonomy and efficiency with "results" from fewer workers. Taylor's recommendation of stable high wages gives way to a performance-based calculus of individual psychological payoffs.

In addition to sanctioning psychological solutions within the management of capitalist production, the federal task force that published the *Work in America* report also represents the degree to which existentialist sensibilities had become part of institutional political culture. The report's concluding section begins by citing a (perhaps apocryphal) statement by Albert Camus: "Without work all life goes rotten. But when work is soulless, life stifles and dies."[111] The report claims its own "analyses" lead "to much the same conclusion." Pervasive "worker alienation" is the "human cost" of "either the absence of work or employment in meaningless work."[112] The sentiments of absurdity have thus been integrated into a federal vocabulary for explaining corporate productivity.

In addition to trading on the terms of existentialist thought and aligning its "analyses" with Camus, *Work in America* expresses a liberal philosophy of management that promotes the opportunity to become one's most meaningful self. Employment security and greater wage parity fall out of the report's calculus. In other words, theorists of American capitalism—including the academics, federal employees, and blue-collar members of the HEW taskforce—had come to employ the terms of self-actualization and absurdity to ameliorate the "blues" plaguing American business in a way they expected to be widely intelligible to an American public.[113]

As this chapter shows, the *Work in America* report was far from alone in promoting this liberal philosophy of management. The Students for a Democratic Society's *Port Huron Statement* likewise advocates for an "economic sphere" in which "work should involve incentives worthier than money or survival. It should be educative, not stultifying; creative, not mechanical; self-directed, not manipulated, encouraging independence."[114] A decade before the *Work in America* report, the radical SDS's "agenda for a generation" construes the workplace as "so personally decisive that the individual must share in its full determination."[115] A new philosophy of liberal management thus influenced a wide spectrum of liberal thought. In both *Work in America* and *The Port Huron Statement*, the economic sphere operates as a handle for governing or enabling private judgments of value in much the same way as the aestheticism of Friedrich Hayek's political philosophy. Furthermore, in a turn on the resurgence of forms of aestheticism during the 1940s, the SDS and the HEW task force both assume that the chief ends of liberal management are the individual's self-direction, not the regulation or maintenance of structural parity in the relation between wages and labor. American liberalism had come to construe opportunities for private judgments of value as the governing moral concern for political movements and institutions.

As many domains of postwar fiction and several schools of management theory formulated alternatives to the gray-flanneled conformity of organizational bureaucracy, these developments inflected public discourse, challenging the postwar welfare order and the social-democratic institutions that could maintain it. These literary and corporate discourses also reframed democratic virtue. A world structured according to the estranging logic of bureaucracy, so went the thinking, requires a corresponding sea change in what it means to live nobly. In one prominent answer to such a demand, authenticity became a cultural ethic, and this ethic reshaped the contours of liberal democratic virtue. As Drucker would put it in one of his more recent expressions, virtue and democracy converge at the opportunity of "managing oneself."[116] In opposition to this theory of self-direction and personal authenticity, the image of gray-flanneled conformity provided a convenient trope for postwar novelists and management theorists alike. Such a trope created space for sensibilities that took the possibilities of the self as liberalism's final horizon—one that, in subsequent decades, would only recede further from view.

NOTES

Introduction

1. It's no secret that 'liberalism' is an inconsistent, ever-changing tradition of political thought. There's no core to liberalism, even if liberals often identify this or that core principle. Duncan Bell's genealogy of the "tradition-construction" of "liberalism" is very useful on this point. Bell's account shows that midcentury liberalism "retrojected" a tradition of coherence for itself. Bell's dynamic account of liberalism and the conceptual emergence of "liberal democracy" explain the evolving content of these terms. I don't police the borders between liberalism and adjacent or overlapping political traditions for this reason. The "liberal tradition" is based on a multitude of non-essential debts and exchanges. See Duncan Bell, "What Is Liberalism?" *Political Theory* 42.6 (2014): 682–715.

2. Alan Brinkley, *The End of Reform: New Deal Liberalism in Recession and War* (New York: Knopf, 1995); Allen J. Matusow, *The Unraveling of America: A History of Liberalism in the 1960s* (New York: Harper & Row, 1984); Dan T. Carter, *The Politics of Rage: George Wallace, the Origins of the New Conservatism, and the Transformation of American Politics* (New York: Simon & Schuster, 1995); Glenn Feldman, *The Great Melding: War, the Dixiecrat Rebellion, and the Southern Model for America's New Conservatism* (Tuscaloosa: University of Alabama Press, 2015); Wendy L. Wall, *Inventing the 'American Way': The Politics of Consensus from the New Deal to the Civil Rights Movement* (New York: Oxford University Press, 2008).

3. Michael Schaller and George Rising, *The Republican Ascendancy: American Politics, 1968–2001* (Wheeling, IL: Harlan Davidson, 2002).

4. See Dwight D. Eisenhower, "The Middle of the Road: A Statement of Faith in America," in *The Welfare State and the National Welfare*, ed. Sheldon Glueck (Cambridge, MA: Addison-Wesley Press, 1952), 132–42; Robert Y. Shapiro and John T. Young, "Public Opinion and the Welfare State: The United States in Comparative Perspective," *Political Science Quarterly* 104.1 (Spring 1989): 74; Hugh A. Wilson, "Eisenhower and the Development of Active Labor Market Policy in the United States: A Revisionist Review," *Presidential Studies Quarterly* 39.3 (Sept. 2009): 519–48.

5. See, for example, Clarke A. Chambers, "Social Security, The Welfare Consensus of the New Deal," in *The Roosevelt New Deal*, ed. Wilbur J. Cohen (Austin: University of Texas, 1986), 145–60; Walter I. Trattner, *From Poor Law to Welfare State: A History of Social Welfare in America*, 6th ed. (New York: Free Press, 1999), 304–35.

6. David Goldfield, *The Gifted Generation: When Government Was Good* (New York: Bloomsbury, 2017), 2. See Henry S. Reuss, *When Government Was Good: Memories of a Life in Politics* (Madison: University of Wisconsin Press, 1999).

7. Qtd. in Rick Perlstein, *Before the Storm: Barry Goldwater and the Unmaking of the American Consensus* (New York: Hill and Wang, 2001), ix.

8. Sheldon S. Wolin, *Politics and Vision: Continuity and Innovation in Western Political Thought*, expanded edition (Princeton, NJ: Princeton University Press, 2004), 552.

9. Thomas Hill Schaub, *American Fiction in the Cold War* (Madison: University of Wisconsin Press, 1991).

10. Wolin, *Politics and Vision*, 553.

11. The inadequacies of postwar liberalism were lost on most contemporary commentators. However, looking back at the years after 1945, John Kenneth Galbraith argues in *The Affluent Society* (1957) that liberalism had a part to play in what he terms the "market revival," or the decline in support for public programs and ascendancy of a privatized ethic for the social arena. Galbraith says, for example, that anti-social-democratic ideas "were meeting no very effective attack from liberals. The main thrust of liberal economic thought flowed in different channels. And it was able, in [Keynesian fiscal policy], to find common cause with the market revival." See John Kenneth Galbraith, *The Affluent Society* (Boston, MA: Houghton Mifflin, 1976), xvii.

12. Michael Edwards, "Philosophy, Early Modern Intellectual History, and the History of Philosophy," *Metaphilosophy* 43.1–2 (Jan. 2012): 84.

13. Raymond Williams, *The English Novel from Dickens to Lawrence* (New York: Oxford University Press, 1970), 11.

14. James F. English, *The Economy of Prestige: Prizes, Awards, and the Circulation of Cultural Value* (Cambridge, MA: Harvard University Press, 2005), 19. For example, a 1957 report in *Publishers Week* records, "The increase in trade book sales during 1956 will top the 7 per cent increase which 1955 registered over 1954." In contrast to the relatively small size of the book trade before World War II, the 1950s enjoyed successive years of significant growth in the economic value of the publishing industry. See "Highlights of 1956 News and Trends in the U.S. Book Industry," *Publishers Weekly*, January 21, 1957, 47.

15. See Carl F. Kaestle, Helen Damon-Moore, Lawrence C. Stedman, Katherine Tinsley, and William Vance Trollinger, Jr. *Literacy in the United States: Readers and Reading since 1880* (New Haven, CT: Yale University Press, 1991), 150–54. This study also notes the increase in library borrowing during the 1950s, which suggests that book reading more generally—not just the publishing industry—grew throughout the 1950s (165).

16. English, *The Economy of Prestige*, 19–20.

17. Evan Brier, *A Novel Marketplace: Mass Culture, the Book Trade, and Postwar American Fiction* (Philadelphia: University of Pennsylvania Press, 2009).

18. Mark Greif, *The Age of the Crisis of Man: Thought and Fiction in America, 1933–1973* (Princeton, NJ: Princeton University Press, 2015), 104.

19. Alan Brinkley provides the following synopsis of the "retreat from reform" that beset New Deal liberalism: "The greatest assault on New Deal reforms [in 1942–43] came from conservatives in Congress, who seized on the war as an excuse to do what many had wanted to do in peacetime: dismantle many of the achievements of the New Deal." See Alan Brinkley, *The Unfinished Nation: A Concise History of the American People*, 3rd ed. (New York: McGraw-Hill, 2000), 831.

20. Richard H. Pells, *The Liberal Mind in a Conservative Age: American Intellectuals in the 1940s and 1950s* (New York: Harper & Row, 1985), 15. As Pells says, this shift had already begun through the wartime emphases of the Roosevelt administration.

21. Franklin D. Roosevelt, "The 'Forgotten Man' Speech," April 7, 1932, Albany, New York, transcript available at http://www.presidency.ucsb.edu/ws/?pid=88408.

22. Ibid.

23. Susan Edmunds, *Grotesque Relations: Modernist Domestic Fiction and the U.S. Welfare State* (New York: Oxford University Press, 2008), 6.

24. John Steinbeck, *The Grapes of Wrath* (New York: Penguin, 1992), 346. Hereafter cited parenthetically.

25. Alan M. Wald, *American Night: The Literary Left in the Cold War Era* (Chapel Hill: University of North Carolina Press, 2012), 92, 93.

26. Sarah D. Wald argues that Steinbeck's novel is not without its own betrayals of political progressivism. According to Wald, *The Grapes of Wrath* relies on the conflation of citizenship and whiteness in its protest against the trials of the Joad family. See Sarah D. Wald, *The Nature of California: Race, Citizenship, and Farming since the Dust Bowl* (Seattle: University of Washington Press, 2016), 57–65. Steinbeck's critique of the shortcomings of the New Deal undeniably had its own failures and weaknesses.

27. Brinkley, *The End of Reform*, 4–5. Many scholars often make distinctions within this "active phase," describing Roosevelt's administration during the 73rd Congress (1933–1935) as the "first" New Deal. It was made up of fifteen acts passed by Congress and signed by the president, many of which were soon hotly contested. For the sake of clarity, I don't employ this legislative distinction. I'm concerned instead with the broad form of liberal thinking from 1933 until the FLSA and the Keynsians won out in 1938.

28. Brinkley, *The End of Reform*, 5.

29. For an anti-capitalist voice in the administration, see Carl Dreher, "The American Way: A Voice from the Left," in *The American Way*, ed. David Cushman Coyle (New York: Harper, 1938), 75–88.

30. Louis Menand, "How the Deal Went Down: Saving Democracy in the Depression," *The New Yorker*, 4 March 4, 2013.

31. Richard Hofstadter, *The Age of Reform: From Bryan to FDR* (New York: Knopf, 1955), 307.

32. Among its failures, the public works programs of the New Deal had devastating environmental consequences and created inadvertent class disparities when trying to solve economic and agricultural problems. See Christopher J. Manganiello, *Southern Water, Southern Power: How the Politics of Cheap Energy and Water Scarcity Shaped a Region* (Chapel Hill: University of North Carolina Press, 2015), 69–91.

33. See Gilbert J. Gall, *Pursuing Justice: Lee Pressman, the New Deal, and the CIO* (Albany: State University of New York Press, 1999). I return to the labor movements of the 1930s and 1940s in the second chapter. It is also worth noting that the less radical American Federation of Labor (AFL) played a significant part in the labor movement in the 1940s, particularly after the CIO broke with the organization in the mid-1930s. See Andrew E. Kersten, *Labor's Home Front: The American Federation of Labor during World War II* (New York: New York University Press, 2006).

34. These banking reforms had their own "contradictory imperatives," as Ellen D. Russell puts it. See Ellen D. Russell, *New Deal Banking Reforms and Keynesian Welfare State Capitalism* (New York: Routledge, 2008).

35. Norman Mailer, "The White Negro: Superficial Reflections on the Hipster," *Dissent*, Summer 1957, 277. Hereafter cited parenthetically.

36. Michael Szalay, *Hip Figures: A Literary History of the Democratic Party* (Stanford, CA: Stanford University Press, 2012), 8.

37. Alan Nadel, *Containment Culture: American Narratives, Postmodernism, and the Atomic Age* (Durham, NC: Duke University Press, 1995); Elaine Tyler May, *Homeward Bound: American Families in the Cold War Era* (New York: Basic Books, 1999), 100–18.

38. Walter Benn Michaels, *The Shape of the Signifier: 1967 to the End of History* (Princeton, NJ: Princeton University Press, 2004), 30.

39. Landon R. Y. Storrs, *The Second Red Scare and the Unmaking of the New Deal Left* (Princeton, NJ: Princeton University Press, 2013).

40. The *Southern Textile Bulletin* offers a record of these worries. See Bart Dredge, "Defending White Supremacy: David Clark and the *Southern Textile Bulletin*, 1911 to 1955," *North Carolina Historical Review* 89.1 (Jan. 2012): 59–91.

41. See J. David Greenstone, *Labor in American Politics* (New York: Knopf, 1969), 408.

42. Ira Katznelson, *Fear Itself: The New Deal and the Origins of Our Time* (New York: Liveright, 2013), 272.

43. See Theodore Rosenof, *Patterns of Political Economy in America: The Failure to Develop a Democratic Left Synthesis, 1933–1950* (New York: Garland, 1983); Dean L. May, *From New Deal to New Economics: The American Liberal Response to the Recession of 1937* (New York: Garland, 1981); and Richard P. Adelstein, "'The Nation as an Economic Unit': Keynes, Roosevelt, and the Managerial Idea," *Journal of American History* 78 (1991): 160–87.

44. Norman Mailer, *The Naked and the Dead* (New York: Picador [1948] 1998), 159. Hereafter cited parenthetically.

45. Norman Mailer, *The Armies of the Night: History as a Novel, the Novel as History* (New York: Penguin, 1994), 54. Hereafter cited parenthetically.

46. Gordon Hutner, *What America Read: Taste, Class and the Novel, 1920–1960* (Chapel Hill: University of North Carolina Press, 2009), 272.

47. Ibid.

48. See John McGowan, *American Liberalism: An Interpretation for Our Time* (Chapel Hill: University of North Carolina Press, 2007), 149.

49. Mical Raz, *What's Wrong with the Poor?: Psychiatry, Race, and the War on Poverty* (Chapel Hill: University of North Carolina Press, 2013), 76–111.

50. Qtd. in "Unconditional War on Poverty," *Social Service Review* 38.1 (Mar. 1964): 73.

51. Qtd. in Brinkley, *The End of Reform*, 48.

52. Kim Phillips-Fein, *Invisible Hands: The Making of the Conservative Movement from the New Deal to Reagan* (New York: Norton, 2009), 20.

53. See Robert Wolfe and Matthew Mendelsohn, "Values and Interests in Attitudes toward Trade and Globalization: The Compromise of Embedded Liberalism," *Canadian Journal of Political Science* 38.1 (Mar. 2005): 45–68.

54. Stephen Schryer, *Fantasies of a New Class: Ideologies of Professionalism in Post-World War II American Fiction* (New York: Columbia University Press, 2011), 6.

55. Ralph Ellison, *Invisible Man* (New York: Vintage, [1952] 1995), 13. Hereafter cited parenthetically.

56. Walker Percy, *The Moviegoer* (New York: Vintage, 1998), 7.

Chapter 1

1. Vladimir Nabokov, *Dear Bunny, Dear Volodya: The Nabokov-Wilson Letters, 1947–1971*, edited by Simon Karlinsky (Berkeley: University of California Press, 2001), 210.

2. Ibid., 232.

3. In the introduction to *Bend Sinister*, written nearly twenty years after its original publication, Nabokov dismisses "automatic comparisons between *Bend Sinister* and Kafka's creations or Orwell's clichés," for such characterizations "would go merely to prove that the automaton could not have read either the great German writer or the mediocre English one" (xii). In the foreword to *Invitation to a Beheading*, Nabokov similarly rejected any affinity between that novel and all "popular purveyors of illustrated ideas and publicistic fiction," listing Orwell as the chief culprit (6).

4. It is important to note the difference between "parody" and "satire." When asked in an interview with Alfred Appel, Jr., whether he makes "a clear distinction between satire and parody," Nabokov answers, "Satire is a lesson, parody is a game" (138). This distinction is consistent with Nabokov's views of literary satisfaction explored throughout the chapter. See Alfred Appel, Jr., and Vladimir Nabokov, "An Interview with Vladimir Nabokov," *Wisconsin Studies in Contemporary Literature* 8.2 (Spring 1967): 127–52.

5. See Alan M. Wald, *The New York Intellectuals: The Rise and Decline of the Anti-Stalinist Left from the 1930s to the 1980s* (Chapel Hill: University of North Carolina Press, 1987), 182–90, 367–71.

6. Lionel Trilling, *The Liberal Imagination: Essays on Literature and Society* (New York: New York Review of Books, 2008), xv, xvii.

7. Ibid., xix.

8. Ibid., xx.

9. Ibid., xxi.

10. Stephen Schryer, *Fantasies of a New Class: Ideologies of Professionalism in Post-World War II American Fiction* (New York: Columbia University Press, 2011), 6. As Schryer convincingly argues, however, this plea to the "new class" of managers is less a rejection of organizational professionalism as a dialectical retention of its contours. That is to say, Trilling construes critics and intellectuals as professional managers of cultural and moral sentiment. While this construal denigrates an activist-managerial state, it retains the notion that intellectuals occupy a privileged position to inform the shape of society.

11. See Sean McCann, "'They Make Their Own Tragedies Too': Harvey Swados and Postwar Liberalism's Discourse of Dependency," in *Literary/Liberal Entanglements: Toward a Literary History for the Twenty-First Century*, ed. Corrinne Harol and Mark Simpson (Toronto: University of Toronto Press, 2017), 309.

12. Vladimir Nabokov, *Strong Opinions* (New York: Vintage, [1973] 1990), 111.

13. Vladimir Nabokov, *Bend Sinister* (New York: Vintage, [1947] 1990), xiii. Hereafter cited parenthetically.

14. Vladimir Nabokov, *Speak, Memory: An Autobiography Revisited* (New York: Vintage, [1967] 1989), 73. Hereafter cited parenthetically. *Speak, Memory* is a revision of Nabokov's earlier autobiography *Conclusive Evidence*, which was first published in 1951.

15. Vladimir Nabokov, *Invitation to a Beheading* (New York: Vintage, 1989), 72. Hereafter cited parenthetically.

16. Following the author's lead, several scholars have paired *Invitation to a Beheading* with *Bend Sinister*. See, for example, David Rampton, *Vladimir Nabokov: A Critical Study of the Novels* (New York: Cambridge University Press, 1984), 31–63.

17. Vladimir Nabokov, "Tyrants Destroyed," in *Tyrants Destroyed and Other Stories* (New York: McGraw-Hill, 1975), 2. Hereafter cited parenthetically.

18. For more on the literary play of the narrative, see L. L. Lee, "*Bend Sinister*: Nabokov's Political Dream," *Wisconsin Studies in Contemporary Literature* 8.2 (Spring 1967): 198–99. See also Michael H. Bengal, "*Bend Sinister*: Joyce, Shakespeare, Nabokov," *Modern Language Studies* 15.4 (1985): 22–27.

19. Trilling, *The Liberal Imagination*, 100.

20. Brian Boyd, *Vladimir Nabokov: The American Years* (Princeton, NJ: Princeton University Press, 1991), 94.

21. Franklin D. Roosevelt, "Fireside Chat," December 29, 1940, Gerhard Peters and John T. Woolley, *The American Presidency Project*. http://www.presidency.ucsb.edu/ws/?pid=15917.

22. Ethan Colton, *Four Patterns of Revolution: Communist U.S.S.R., Fascist Italy, Nazi Germany, New Deal America* (New York: Association Press, 1935), 248.

23. Friedrich Hayek, *The Road to Serfdom*, vol. 2 of *The Collected Works of F. A. Hayek* (Chicago: University of Chicago Press, [1944] 2007), 42. Hereafter cited parenthetically.

24. Bruce Caldwell notes that the American edition sold 17,000 copies in the month of September, while over 1 million reprints of the book were eventually sold. Perhaps more importantly, *The Reader's Digest*, which had a circulation of between 9 and 10 million readers, published a 20-page condensation of the book. *Look* magazine even published a cartoon edition in February 1945. For more about the circulation of *The Road to Serfdom* and the various uses to which the book was put, see Bruce Caldwell, Introduction to *The Road to Serfdom* (Chicago, University of Chicago Press, [1944] 2007), 18–23.

25. Robert Putnam, *Bowling Alone: The Collapse and Revival of American Community* (New York: Simon & Schuster, 2000).

26. Leo Strauss and Joseph Cropsey, eds., *History of Political Philosophy* (Chicago: University of Chicago Press, 1987), 181.

27. Bhikhu Parekh, "Putting Civil Society in Its Place," in *Civil Society: Views and Reviews*, ed. G. K. Rathod (New Delhi: Viva Books, 2012), 16.

28. See also Charles Taylor, *Modern Social Imaginaries* (Durham, NC: Duke University Press, 2004), 3–10, 83–99. In the Hobbesian view, human beings band together out of self-interest, and this civic affiliation eventually necessitates (or, in some cases, is subjugated by) a formalized government that protects the interests of its citizens. For Locke, on the other hand, the rational associational life of human beings manifests a social contract, which in turn justifies the state.

29. For more on the important contributions of Hegel and Marx, see G. W. F. Hegel, *Philosophy of Right* (Oxford: Oxford University Press, 1952), 266–76. See also Michael W. Foley and Bob Edwards, Introduction to "Beyond Tocqueville: Civil Society and Social Capital in Comparative Perspective," *American Behavioral Society* 42.1 (Sept. 1998), 6–7; Michael Edwards, *Civil Society*, 2nd ed. (Cambridge, UK: Polity Press, 2009), 8–20.

30. See Alexis de Tocqueville, "Political Associations in the United States," in *Democracy in America* (New York: Penguin, 2003), 219–27. In an earlier moment of optimism, Tocqueville concludes, "Therefore, in reality it is the people who rule. Although they have a representative government, it is quite clear that the opinions, bias, concerns, and even the

passions of the people can encounter no lasting obstacles preventing them from exercising a day-to-day influence upon the conduct of society" (201–2). Tocqueville believes such civic associations are the means for securing popular self-governance.

31. Ibid., 227, italics added.

32. See, for example, Michael Walzer, "The Idea of Civil Society: A Path to Social Reconstruction," in *Community Works: The Revival of Civil Society in America*, ed. E. J. Dionne (Washington, DC: Brookings Institute Press, 1998); see also William Galston, "Liberal Egalitarianism: A Family of Theories, Not a Single View," in *Civil Society and Government*, ed. R. Post and N. Rosenblum (Princeton,NJ: Princeton University Press, 2002).

33. On the consonance between Gramsci and Dewey, see Cornel West, *The American Evasion of Philosophy: A Genealogy of Pragmatism* (Madison: University of Wisconsin Press, 1989), 218–19. See also Edwards, *Civil Society*, 9.

34. See John Dewey, *The Public and Its Problems* (New York: Holt, 1927), 101.

35. Ibid., 102.

36. Ibid., 106.

37. Ibid., 106.

38. Hannah Arendt provides a nuanced distinction between the ideas of "public life" and "society" or the "social." See Hannah Arendt, *The Human Condition* (Chicago: University of Chicago Press, 1958). On the issue of Arendt as a theorist of "civil society," see John McGowan, *Hannah Arendt: An Introduction* (Minneapolis: University of Minnesota Press, 1998), 158–61.

39. Frederick Powell, *The Politics of Civil Society: Neoliberalism or Social Left?* (Bristol, UK: Policy Press, 2007), 63–85.

40. Ibid., 85.

41. Ibid., 88.

42. Ibid., 91.

43. Hannah Arendt, *On Revolution* (New York: Penguin Books, [1963] 1977), 221.

44. Arendt, *The Human Condition*, 40.

45. Arendt, *The Origins of Totalitarianism*, 2nd ed. (New York: Meridian Books, [1951] 1958), 43–45.

46. Hannah Arendt, *On Violence* (New York: Harcourt Brace Jovanovich, 1969), 38–39.

47. Arendt, *On Revolution*, 269.

48. Powell, *Politics of Civil Society*, 140. In another form of skepticism regarding the possibilities of civil society, some theorists have argued that such civic associations frequently rely on exclusionary tactics to establish a consensus political order, such that their political aims have often facilitated the segregation or marginalization of minority groups. See Partha Chatterjee, *The Politics of the Governed: Reflections on Popular Politics in Most of the World* (New York: Columbia University Press, 2004), 4; Partha Chatterjee, "Beyond the Nation? Or Within?" *Social Text* 56 (Autumn 1998): 57–69; Nicolas Martin, "The Dark Side of Political Society: Patronage and the Reproduction of Social Inequality," *Journal of Agrarian Change* 14.3 (2014): 419–34.

49. Arendt's valorization of spontaneity, or what she calls "natality" in *The Human Condition*, underwrites her view of genuine political community as necessarily being antithetical to such bureaucratic structures. See her definition of natality in Arendt, *The Human Condition*, 9.

50. As Jesse Larner says about Hayek, his influence on American political thought was immediate but also extended most forcefully into the 1980s: "Ronald Reagan and

Margaret Thatcher cited his ideas as central to the social revolutions they hoped to spark. Antigovernment ideologues admire him as one of those few who kept Adam Smith's fires burning during the dark reign of John Maynard Keynes in the West." See Jesse Larner, "Who's Afraid of Friedrich Hayek? The Obvious Truths and Mystical Fallacies of a Hero of the Right," *Dissent* (Winter 2008), 85.

51. Regarding the relation between Hayek's political theory and "civil society," see Steven Horowitz, "The Functions of the Family in the Great Society," *Cambridge Journal of Economics* 29 (2005): 669–84. Regarding Hayek's notion of the "spontaneous order" and its underlying aestheticism, see Charles McDaniel, "Friedrich Hayek and Reinhold Niebuhr on the Moral Persistence of Liberal Society," *Journal of Interdisciplinary Studies* 16 (2004): 133–56.

52. Hayek, *The Road to Serfdom*, 125.

53. Ibid.

54. This recalls John Locke's theory of natural rights. See John Locke, *Second Treatise*, in *Two Treatises of Government, and A Letter Concerning Toleration* (New Haven, CT: Yale University Press, 2004), §123. In this remark Locke describes the "lives, liberties, and estates" of individuals as a "property" of the self. Liberty is therefore innate and, more importantly, a possession that may be violated by tyranny.

55. Hayek, *The Road to Serfdom*, 125.

56. In his later foreword to the 1956 American paperback edition, Hayek changes the rationale for conflating "economic planning" and "social control." In *The Road to Serfdom*, Hayek argues that the economic arena is an avenue for divesting freedom from individuals, as if the liberty to determine "value" were a possession of the self. Economic planning is a violation of an innate characteristic of the self. Yet Hayek later implies that *economic conditions* actually determine the private arena, as if such material conditions conform the individual to a pattern of either freedom or oppression. For example, he says in the later foreword, "the most important change which extensive government control produces is a psychological change, an alteration in the character of the people" (48). Still, despite the curiously materialist assumptions of Hayek's later claim, he remains concerned with the effects of economic planning upon the private lives of individuals.

57. Ibid., 126.

58. Ibid.

59. Opposition to "collectivism" gathered such force that it even appeared in the public addresses of ex-President Herbert Hoover in 1949. See Herbert Hoover, "The Last Miles to Collectivism," in *The Welfare State and the National Welfare* (Cambridge, MA: Addison-Wesley Press, 1952), 161–85.

60. For more on Arendt's aestheticism, see the convincing argument in Dana R. Villa, "Beyond Good and Evil: Arendt, Nietzsche, and the Aestheticization of Political Action," *Political Theory* 20.2 (May 1992): 274–308.

61. Adam B. Seligman, "Civil Society as Idea and Ideal," in *Alternative Conceptions of Civil Society*, ed. Simone Chambers and Will Kymlicka (Princeton, NJ: Princeton University Press, 2002), 13.

62. Mark McGurl associates Nabokov's view of literature and reading, and his notion of an enclosed system of literary pleasure, with the institution of universities in the postwar era—a dependence that led writers and critics to assert programs of literature and, more generally, higher education itself to be an independent, enclosed system. See Mark

McGurl, *The Program Era: Postwar Fiction and the Rise of Creative Writing* (Cambridge, MA: Harvard University Press, 2009), 4–11.

63. Appel, "An Interview with Vladimir Nabokov," 134–36.

64. Ibid., 127.

65. See Appel's note on p. 136.

66. Saul Maloff, "The World of Rococo," *The Nation* (June 16, 1962): 541–42; Mary McCarthy, "A Bolt from the Blue," *The New Republic* (June 4, 1962): 15–34; Dwight Macdonald, "Virtuosity Rewarded, Or Dr. Kinbote's Revenge," *Partisan Review* 29 (Summer 1962): 437–42; and Frank Kermode, "Zemblances," *New Statesman*, November 9, 1962, 671–72. As an example of mass-market coverage of Nabokov—precipitated in large part by the release of Stanley Kubrick's film version of *Lolita* (1962)—see "Lolita's Creator—Author Nabokov, a 'Cosmic Joker,'" *Newsweek*, June 25, 1962, 51–54. See also Pells, *The Liberal Mind in a Conservative Age*, 14–16.

67. Vladimir Nabokov, *Lolita* (New York: Vintage, [1955] 1989), 283. Hereafter cited parenthetically.

68. Ibid., xxi.

69. Dana Brand, "The Interaction of Aestheticism and American Consumer Culture in Nabokov's *Lolita*," *Modern Language Studies* 17.2 (Spring 1987): 19.

70. Ibid.

71. Eric Naiman, *Nabokov, Perversely* (Ithaca, NY: Cornell University Press, 2010).

72. Vladimir Nabokov, "Good Readers and Good Writers," in *Lectures on Literature*, ed. Fredson Bowers (New York: Harcourt, 1980), 4. Hereafter cited parenthetically.

73. Friedrich Nietzsche, *The Gay Science*, trans. Josefine Nauckhoff (New York: Cambridge University Press, 2001). Hereafter cited parenthetically.

74. Jennifer Ratner-Rosenhagen, *American Nietzsche: A History of an Icon and His Ideas* (Chicago: University of Chicago Press, 2011), 220.

75. Ibid., 221, 220.

76. Ibid., 222.

77. Ibid., 223.

78. Ibid., 221.

79. Qtd. in Ratner-Rosenhagen, *American Nietzsche*, 224.

80. Ibid., 226.

81. In complement to the comparison between Nietzsche and Nabokov, Corey Robin has traced an "elective affinity" between Nietzsche and Friedrich Hayek on the grounds of a comparable aestheticism. Robin's mapping of these "elective affinities" suggests yet another dimension to the resurgence of aestheticism as a feature of changes in postwar political culture. See Corey Robin, "Nietzsche's Marginal Children: On Friedrich Hayek," *The Nation*, May 7, 2013, available at http://www.thenation.com/article/nietzsches-marginal-children-friedrich-hayek/.

82. John Crowe Ransom, *The New Criticism* (Norfolk, CT: New Directions, 1941), xi.

83. Gerald Graff, *Professing Literature: An Institutional History* (Chicago: University of Chicago Press, 1987), 173.

84. Schryer, *Fantasies of the New Class*, 30.

85. John Crowe Ransom, "Reconstructed but Unregenerate," in *I'll Take My Stand* (Baton Rouge: Louisiana State University Press, 1978), 10.

86. Brooks, *The Well Wrought Urn*, 76.

87. Ransom, *The New Criticism*, 279–281.

88. Schryer, *Fantasies of the New Class*, 41.

89. Ibid., 32.

90. Amy Reading, "Vulgarity's Ironist: New Criticism, Midcult, and Nabokov's *Pale Fire*," *Arizona Quarterly: A Journal of American Literature, Culture, and Theory* 62.2 (Summer 2006): 83.

91. Alan Brinkley, *The End of Reform: New Deal Liberalism in Recession and War* (New York: Knopf, 1995), 15.

92. Ibid., 154. See also Wendy L. Wall, *Inventing the "American Way": The Politics of Consensus from the New Deal to the Civil Rights Movement* (New York: Oxford University Press, 2008), 163–200.

93. Brinkley, *The End of Reform*, 154.

Chapter 2

1. Friedrich Nietzsche, *On the Genealogy of Morals*, trans. Douglas Smith (New York: Oxford University Press, 2008), 28.

2. Ibid., 32.

3. In addition to Nietzsche, the "underground" narrative frame of *Invisible Man* owes a conspicuous debt to another proto-existentialist, Fyodor Dostoyevsky, who also repudiated the progressive politics of his day. The Ellison-Dostoyevsky connection is a well-established one. See Dale E. Peterson, "Underground Notes: Dostoevsky, Bakhtin, and the African American Novel," *Bucknell Review: A Scholarly Journal of Letters, Arts and Sciences* 43.2 (2000): 31–46; Maria R. Bloshteyn, "Rage and Revolt: Dostoevsky and Three African-American Writers," *Comparative Literature Studies* 38.4 (2001): 277–309; Paul W. Nisly, "A Modernist Impulse: *Notes from Underground* as Model," *College Literature* 4.2 (Spring 1977): 152–58.

4. Arnold Rampersad, *Ralph Ellison: A Biography* (New York: Knopf, 2007), 190–91.

5. The American encounter with European avant-garde and modernist art during the war subsequently transformed American art during the postwar decades. See Lisa Phillips, *The American Century: Art & Culture, 1950–2000* (New York: Whitney Museum of American Art, 1999), 14; Mark Stevens and Annalyn Swan, *De Kooning: An American Master* (New York: Knopf, 2004), 267–70; Robert Genter, *Late Modernism: Art, Culture, and Politics in Cold War America* (Philadelphia: University of Pennsylvania, 2010), 197–235; J. M. Berstein, *Against Voluptuous Bodies: Late Modernism and the Meaning of Painting* (Stanford CA: Stanford University Press, 2006), 165–92; Erika Lee Doss, *Benton, Pollock, and the Politics of Modernism: From Regionalism to Abstract Expressionism* (Chicago: University of Chicago Press, 1991), 67–151.

6. Andrew Hoberek, *The Twilight of the Middle Class: Post-World War II American Fiction and White-Collar Work* (Princeton, NJ: Princeton University Press, 2005), 55.

7. Rampersad, *Ralph Ellison*, 93.

8. Michael Denning situates Ellison's career during the 1930s and 1940s within what he calls the "cultural front," or the cultural activities of popular front politics. Ellison edited *The Negro Quarterly* with Angelo Herndon, a prominent communist intellectual, and he published almost exclusively in politically progressive magazines, such as his story "Slick Gonna Learn," published in 1939 in *Direction*, and "The Birthmark," published in

1940 in *New Masses*, which was explicit about its association with the CPUSA. Michael Denning, *The Cultural Front: The Laboring of American Culture in the Twentieth Century* (New York: Verso, 1998), 332.

9. Foley's first articles on Ellison and leftist politics generated a great deal of interest in a subject that more or less had remained dormant for three decades. See Barbara Foley, "The Rhetoric of Anticommunism in *Invisible Man*," *College English* 59 (1997): 530–47; and "Ralph Ellison as Proletarian Journalist," *Science and Society* 62 (1998–99): 537–56. Foley has recently expanded her argument and responded to her critics in *Wrestling with the Left: The Making of Ralph Ellison's* Invisible Man (Durham, NC: Duke University Press, 2010).

10. Foley, *Wrestling with the Left*, 7.

11. Rampersad, *Ralph Ellison*, 142.

12. Qtd. in Rampersad, *Ralph Ellison*, 243.

13. Raymond A. Mazurek, "Writer on the Left: Class and Race in Ellison's Early Fiction," *College Literature* 29.4 (Fall 2002): 110.

14. One way in which the novel expresses its democratic sympathies is through celebrating certain kinds of vernacular American culture. Regarding the novel's interest in the vernacular, see the influential argument in Houston A. Baker, Jr., *Blues, Ideology, and Afro-American Literature: A Vernacular Theory* (Chicago: University of Chicago Press, 1984), 185–95.

15. Denning, *The Cultural Front*, xviii.

16. This expansive spectrum is remarkable for many reasons, not least of which is that most varieties of socialism and communism have positioned themselves as ideologically opposed to liberal democracy. The liberalism that Marx opposed in the nineteenth century, and the left-of-center liberalism that the nonliberal left opposed after 1968, were, of course, remarkably different from one another. Yet these later oppositional stances occurred under conditions very different from those governing the more capacious liberalism of the 1930s. The uneasy coalition between these competing (but also overlapping) political philosophies attests to the fact that American liberalism had an expansive capacity for pragmatic co-operation during the 1930s. For more on this complicated issue, see Seymour Martin Lipset and Gary Marks, *It Didn't Happen Here: Why Socialism Failed in the United States* (New York: Norton, 2000), 203–36.

17. Wall, *Inventing the "American Way,"* 28.

18. Aaron D. Purcell, *White Collar Radicals: TVA's Knoxville Fifteen, the New Deal, and the McCarthy Era* (Knoxville: University of Tennessee Press, 2009).

19. Marcel Cornis-Pope, *Narrative Innovation and Cultural Rewriting in the Cold War Era and After* (New York: Palgrave, 2001). For Cornis-Pope, the postmodern texts beginning in the late 1960s, particularly works by Pynchon and Morrison, are a reaction against the Cold War era's trademark binaries.

20. Gilbert J. Gall, *Pursuing Justice: Lee Pressman, the New Deal, and the CIO* (Albany: State University of New York Press, 1999), 128.

21. Ibid., 129.

22. Ibid., 4.

23. The Landrum-Griffin Act of 1959 was another blow to labor unions during the postwar decades. It created controls on the internal affairs of unions. Among other regulations weakening the power of organized labor, Landrum-Griffin strengthened the Taft-Hartley Act by barring members of the Communist Party from holding union office.

24. Landon R. Y. Storrs, *The Second Red Scare and the Unmaking of the New Deal Left* (Princeton NJ: Princeton University Press, 2013), 147.

25. Ibid., 2.

26. As yet another example, Carol Anderson has shown how the Truman administration often practiced merely "symbolic equality" by failing to provide significant funding or create strong enforcement mechanisms for its civil rights initiatives. See Carol Anderson, *Eyes Off the Prize: The United Nations and the African American Struggle for Human Rights, 1944–1955* (New York: Cambridge University Press, 2003).

27. Earl Latham, *The Communist Controversy in Washington: From the New Deal to McCarthy* (Cambridge: Harvard University Press, 1966).

28. Purcell, *White Collar Radicals*, 136.

29. The image and text are available from the University of Minnesota at https://umedia. lib.umn.edu/node/45882. See Carlos Bulosan, "Freedom from Want," in *The Concise Heath Anthology of American Literature*, ed. Paul Lauter (Boston: Wadsworth, 2014), 947.

30. Ibid., 948.

31. Bulosan, "Freedom from Want," 948.

32. Denning, *The Cultural Front*, 274.

33. E. San Juan Jr., "Carlos Bulosan," in *The American Radical*, ed. Mari Jo Buhle, Paul Buhle, and Harvey J. Kaye (New York: Routledge, 1994), 253–54.

34. See Nadel, *Containment Culture*, 13–37.

35. See Barbara Foley, "Reading Redness: Politics and Audience in Ralph Ellison's Early Short Fiction," *JNT: Journal of Narrative Theory* 29 (1999): 323–39.

36. Francis Fukuyama, *The End of History and the Last Man* (New York: Free Press, 1992).

37. Chester Himes, *Lonely Crusade* (New York: Thunder's Mouth Press, 1997), 305.

38. Himes's novel offers in the place of leftist politics what Justus Nieland describes as "universalizing" noir humanism, which is a close cousin of the existential humanism that I attribute to Ellison later in this chapter. See Justus Nieland, "Everybody's Noir Humanism: Chester Himes, *Lonely Crusade*, and the Quality of Hurt," *African American Review* 43.2–3 (Summer/Fall 2009): 277–93.

39. Michel Fabre, *The Unfinished Quest of Richard Wright* (Urbana: University of Illinois Press, 1993), 229.

40. Hazel Rowley, *Richard Wright: The Life and Times* (New York: Henry Holt, 2001), 263.

41. Wright's *American Hunger* was significantly edited by his publisher, Harper, before being published as *Black Boy* in 1945. The unredacted version was not published until 1993. For the restored version, see Richard Wright, *Black Boy: A Story of Childhood and Youth* (New York: Buccaneer, 1993), 295–96.

42. Wright first published the essay in *Atlantic Monthly* 174.1 (1944). Reprinted in *The God That Failed,* ed. Richard Crossman (New York: Columbia University Press, 2001), 118.

43. Ibid., 125.

44. Ibid., 128.

45. Ibid., 118, 131.

46. Richard Wright, *The Outsider* (New York: Perennial, 2003), 241.

47. Richard Wright, *Native Son* (New York: Harper, [1940] 2005), 12.

48. Richard Wright, "How 'Bigger' Was Born," [1940] In *Native Son* (New York: Harper, 2005), 446.

49. Ralph Ellison, "Richard Wright's Blues," *Antioch Review* 3.2 (1945). Reprinted in *Shadow and Act* (New York: Vintage, [1964] 1995), 82.

50. Ibid., 83.

51. Susan Louise Edmunds, "'Just Like Home': Richard Wright, Harriet Beecher Stowe, and the New Deal," *American Literature* 86.1 (Mar. 2014): 61–86.

52. Fabre, *The Unfinished Quest*, 121–39, 165–68. See also Michael Szalay, *New Deal Modernism: American Literature and the Invention of the Welfare State* (Durham, NC: Duke University Press, 2000), 215–17.

53. Lizabeth Cohen, *A Consumer's Republic: The Politics of Mass Consumption in Postwar America* (New York: Random House, 2003).

54. Ralph Ellison, "Remembering Richard Wright" [1971], in *Going to the Territory* (New York: Vintage, [1986] 1995), 204, 205.

55. See Keith T. Poole and Howard Rosenthal, *Congress: A Political-Economic History of Roll Call Voting* (New York: Oxford University Press, 1997), 109–11, 230.

56. As only one example, Eric Schickler, Kathryn Pearson, and Brian Feinstein argue that certain segments of the Democratic Party's voting bloc, particularly CIO unionists and the burgeoning civil rights movement, began to demand changes from congressional Democrats. Pressure on democratic institutions did in fact have demonstrable institutional consequences. See Eric Schickler, Kathryn Pearson, and Brian D. Feinstein, "Congressional Parties and Civil Rights Politics from 1933 to 1972," *Journal of Politics* 72.3 (July 2010): 672–89.

57. Ralph Ellison, "The Myth of the Flawed White Southerner" [1968], in *Going to the Territory* (New York: Vintage, [1986] 1995), 76–87.

58. George Cotkin, *Existential America* (Baltimore, MD: Johns Hopkins University Press, 2003), 92.

59. Ibid.

60. *Funny Face*. Directed by Stanley Donen. Hollywood, CA: Paramount Pictures, 1957.

61. Cotkin, *Existential America*, 105–33.

62. Ibid., 161–83.

63. Letter to Wright quoted in Rampersad, *Ralph Ellison*, 190–91.

64. Jean Wahl, "Existentialism: A Preface," *New Republic*, September 30, 1945, 442–44.

65. "Existentialism," *Time*, January 28, 1946, 28–29; John L Brown, "Paris, 1946— And Its Three Warring Literary Philosophies." *New York Times*, September 1, 1946, 9, 12; Simone de Beauvoir, "Strictly Personal: Jean-Paul Sartre," *Harper's Bazaar*, trans. Malcolm Cowley, January 1946, 113. Admittedly, many early essays disseminating existentialism were far from enthusiastic about the movement. See Albert Guerard, "French and American Pessimism," *Harper's*, September 1945, 276; Bernard Fizell, "Existentialism: Postwar Paris Enthrones a Bleak Philosophy of Pessimism," *Life*, 7 June 7, 1946, 59; Oliver Barres, "In the Deeps of Despair," *Saturday Review of Literature*, May 31, 1947, 14.

66. See Paul Tillich, *A History of Christian Thought: From Its Judaic and Hellenistic Origins to Existentialism* (New York: Simon & Schuster, [1967–68], 1972).

67. Jacques Barzun, "Ça Existe: A Note on the New Ism," *American Scholar* 15.4 (Oct. 1946): 449–54. For another scholarly evaluation, see Brand Blanshard, "From the Commissioner's Mailbag," *Philosophical Review* 54 (May 1945): 210–16.

68. Ann Fulton, *Apostles of Sartre: Existentialism in America, 1945–1963* (Evanston, IL: Northwestern University Press, 1999).

69. Ibid., 67.

70. While the use of existentialism by postwar writers was at odds with the forms of philosophy dominant in American philosophy departments, Michael LeMahieu shows that logical positivism (a prominent subset in the wider analytic tradition) consistently influenced the postwar literary arena. According to this reading, the cultural cachet of existentialism may be entangled with (rather than in opposition to) the "erasure" of logical positivism. See Michael LeMahieu, *Fictions of Fact and Value: The Erasure of Logical Positivism in American Literature, 1945–1975* (New York: Oxford University Press, 2013).

71. Fulton, *Apostles of Sartre*, 73.

72. Ibid.

73. Ibid., 74–75.

74. Stark Young, "Weaknesses," *The New Republic*, December 9, 1946, 764.

75. Hilary Holladay, *Ann Petry* (New York: Twayne, 1996), 14.

76. Ann Petry, *The Street* (New York, Boston: Houghton Mifflin, [1946] 1991), 7.

77. Heather J. Hicks, "Rethinking Realism in Ann Petry's *The Street*," *MELUS* 27.4 (Winter 2002): 90.

78. Bill V. Mullen, "Object Lessons: Fetishization and Class Consciousness," in *Revising the Blueprint: Ann Petry and the Literary Left*, ed. Alex Lubin (Jackson: University of Mississippi Press, 2007), 35–48.

79. Saul Bellow, *The Adventures of Augie March* (New York: Penguin, 2006), 418. Hereafter cited parenthetically.

80. James Atlas, *Bellow: A Biography* (New York: Random House, 2000), 94.

81. Saul Bellow, *Dangling Man* (New York: Penguin, [1944] 1996), 12.

82. Zachary Leader, *The Life of Saul Bellow: To Fame and Fortune, 1915–1964* (New York: Knopf, 2015), 233–34.

83. Qtd. in Atlas, *Bellow*, 141–42.

84. Sean McCann, *A Pinnacle of Feeling: American Literature and Presidential Government* (Princeton, NJ: Princeton University Press, 2008), 107.

85. Ibid., 105.

86. Bulosan, "Freedom from Want," 949.

87. See also the juxtaposition between *Augie March* and the naturalism of James Farrell—a contrast analogous to those sketched in this chapter—in Schryer, *Fantasies of the New Class*, 20–24.

Chapter 3

1. Patricia Highsmith, *A Game for the Living* (New York: Atlantic Monthly Press, [1958] 1988), 5. Hereafter cited parenthetically.

2. Nathan Hale, Jr., *The Rise and Crisis of Psychoanalysis in the United States: Freud and the Americans, 1917–1985* (New York: Oxford University Press, 1995), 276.

3. Whether anyone actually read Auden's labyrinthine poem—it was reprinted four times within two years of its appearance and won the Pulitzer Prize for poetry in 1948—at least its titular notion became the centerpiece of American intellectual life for several years. Jacques Barzun praised *The Age of Anxiety* in the pages of *Harper's* magazine, noting that "the very title . . . roots it in our generation" (Jacques Barzun, "Workers in Monumental Brass," *Harper's*, September 1947, 195.) The influence of *The Age of Anxiety* quickly spread beyond its appreciative critics. It inspired Leonard Bernstein's Symphony no. 2 for Piano and

Orchestra, *The Age of Anxiety* (1949). Jerome Robbins also choreographed a spinoff ballet in 1950, and there were several attempts at stage versions of the poem. Such resonances lead Alan Jacobs, one of Auden's editors, to proclaim that *The Age of Anxiety* provided a "terse and widely applicable diagnostic phrase." See Alan Jacobs, Introduction to *The Age of Anxiety: A Baroque Eclogue* by W. H. Auden (Princeton, NJ: Princeton University Press, 2011), xli. Arthur Schlesinger also takes up the phrase and features it prominently in *The Vital Center* (1949), and General Dwight D. Eisenhower, then the president of Columbia University, remarked in 1949, "We are seldom free from anxiety as each day's events crown instantly upon our attention" (Eisenhower, "The Middle of the Road,": A Statement of Faith in America," in *The Welfare State and the National Welfare*, ed. Sheldon Glueck [Cambridge, MA: Addison-Wesley Press, 1952], 152).

4. Peter Gay, *Freud: A Life for Our Time* (New York: Norton, 2006), 211.

5. Ibid., 186.

6. Ibid., 213.

7. Ibid., 211.

8. John Burnham, "A Shift in Perspective," in *After Freud Left: A Century of Psychoanalysis in America*, ed. John Burnham (Chicago: University of Chicago Press, 2012), 157.

9. Dorothy Ross, "Freud and the Vicissitudes of Modernism in the United States, 1940–1980," in *After Freud Left: A Century of Psychoanalysis in America,* ed. John Burnham (Chicago: University of Chicago Press, 2012), 164.

10. Irving Howe, "The Idea of the Modern," in *Literary Modernism*, ed. Irving Howe (Greenwich, CT: Fawcett, 1967), 14.

11. Ross, "Freud and the Vicissitudes of Modernism," 166.

12. Burnham, "A Shift in Perspective," 159.

13. Richard Yates, *Revolutionary Road* (New York: Vintage, [1961] 2007), 65.

14. Ibid., 66.

15. On the proliferation of televisions among American households in the 1950s, see Sue Bowden and Avner Offer, "Household Appliances and the Use of Time: The United States and Britain since the 1920s," *Economic Historical Review* 47 (1994): 729, table 1. Bowden and Offer estimate that by 1955 black-and-white televisions had "penetrated" approximately 75 percent of households. On the issue of the consolidation of audiences, see Evan Brier, *A Novel Marketplace: Mass Culture, the Book Trade, and Postwar American Fiction* (Philadelphia: University of Pennsylvania Press, 2009), 1–3.

16. See Constantine Sandis, "Hitchcock's Conscious Use of Freud's Unconscious," *Europe's Journal of Psychology* 3 (2009): 56–81.

17. Alfred Hitchcock, dir., "Revenge," *Alfred Hitchcock Presents*, season 1, episode 1 (Aired October 2, 1955; Los Angeles: Universal Studios, 2005), DVD.

18. See also Jonathan Freedman, "From *Spellbound* to *Vertigo*: Alfred Hitchcock and Therapeutic Culture in America," in *Hitchcock's America*, ed. Jonathan Freedman and Richard Millington (New York: Oxford University Press, 1999), 77–98.

19. James L. Baughman, *Same Time, Same Station: Creating American Television, 1948–1961* (Baltimore, MD: Johns Hopkins University Press, 2007), 149.

20. Ibid., 188.

21. Similarly, David Thomson argues that Hitchcock's *Psycho* (1960) established a pattern for representing violence, sex, and desire, creating expectations that would comprise

one of the most influential templates for subsequent filmic representations of these phe-nomena. See David Thomson, *The Moment of* Psycho: *How Alfred Hitchcock Taught America to Love Murder* (New York: Basic Books, 2009).

22. Alexander Lobrano, "Patricia Highsmith: Serial Thriller," *The Lively Arts* 20, October 20, 1989, n. p.

23. Andrew Wilson, *Beautiful Shadow: A Life of Patricia Highsmith* (New York: Bloomsbury, 2003), 40–41.

24. Qtd. in ibid., 70.

25. Lionel Trilling, *Freud and the Crisis of Our Culture* (Boston: Beacon Press, 1955), 12.

26. Anatole Broyard, *Kafka Was the Rage: A Greenwich Village Memoir* (New York: Carol Southern Books, 1993), 45.

27. Wilson, *Beautiful Shadow*, 149–53.

28. Ibid., 118.

29. Ibid., 126, 158.

30. Patricia Highsmith, *Strangers on a Train* (New York: Norton, [1950] 2001), 140. Hereafter cited parenthetically.

31. See Friedrich Nietzsche, *Beyond Good and Evil: Prelude to a Philosophy of the Future*, trans. R. J. Hollingdale (New York: Penguin, [1886] 2003). Nietzsche's subsequent volume, *On the Genealogy of Morals* (1887), is a more cohesive and compelling account of the religious heritage of "good" and "evil" in the modern humanistic tradition.

32. Wilson, *Beautiful Shadow*, 211.

33. Friedrich Nietzsche, *Ecce Homo*, trans. Anthony M. Ludovic (New York: Macmillan, 1911), 131.

34. Julian Symons, *The Modern Crime Story* (Edinburgh: Tragara Press, 1980), 14.

35. *New York Herald Tribune*, 16 April 16, 1950, 26.

36. Joshua Lukin, "Identity-Shopping and Postwar Self-Improvement in Patricia Highsmith's *Strangers on a Train*," *Journal of Modern Literature* 33.4 (Summer 2010): 21–23.

37. Theodore Dreiser, *Sister Carrie* (New York: Modern Library, [1900] 1917), 4. Hereafter cited parenthetically.

38. Jack Salzman, "The Critical Recognition of *Sister Carrie*, 1900–1907," *Journal of American Studies* 3.1 (July 1969): 123–33.

39. Kevin J. Hayes, "Editing Naturalism," in *The Oxford Handbook of American Literary Naturalism*, ed. Keith Newlin (New York: Oxford University Press, 2011), 397, 399–400.

40. Malcolm Cowley, "Naturalism in American Literature," in *Evolutionary Thought in America*, ed. Stow Persons (New Haven, CT: Yale University Press, 1950). Reprinted in *American Naturalism*, ed. Harold Bloom (Philadelphia: Chelsea House, 2004), 49–79.

41. Philip Rahv, "Notes on the Decline of Naturalism," *Partisan Review* 9 (Nov.–Dec. 1942). Reprinted in Philip Rahv, *Literature and the Sixth Sense* (New York: Houghton Mifflin, 1969), 76–87.

42. Ibid., 84.

43. Ibid., 76.

44. Ibid., 76–77.

45. Ibid., 81.

46. Ibid., 86.

47. Hoberek's *The Twilight of the Middle Class* shows how such ostensibly inward turns had very definite public links. Rahv's view of the "inward turn," I'm arguing, was

part of concentric public anxieties about organizational politics more generally and social democratic institutions in particular.

48. Edward Stone, ed., *What Was Naturalism?: Materials for an Answer* (New York: Appleton-Century-Crofts, 1959).

49. Ibid., ix.

50. Ibid., viii.

51. Christophe den Tandt, "Refashioning American Literary Naturalism: Critical Trends at the Turn of the Twenty-First Century," in *The Oxford Handbook of American Literary Naturalism*, ed. Keith Newlin (New York: Oxford University Press, 2011), 405.

52. James Burkhart Gilbert, *Writers and Partisans: A History of Literary Radicalism in America* (New York: Columbia University Press, 1992).

53. Andrew J. Dvosin, Preface to *Essays on Literature and Politics, 1932–1972* (New York: Houghton Mifflin, 1978), xiii.

54. Gilbert, *Writers and Partisans*, 193.

55. Ibid., 192.

56. Mark Greif offers a more generous, but nonetheless "anxious," portrayal of *Partisan Review*. See Greif, *The Age of the Crisis of Man: Thought and Fiction in America, 1933–1973* (Princeton, NJ: Princeton University Press, 2015), 66–73.

57. Lawrence H. Schwartz, *Creating Faulkner's Reputation: The Politics of Modern Literary Criticism* (Knoxville: University of Tennessee Press, 1988), 117.

58. Ibid., 121–22.

59. Ibid., 125–41.

60. See William McBride, "Existentialism as a Cultural Movement," in *The Cambridge Introduction to Existentialism* (New York: Cambridge University Press, 2012), 50–69. McBride marks the widespread dissemination of existentialism as a "cultural force" by the mid-1950s.

61. See Jessica Grogan, *Encountering America: Humanistic Psychology, Sixties Culture, and the Shaping of the Modern Self* (New York: Harper, 2013), 75–79.

62. Rollo May, ed., *Existence* (New York: Basic, 1958). See the short book review of *Existence*, which explains that May simply presents European trends for general psychiatrists and other psychological professionals, in *Psychiatric Quarterly* 32.4 (1958): 870.

63. Grogan, *Encountering America*, 79.

64. Erich Fromm, *Escape from Freedom* (New York: Avon, [1941] 1969).

65. Rollo May, *The Meaning of Anxiety*, 2nd ed. (New York: W. W. Norton, [1950] 1977), 12. See also Bruno Bettelheim, *Surviving and Other Essays* (New York: Knopf, 1979); Arthur Schlesinger, Jr., *The Vital Center: The Politics of Freedom* (Boston: Houghton Mifflin, 1949). During Guy's confession to Owen Markham, he asserts, "And listen, I believe any man can be broke down. . . . It might take different methods from the ones Bruno used on me, but it could be done. What else do you think keeps the totalitarian states going?" (276). While it is uncertain whether Highsmith had yet read Fromm and, as a result, if Guy's psychologizing of totalitarianism is indebted to his work, Highsmith was later drawn to Fromm's psychoanalytical readings of love and sadism. See Wilson, *Beautiful Shadow*, 346–47, 427.

66. Robert Genter, *Late Modernism: Art, Culture, and Politics in Cold War America* (Philadelphia: University of Pennsylvania, 2010), 91.

67. Simon Jarvis, *Adorno: A Critical Introduction* (New York: Routledge, 1998), 84. Qtd. in Genter, *Late Modernism*, 91.

68. Louis Menand, "Freud, Anxiety, and the Cold War," in *After Freud Left: A Century of Psychoanalysis in America*, ed. John Burnham (Chicago: University of Chicago Press, 2012), 200–202.

69. Ibid., 202.

70. Ibid., 206.

71. Florence Dore, *The Novel and the Obscene: Sexual Subjects in American Modernism* (Stanford: Stanford University Press, 2005), 38.

72. Mary Margaret McCabe, *Plato and His Predecessors: The Dramatization of Reason* (New York: Cambridge University Press, 2000).

73. E. R. Dodds, "Plato and the Irrational," *Journal of Hellenic Studies* 65 (1945): 16.

74. Walter Benn Michaels claims that Carrie becomes "the body of desire in capitalism," a character whose sexuality and mental life are coded with the logic of urban capitalist society. See Walter Benn Michaels, *The Gold Standard and the Logic of Naturalism: American Literature at the Turn of the Century* (Berkeley: University of California Press, 1987), 56.

75. Russell Harrison, *Patricia Highsmith* (New York: Twayne, 1997), 14.

76. See Malin Lavon Walther, "Re-Wrighting *Native Son*: Gwendolyn Brooks's Domestic Aesthetic in *Maud Martha*," *Tulsa Studies in Women's Literature* 13.1 (Spring 1994): 143–45.

77. Gwendolyn Brooks, *Maud Martha* (Chicago, IL: Third World Press, 1993), 5.

78. Megan K. Ahern, "Creative Multivalence: Social Engagement beyond Naturalism in Gwendolyn Brooks's *Maud Martha*," *African American Review* 47.2–3 (Summer/Fall 2014): 316.

79. Edward A. Shannon, "Where Was the Sex?: Fetishism and Dirty Minds in Patricia Highsmith's *The Talented Mr. Ripley*," *Modern Language Studies* 34 (Spring–Autumn 2004): 17.

80. Ibid., 18.

81. See Wilson, *Beautiful Shadow*, 158.

82. Søren Kierkegaard, *A Kierkegaard Anthology*, ed. Robert Bretall (Princeton, NJ: Princeton University Press, 1946), 353.

83. Ibid.

84. Ibid.

85. Jennifer Fleissner, *Women, Compulsion, Modernity: The Moment of American Naturalism* (Chicago: University of Chicago, 2004).

86. Harrison, *Patricia Highsmith*, 20.

87. Jean-Paul Sartre, *Being and Nothingnes*, trans. Hazel Barnes (New York: Washington Square Press, 1953), 607.

88. US Department of Labor, "The Negro Family: The Case for National Action" (1965), www.dol.gov/oasam/programs/history/webid-meynihan.htm. References to the report refer to the unpaginated chapter divisions.

89. Chapter IV, "The Tangle of Pathology," n. p.

90. Chapter II, "The Negro American Family," n. p.

91. The research cited by Marshall, which Clark conducted with his wife, Mamie, may be found in Kenneth Clark and Mamie Clark, "Racial Identification and Preference in Negro Children," in *Readings in Social Psychology*, ed. Eleanor Maccoby, Theodore M. Newcomb, and Eugene L. Hartle (New York: Holt, 1952), 602–11.

92. James T. Patterson, Brown v. Board of Education: *A Civil Rights Milestone and Its Troubled Legacy* (New York: Oxford University Press, 2001), 43.

93. Ibid., 44.

94. Richard Kluger, *Simple Justice: The History of* Brown v. Board of Education *and Black America's Struggle for Equality* (New York: Vintage, 2004), 357, 557–87. See also Patterson, Brown v. Board of Education, 68–69.

95. Sean McCann, *Gumshoe America: Hard-Boiled Crime Fiction and the Rise and Fall of New Deal Liberalism* (Durham NC: Duke University Press, 2000), 5.

96. Ibid., 193.

Chapter 4

1. Walker Percy, *The Moviegoer* (New York: Vintage, 1998), 228. Cited parenthetically and hereafter.

2. For example, see Lewis A. Lawson, "From Tolstoy to Dostoyevsky in *The Moviegoer*," *The Mississippi Quarterly* 56.3 (Summer 2003), 412; Philip E. Simmons, "Toward the Postmodern Historical Imagination: Mass Culture in Walker Percy's *The Moviegoer* and Nicholson Baker's *The Mezzanine*," *Contemporary Literature* 33.4 (Winter 1992): 601–24; Robert Lacy, "*The Moviegoer*, Fifty Years After," *Southern Review* 47.1 (Winter 2011): 49–54; Martyn Bone, "The Postsouthern 'Sense of Place' in Walker Percy's *The Moviegoer* and Richard Ford's *The Sportswriter*," *Critical Survey* 12.1 (2000): 64–81.

3. Walker Percy, "The Loss of the Creature," in *The Message in the Bottle: How Queer Man Is, How Queer Language Is, and What One Has to Do with the Other* (New York: Picador, [1975] 2000), 50. Hereafter cited parenthetically.

4. See Paul Elie, *The Life You Save May Be Your Own: An American Pilgrimage* (New York: Farrar, Straus and Giroux, 2003), 213ff.

5. Farrell O'Gorman, *Peculiar Crossroads: Flannery O'Connor, Walker Percy, and Catholic Vision in Postwar Southern Fiction* (Baton Rouge: Louisiana State University Press, 2004), 79.

6. Walker Percy, *Love in the Ruins: The Adventures of a Bad Catholic at a Time Near the End of the World* (New York: Picador, 1971), 236, 328. Hereafter cited parenthetically.

7. Flannery O'Connor, *Mystery and Manners: Occasional Prose*, ed. Sally Fitzgerald and Robert Fitzgerald (New York: Farrar, Straus and Giroux, 1997), 146.

8. Flannery O'Connor, *Everything That Rises Must Converge*, in *Collected Works* (New York: Library of America, 1988), 654. Hereafter cited parenthetically.

9. Jean-Paul Sartre, *Nausea*, trans. Lloyd Alexander (New York: New Directions, 1964), 130.

10. Ibid.

11. Ibid.

12. Ibid., 19–20.

13. Flannery O'Connor, *The Habit of Being*, ed. Sally Fitzgerald (New York: Farrar, Straus, and Giroux, 1979), 24, 27.

14. Flannery O'Connor, *Wise Blood*, in *Collected Works*, 11. Hereafter cited parenthetically.

15. As William Rodney Allen explains, Haze discovers that "the world is his prison" and he consequently—absurdly—blinds himself, which is simultaneously an act of religious

devotion and existential despair. See William Rodney Allen, "The Cage of Matter: The World as Zoo in Flannery O'Connor's *Wise Blood*," *American Literature* 58.2 (May 1986): 268.

16. Jean-Paul Sartre, *Existentialism Is a Humanism*, trans. Carol Macomber (New Haven, CT: Yale University Press, 2007), 40. Hereafter cited parenthetically.

17. Percy's well-known debt to Søren Kierkegaard is explored in Bradley R. Dewey, "Walker Percy Talks about Kierkegaard: An Annotated Interview," *Journal of Religion* 54.3 (July 1974): 273–98. I emphasize Sartre and not Kierkegaard because the form of consciousness underlying *The Moviegoer* resonates more with the essays of the former. Also, in Dewey's interview with Percy, the author notes that he encountered Kierkegaard through other existentialists, particularly Sartre—an inheritance that has been neglected in scholarship on Percy.

18. Sartre gives the following explanation of "bad faith": "If we define man's situation as one of free choice, in which he has no recourse to excuses or outside aid, then any man who takes refuge behind his passions, any man who fabricates some deterministic theory, is operating in bad faith" ("Existentialism," 47). For Sartre, bad faith is the refusal to confront the metaphysical meaninglessness of the world or (as a derivation of that truth) the radical possibilities of choice available to each individual.

19. Alan Brinkley, *The End of Reform: New Deal Liberalism in Recession and War* (New York: Knopf, 1995) , 31.

20. Ibid., 174.

21. See Lizabeth Cohen, *A Consumer's Republic: The Politics of Mass Consumption in Postwar America* (New York: Random House, 2003), 257–89.

22. Daniel Horowitz, *Consuming Pleasure: Intellectual and Popular Culture in the Postwar World* (Philadelphia: University of Pennsylvania Press, 2012), 19.

23. Ibid., 368.

24. Ibid., 124.

25. Ibid., 125.

26. Daniel T. Rodgers, *Atlantic Crossings: Social Politics in a Progressive Age* (Cambridge, MA: Belknap Press, 1998), 445.

27. The two principle exceptions to this description are the Democrats' support for civil rights and the Republican creation of the EPA in 1970. However, as I have argued, these postwar forms of federal interventionism consistently drop the concentration of economic power as a constitutive element of their discourse. The elision of the economic and the transmutation of political crises as *social* issues serve as one of the hallmarks of the welfare state's transformation in the United States.

28. This may also have been bound up with the rise of new polling technologies and measurable notions of public opinion, not just the actuarial science of social security. See Benjamin Mangrum, "Aggregation, Public Criticism, and the History of Reading 'Big Data.'" Forthcoming in *PMLA* (October 2018).

29. Brinkley, *The End of Reform*, 271.

30. For the cultural consequences of this notion of social welfare in the 1930s and 1940s, see Michael Szalay, *New Deal Modernism: American Literature and the Invention of the Welfare State* (Durham NC: Duke University Press, 2000).

31. Mark McGurl, *The Program Era: Postwar Fiction and the Rise of Creative Writing* (Cambridge, MA: Harvard University Press, 2009), 330.

32. Ibid., 331.

33. Interview with James Boulware, *Walker Percy Remembered: A Portrait in the Words of Those Who Knew Him*, ed. David Horace Harwell (Chapel Hill: University of North Carolina Press, 2006), 23.

34. Walker Percy, "A Southern View," *Signposts in a Strange Land* (New York: Picador, 2000), 93.

35. Ibid.

36. Walker Percy, "The Southern Moderate," *Signposts in a Strange Land* (New York: Picador, 2000), 94.

37. Ibid., 96.

38. Ibid.

39. Ibid.

40. Jay Tolson, *Pilgrim in the Ruins: A Life of Walker Percy* (New York: Simon & Schuster, 2007), 250.

41. Ibid., 345.

42. Ibid., 444, 180.

43. Rpt. in Percy, *Signposts in a Strange Land*, 46.

44. Letter from Walker Percy to Richard Faust, August 14, 1987. Qtd. in Patrick H. Samway, *Walker Percy: A Life* (New York: Farrar, Straus and Giroux, 1997), 395.

45. Interview with James Boulware, *Walker Percy Remembered*, 23.

46. Ibid.

47. Walker Percy, *Lancelot* (New York: Farrar, Straus, Giroux, 1977), 58. Hereafter cited parenthetically.

48. Harold D. Clarke and Motoshi Suzuki, "Partisan Dealignment and the Dynamics of Independence in the American Electorate, 1953–88," *British Journal of Political Science* 24.1 (Jan. 1994): 57–77.

49. Helmut Norpoth and Jerrold G. Rusk, "Partisan Dealignment in the American Electorate: Itemizing the Deductions since 1964," *American Political Science Review* 76.3 (Sept. 1982): 522–37.

50. See Norman H. Nie, Sidney Verba, and John R. Petrocik, *The Changing American Voter*, enlarged edition (Cambridge: Harvard University Press, 1999), 43–46.

51. For an analysis of trends into the twenty-first century, see Russell J. Dalton, "Partisan Mobilization, Cognitive Mobilization, and the Changing American Electorate," *Electoral Studies* 26.2 (June 2007): 274–86.

52. See Russell J. Dalton, Ian McAllister, and Martin P. Wattenberg, "The Consequences of Partisan Dealignment," in *Parties without Partisans: Political Change in Advanced Industrial Democracies*, ed. Russell J. Dalton and Martin P. Wattenberg (New York: Oxford University Press, 2002), 37–63.

53. Bruce E. Keith, David B. Magleby, Candice J. Nelson, Elizabeth Orr, Mark C. Westlye, and Raymond E. Wolfinger, *The Myth of the Independent Voter* (Berkeley: University of California Press, 1992).

54. See Marc J. Hetherington, "Resurgent Mass Partisanship: The Role of Elite Polarization," *American Political Science Review* 95.3 (Sept. 2001): 619–31.

55. Paul Krugman, "Democrats Being Democrats," *New York Times*, June 15, 2015, http://nyti.ms/1Gnutgi.

56. Harold L. Wilensky, *American Political Economy in Global Perspective* (New York: Cambridge University Press, 2012), 199.

57. Walker Percy, "Symbol, Consciousness, and Intersubjectivity," *Journal of Philosophy* 55.15 (July 1958): 640. Percy reprinted the essay in *The Message in the Bottle*, but I cite here the earlier version because of its proximity to the publication of *The Moviegoer*.

58. Karl Marx and Friedrich Engels, "The Communist Manifesto," in *Karl Marx: Selected Writings*, ed. Lawrence H. Simon (Indianapolis: Hackett, 1994), 168.

59. Raymond Aron, *The Opium of the Intellectuals* (New Brunswick, NJ: Transaction, [1955] 2009), 328.

60. Thomas R. Flynn, *Sartre and Marxist Existentialism: The Test Case of Collective Responsibility* (Chicago: University of Chicago Press, 1984), 173.

61. George Cotkin, *Existential America* (Baltimore, MD: Johns Hopkins University Press, 2003), 105.

62. Hannah Arendt, "What Is Existenz Philosophy?" *Partisan Review* 13 (1946): 40.

63. Clement Greenberg, "Jean Dubuffet and French Existentialism," in *Clement Greenberg: The Collected Essays and Criticism*, vol. 2: *Arrogant Purpose, 1945–1949* (Chicago: University of Chicago Press, 1988), 92.

64. Marjorie Grene, *Dreadful Freedom: A Critique of Existentialism* (Chicago: University of Chicago Press, 1948), 14.

65. Hazel E. Barnes, *The Literature of Possibility: A Study in Humanistic Existentialism* (Lincoln: University of Nebraska Press, 1959), 171.

66. Cotkin, *Existential America*, 135.

67. William Barrett, *Irrational Man: A Study in Existential Philosophy* (New York: Doubleday, 1958), 19.

68. Jerry Rubin, "Alliance for Liberation," *Liberation* 11 (Apr. 1966): 9, 11. Qtd. in Cotkin, *Existential America*, 227.

69. See Cotkin, *Existential America*, 225–51.

70. Tod Gitlin, *The Sixties: Years of Hope, Days of Rage* (New York: Bantam, 1989), 84.

71. See Dwight Macdonald, "The Lady Doth Protest," *Reporter*, April 14, 1953, 36; William Phillips, "A French Lady on the Dark Continent: Simone de Beauvoir's Impressions of America," *Commentary* 16 (July 1953): 28–29.

72. Sandra Dijkstra, "Simone de Beauvoir and Betty Friedan: The Politics of Omission," *Feminist Studies* 6.2 (Summer 1980): 290–303.

73. Daniel Horowitz, *Betty Friedan and the Making of the Feminine Mystique: The American Left, the Cold War, and Modern Feminism* (Amherst: University of Massachusetts Press, 1998), 201.

74. Ibid., 2.

75. *The Port Huron Statement: Sources and Legacies of the New Left's Founding Manifesto*, ed. Richard Flacks and Nelson Lichtenstein (Philadelphia: University of Pennsylvania Press, 2015), 241.

76. Ibid., 240, 242.

77. Ibid., 242.

78. Doug Rossinow, *The Politics of Authenticity: Liberalism, Christianity, and the New Left in America* (New York: Columbia University Press, 1998), 15.

79. *The Port Huron Statement*, 242.

80. To some, the phrase "radical liberals" is as much of an oxymoron as "fashionable tube socks." However, the constituent assumptions of the New Left clearly situate them within the wider tradition of liberalism. In addition to the case Rossinow makes in

The Politics of Authenticity, see also Kevin Mattson, *Intellectuals in Action: The Origins of the New Left and Radical Liberalism, 1945–1970* (University Park: Pennsylvania State University Press, 2002), especially 97–144.

81. See Fulton, *Apostles of Sartre*, 112–13. Regarding presidential media coverage, see President Carter's infamous "malaise" speech on July 15, 1979. Carter describes the country's failure to address the decade's oil crisis, sluggish economy, and rising inflation as symptoms of its psychological state. The transcript of Carter's speech may be accessed at the American Presidency Project at the University of California Santa Barbara. See Jimmy Carter, "Address to the Nation on Energy and National Goals: 'The Malaise Speech,'" July 15, 1979, http://www.presidency.ucsb.edu/ws/?pid=32596.

82. Walker Percy, *The Last Gentleman* (New York: Picador, 1966), 20. Hereafter cited parenthetically.

83. Jean-Paul Sartre, *No Exit*, trans. Paul Bowles (New York: Samuel French, 1958), 21.

Chapter 5

1. Sloan Wilson, *The Man in the Gray Flannel Suit* (New York: Simon and Schuster, 1955), 300. Hereafter cited parenthetically.

2. Jonathan Franzen, Introduction to *The Man in the Gray Flannel Suit* by Sloan Wilson (New York: Four Walls Eight Windows, 2002), v.

3. Alfred Chandler, Jr., *The Visible Hand: The Managerial Revolution in American Business* (Cambridge, MA: Harvard Univ. Press, 1977), 9. The distinction between "vertical" and "horizontal" growth seems to have originated with Chandler. Horizontal growth refers to the merger of related firms or producers in a sector, while vertical growth involves the acquisition of various stages in the production process, which was often motivated either by an attempt to cut off a competitor's supply line or to integrate the processes of mass production and mass distribution.

4. Ibid., 1.

5. Ibid.

6. James Burnham, *The Managerial Revolution: What Is Happening in the World* (New York: Van Rees Press, 1941).

7. Yehouda Shenlav, *Manufacturing Rationality: The Engineering Foundations of the Managerial Revolution* (New York: Oxford Univ. Press, 1999), 3.

8. Robert R. Locke, *Management and Higher Education since 1940: The Influence of American and Japan on West Germany, Great Britain and France* (Cambridge: Cambridge University Press, 1989).

9. William Lazonick, *Competitive Advantage on the Shop Floor* (Cambridge, MA: Harvard University Press, 1990), 229.

10. Frederick Winslow Taylor, *The Principles of Scientific Management* (New York: Cosimo, 2006), 1.

11. Jean-François Chanlat, "Management Theory," in *Blackwell Encyclopedia of Sociology*, ed. George Ritzer (New York: Blackwell, 2007). *Blackwell Reference Online*, http://www.blackwellreference.com.

12. Marc Doussard, *Degraded Work: The Struggle at the Bottom of the Labor Market* (Minneapolis: University of Minnesota Press, 2013), 144. Doussard identifies the return of this compensation-work model during the 2000s' construction boom in the United

States—a shift that interestingly occurs within the heyday of so-called post-Fordist wages, which developed during the late twentieth century. While pre-Fordist wages are divorced from guaranteed income, post-Fordist wages are distinct from a stable correspondence between earnings and labor. As Doussard's study frequently suggests, it is perhaps best not to think of these three categories temporally, for they each predate Ford's assembly line.

13. Ibid., 87.

14. Among its many problems, the efficiency school of management had a fraught relation to organized labor. For instance, Henry Ford apparently advised workers in 1937 to "stay out of union labor organizations" because "international financiers are behind the labor unions" and the former "want to control industry and kill competition." See "Ford Scores Labor Unions: International Bankers Declared Behind Them; High Court Plan Hit," *Los Angeles Times*, February 20, 1937, 5

15. The Great Depression and the Second World War, more than anything else, leveled the economic scales in the United States. As Claudia Goldin and Robert A. Margo have shown, the wage structure underwent "a long-run roller coaster ride since 1940—with inequality falling precipitously during the 1940s, rising slightly in the 1950s and 1960s, and finally increasing sharply from the 1970s." See Claudia Goldin and Robert A. Margo, "The Great Compression: The Wage Structure in the United States at Mid-Century," *Quarterly Journal of Economics* 107.1 (1992): 3.

16. Chanlat, "Management Theory," *Blackwell Reference Online*.

17. I'm implying this view is mistaken. Let me explain why. Fligstein's critique of labor law assumes the rationality of corporate behavior, but it overlooks the rationality of interested parties—namely, citizens without substantial economic power—who look for federal protections within a consumer economy. In other words, Fligstein's view privileges corporate behavior and has a selective application of rational decision-making, thus occluding what's very reasonable about the progressive desire for regulation. The governing ideal of corporations having "rational self-interest" is a form of selective ignorance at best, and a Janus-faced fiction at worst.

18. Neil Fligstein, *The Transformation of Corporate Control* (Cambridge, MA: Harvard University Press, 1990), 2.

19. Louis Hyman, "Rethinking the Postwar Corporation: Management, Monopolies, and Markets," in *What's Good for Business: Business and American Politics since World War II*, edited by Kim Phillips-Fein and Julian E. Zelizer (New York: Oxford University Press, 2012), 197.

20. Ibid.

21. The phenomenon of disinvestment—in effect, the breaking up and selling off of subsidiary companies, usually for the sake of shareholder profit—became commonplace in the 1980s.

22. Fligstein, *The Transformation of Corporate Control*, 28.

23. Ibid.

24. Mark S. Mizruchi, *The Fracturing of the American Corporate Elite* (Cambridge MA: Harvard University Press, 2013), 81–110.

25. Ibid., 164–79.

26. Fligstein, *The Transformation of Corporate Control*, 29.

27. Lazonick, *Competitive Advantage on the Shop Floor*, 214.

28. Fligstein, *The Transformation of Corporate Control*, 116; Sukkoo Kim, "The Rise of Multiunit Firms in U.S. Manufacturing," *Explorations in Economic History* 36 (1999): 360–86. Kim, in contrast to a later argument by Alfred Chandler, suggests that "economies of marketing" had as much of a share in the success of the modern managerial firm than the "scale and scope" of mergers, integration, and organizational change. See Alfred Chandler, *Scale and Scope: The Dynamics of Industrial Capitalism* (Cambridge, MA: Harvard University Press, 1990), 47–48.

29. Harold Koontz, "Making Sense of Management Theory," *Harvard Business Review* 40 (July–Aug. 1962): 25.

30. Ibid., 24.

31. Stephen P. Waring, *Taylorism Transformed: Scientific Management Theory since 1945* (Chapel Hill: University of North Carolina Press, 1991), 7.

32. Ibid.

33. Max Weber, *From Max Weber: Essays in Sociology*, ed. H. B. Gerth and C. W. Mills (New York: Oxford University Press, 1946), 215–16.

34. According to Waring's taxonomy, there were two main schools of postwar management theory: the post-Taylorist bureaucrats and the post-Mayoist corporatists. In Waring's gloss, "Post-Taylorite bureaucratic thinkers believed in the basic rationality and legitimacy of centralized power and specialized tasks." The corporatists, in contrast, "questioned some aspects of the rationality and legitimacy of bureaucratic forms of managerial capitalism. . . . They sought to explain the dysfunctions of bureaucracy and to develop 'democratic' styles of leadership and participative methods of management that could bring harmony to the workplace or at least reduce conflict" (7).

35. Daniel A. Wren and Arthur G. Bedeian, *The Evolution of Management Thought*, 6th ed. (New York: John Wiley & Sons, 2009), 283.

36. Elton Mayo, *The Human Problems of an Industrial Civilization* (New York: Macmillian, 1933).

37. See Frederick G. Lesieur, ed., *The Scanlon Plan: A Frontier in Labor-Management Cooperation* (Cambridge, MA: Cambridge Technology Press of Massachusetts Institute of Technology, 1958).

38. Waring, *Taylorism Transformed*, 104–5.

39. See Mayo, *The Human Problems of an Industrial Civilization*.

40. For example, see Leland P. Bradford and Ronald Lippitt, "Roleplaying in Supervisory Training," *Personnel* 22 (1946): 358–69.

41. Waring, *Taylorism Transformed*, 120.

42. This theory advocates participation between managers and employees in establishing corporate or divisional goals—a more muted form of the autonomy and self-actualization that Abraham Maslow and others would later propose.

43. Peter F. Drucker, *Concept of the Corporation* (New York: John Day, 1946).

44. Peter F. Drucker, *The Practice of Management* (New York: Harper, 1954), 303, 136.

45. Peter F. Drucker, *Management: Tasks, Responsibilities, Practices* (New York: Harper & Row [1974] 1993), 441.

46. Ronald Lippitt and Leland Bradford, "Building a Democratic Work Group," *Personnel* 22 (1945): 142–52. For the seeds of this postwar managerial practice, see Kurt Lewin, Ronald Lippitt, and Ralph K. White, "Patterns of Aggressive Behavior in Experimentally Created 'Social Climates,'" *Journal of Psychology* 10 (1939): 271–99.

47. Waring, *Taylorism Transformed*, 113.

48. However, as Waring notes, other "intellectual pioneers" included "social scientists at universities: Douglas McGregor at MIT, Chris Argyris at Yale, Rensis Likert at the Institute for Social Research at Michigan, and Frederick Herzberg at Case Western Reserve." See Waring, *Taylorism Transformed*, 133.

49. Abraham H. Maslow, "A Theory of Human Motivation," *Psychological Review* 50 (1943): 380.

50. See Abraham Maslow, *Motivation and Personality* (New York: Harper & Row, 1954).

51. Wren and Bedeian, *The Evolution of Management Thought*, 340.

52. Waring, *Taylorism Transformed*, 134–35.

53. Many academic accounts of management theory either downplay or deny the importance of Maslow and the humanistic psychology moment. See, for example, Ivar Berg, Marcia Freedman, and Michael Freeman, *Managers and Work Reform: A Limited Engagement* (New York: Free Press, 1978), 8–14.

54. Abraham Maslow, *Eupsychian Management: A Journal* (Homewood, IL: Irwin-Dorsey, 1965), 66. The book was significantly revised, supplemented with Maslow's journal entries, and republished as Abraham H. Maslow, *Maslow on Management* (New York: John Wiley & Sons, 1998). The revision and republication suggests that, contrary to the claims of many academic theorists and historians of management practice, Maslow's work continued to enjoy a market of readers well into the 1990s.

55. Ibid., 1.

56. Frederick Herzberg, "One More Time: How Do You Motivate Employees?" *Harvard Business Review* 46 (Jan. 1968): 53–62. Reprinted in "Best of HBR," *Harvard Business Review* (Jan. 2003): 87.

57. Ibid., 93.

58. Ibid., 91.

59. Ibid., 91.

60. Catherine Jurca, *White Diaspora: The Suburb and the Twentieth-Century American Novel* (Princeton, NJ: Princeton University Press, 2001), 133.

61. Ibid., 136.

62. Ibid., 139.

63. The data tool may be accessed at www.bls.gov/data/inflation_calculator.htm.

64. US Department of Commerce, Current Population Reports, "Consumer Income," Washington, DC, October 7, 1955, n. p. Available at http://www2.census.gov/prod2/popscan/p60-018.pdf.

65. In William Whyte's dismissive summary of the novel, for instance, he explains, "In this story of a man 'heroically reconverting' to civilian life, hero Tom Rath is offered a big-money job by his boss." See William H. Whyte, Jr., *The Organization Man* (New York: Simon & Schuster, 1956), 251.

66. Evan Brier, *A Novel Marketplace: Mass Culture, the Book Trade, and Postwar American Fiction* (Philadelphia: University of Pennsylvania Press, 2009), 89.

67. Ibid., 91.

68. Sean McCann, *A Pinnacle of Feeling: American Literature and Presidential Government* (Princeton, NJ: Princeton University Press, 2008), 106.

69. Ibid., 107.

70. Ibid., 110.

71. Saul Bellow, *Henderson the Rain King* (New York: Penguin, 1996), 233. Hereafter cited parenthetically.

72. Martin Heidegger, *Being and Time*, trans. John Macquarrie and Edward Robinson (New York: Harper and Row, 1962), 67.

73. Ibid., 438.

74. Ibid., 437.

75. Saul Bellow, *Seize the Day* (New York: Penguin, 2003), 60.

76. Jack Kerouac, *On the Road* (New York: Penguin, 1999), 135.

77. Alan Watts, *This Is It: And Other Essays on Zen and Spiritual Experience* (New York: Vintage, 1973), 101.

78. Maria Bloshteyn, "Dostoevsky and the Beat Generation," *Canadian Review of Comparative Literature/Revue Canadienne de Littérature Comparée* (June–Sept. 2001): 218.

79. Leerom Medovoi, *Rebels: Youth and the Cold War Origins of Identity* (Durham, NC: Duke University Press, 2005) 217.

80. The Beats' interests in Whitman and the surrealists have been well documented, but Bloshteyn is among the first to trace Dostoevsky's influence across the letters and writings of Kerouac, Burroughs, Ginsberg, and others during the 1940s and 1950s. The Russian writer's influence was fundamental to the Beats during these decades. As Ginsberg recounts, for example, "The first sort of meeting of minds that Kerouac and I had was over the fact that we both read Dostoevsky's *Idiot*. And we identified with Alyosha or Myshkin. And Burroughs was very interested in [Dostoevsky's] nutty-man-confessional." Qtd. in Bloshteyn, "Dostoevsky and the Beat Generation," 220.

81. John Clellon Holmes, "The Game of the Name," in *The Portable Beat Reader* (New York: Penguin, 1992), 621.

82. Ibid.

83. Ken Kesey, *One Flew Over the Cuckoo's Nest* (New York: Penguin, 2003), 30. Hereafter cited parenthetically.

84. Robert Faggen, Introduction to *One Flew Over the Cuckoo's Nest*, xvii.

85. Kurt Vonnegut, *Player Piano* (New York: Dial, 2006), 92.

86. Paul Kurt Ackerman, "A History of Critical Writing on Franz Kafka" *German Quarterly* 23.2 (Mar. 1950): 108–9.

87. Franz Kafka, *A Franz Kafka Miscellany* (New York: Twice a Year Press, 1940).

88. Ackerman, "A History of Critical Writing on Franz Kafka," 110.

89. Hannah Arendt, "Franz Kafka: A Revaluation (On the occasion of the twentieth anniversary of his death)," *Partisan Review* 2 (Fall 1944): 412–22.

90. Hannah Arendt, "Franz Kafka, Appreciated Anew," in *Reflections on Art and Literature*, ed. Susannah Young-Ah Gottlieb (Palo Alto, CA: Stanford University Press, 2007), 108.

91. See, for example, Hannah Arendt, *The Human Condition* (Chicago: University of Chicago Press, 1958), 9.

92. Arendt, "Franz Kafka, Appreciated Anew," 108–109.

93. See Howard Caygill, "The Fate of the Pariah: Arendt and Kafka's 'Nature Theatre of Oklahoma," *College Literature* 38.1 (Winter 2011): 1–14. The terms "comedic" and "comedy" follow the sense of Dante's *la commedia*, which signifies an ascent from a damnable state or the resolution of some fundamental conflict.

94. Challenging the comedic interpretation even of the early "Nature Theatre of Oklahama," Caygill explains that Kafka's own view of the chapter was "located within the matrix of the racism of the new world and the transportation and implied extermination of the pariahs" (7). Rather than a utopia, Kafka's early "Nature Theatre" becomes a harbinger of the concentration camp.

95. Tracy Daugherty, *Just One Catch: A Biography of Joseph Heller* (New York: St. Martin's Press, 2011), 150.

96. Ibid., 186.

97. See Hugh Rockoff, *America's Economic Way of War: War and the U.S. Economy from the Spanish-American War to the Persian Gulf War* (New York: Cambridge University Press, 2012), 155–241.

98. Brinkley, *End of Reform*, 177.

99. Eisenhower, the chief engineer of this expansion, says, "This conjunction of an immense military establishment and a large arms industry is new in the American experience. The total influence—economic, political, even spiritual—is felt in every city, every Statehouse, every office of the Federal government. . . . In the councils of government, we must guard against the acquisition of unwarranted influence, whether sought or unsought, by the military-industrial complex."

100. Brier notes, "[I]n a novel that seems to have no place for the suffering, belief-producing artist, it is Hopkins himself who assumes that role. Hopkins's job requires all of the suffering, the detachment, the avoidance of family that artist-characters of other postwar novels—not just Holden Caulfield and Sal Paradise but also Bowles's Port (dead in the Sahara), Bradbury's Clarisse (killed by the government)—exhibit" (100). Hopkins is even repeatedly described as a "genius."

101. Daniel T. Rodgers identifies "fracture" as the general template of the decades surround the 1980s. See Daniel T. Rodgers, *Age of Fracture* (Cambridge MA: Harvard University Press, 2011).

102. US Department of Health, Education, and Welfare, *Work in America: Report of a Special Task Force to the Secretary of Health, Education, and Welfare*, (Washington, DC: December 1972), x, xi. The report, also prepared by the W. E. Upjohn Institute for Employment Research, was widely published and its first edition was sold out in a number of days. MIT Press released an edition of the report in 1973.

103. Ibid.

104. See Carter, "Address to the Nation on Energy and National Goals: 'The Malaise Speech,'" http://www.presidency.ucsb.edu/ws/?pid=32596.

105. Ibid., xi.

106. Ibid., x.

107. US Department of Health, Education, and Welfare, *Work in America*, xi.

108. Irving Kristol, "Is the American Worker 'Alienated'?" *Wall Street Journal*, January 18, 1973, 12. Not only did Kristol express disgust at the notion of worker "alienation," but also he and other conservative commentators rejected the report's policy implications regarding employment. *Work In America* maintains, for example, "If our society provided stable employment at above-poverty level wages for all men, and if all women could therefore look forward to marrying men who could serve them in the provider role and for whom they could serve in the homemaker role, then it is likely that fewer girls would become pregnant before marriage, that lower-class couples would marry at a somewhat later age, that

relationships in lower-class marriages would be less tense, [etc.]. All these tendencies would be strengthened if women, too, could readily find stable part- and full-time employment" (147–48). The ostensible benefits of employment standards for a guaranteed living wage (i.e., minimum wage policy) pertain to conventional domestic roles ("provider" and "home-maker"). If the latter was an olive branch to cultural conservatives, the former would be an unrealized hope for American liberals as the minimum wage reached its (inflation-adjusted) peak in 1968.

109. The influential idea of "human capital" was first theorized in Gary S. Becker, *Human Capital: A Theoretical and Empirical Analysis with Special Reference to Education* (Chicago: University of Chicago Press, 1964).

110. US Department of Health, Education, and Welfare, *Work in America*, 150.

111. Qtd. in ibid., 149.

112. Ibid.

113. Ibid., 25.

114. *The Port Huron Statement*, 243.

115. Ibid., 239, 243.

116. Peter F. Drucker, *Managing Oneself* (Boston: Harvard Business School, 2008).

INDEX

absurdity
  American literary uses of, 26, 37, 48, 107, 109–
    111, 123, 135, 155–156, 160–162, 185n15
  existential idea of, 109–110, 128, 132
  as political concept, 10, 14–15, 159–160, 165
activist-managerial state. *See* New Deal *and*
    social democracy
aestheticism, 17–18, 19, 21, 22–48, 86–87,
    133, 175n81
  critiques of, 40–42, 74
  definition of, 23, 30
  and the economy, 118, 165–166, 174n51
  as governing value for criticism, 23–25, 44–47
  and literary form, 23, 27–28, 39, 45–46, 60, 67,
    75, 95, 108–109, 112–113, 150, 154
  and political action, 33–34, 174n60
  and postwar reception history, 43–44, 92–93,
    128–132, 158–163
  relationship between civil society and,
    30, 34–36
  resurgence during postwar decades, 23, 128
  and totalitarianism, 25–29, 43–44
alienation, 49–51, 67, 126
  as diagnosis for social phenomena, 78, 98–100,
    140–141, 157–158, 163–165, 194n108
  as individual rather than structural, 19, 54, 76,
    84, 98, 106, 113–118, 129–130, 147, 150
  popular discourse of, 67–68
  as product of structural inequality, 14, 16, 47,
    57–58, 63–64, 70–71, 91–92
  as result of organizations and bureaucracies,
    15–17, 20, 60–61, 65, 107–108, 129–132,
    135–136, 157–159
anxiety, 2, 3, 27, 42, 47, 64, 67, 77–106,
    107–108, 123–124, 146–149, 183n56
  as diagnostic term for social phenomena, 73,
    89–90, 105, 180n3
  as image of postwar liberalism, 17, 20, 43, 54,
    95–96, 129, 154, 189n81
  raced presuppositions of, 11, 88–89
  regarding the mediation of reality,
    111–116, 154
  regarding political tyranny, 25, 28, 43, 44,
    54–56, 128, 159–160, 182n47
Arendt, Hannah, 3, 18, 23, 30, 48
  aestheticism of, 33–36, 128, 174n60
  on Franz Kafka, 159–161, 194n94

  opposition to welfare state, 33–36, 159–160
  and political action, 34–35, 44, 159, 173n49
  on totalitarianism, 22–23
Auden, W. H., 78, 158, 180n3
authenticity, 21, 42, 67–70, 77, 106, 107–133,
    151–153
  as antithesis of collectivism, 35–36, 42, 43,
    74–76, 86–87
  as corporate ethic, 20, 134–135, 145–149,
    163–166
  as fundamental epistemic commitment, 108,
    112–117, 124–126, 129
  and individual estrangement, 20, 54, 86–90,
    95–96, 100–103, 107, 114–115, 118,
    147–149
  as locus for political action, 11, 19, 50–51, 54,
    67, 162–163
  and the New Left, 131–132, 155, 165
  and partisan disaffiliation, 118–126
  in tension with intersubjectivity and solidarity,
    126–128, 132–133
  within theories of labor, 145, 163–166

Barrett, William, 50, 69, 128, 129, 132
Barzun, Jacques, 69, 180n3
Beat movement, 154–155, 193n80
Bellow, Saul, 3, 18, 50, 77, 154, 163
  Adventures of Augie March, 5, 19, 71–76,
    153, 180n87
    and the political implications of form,
      74–75, 150
  break with European existentialists, 72
  Dangling Man, 71–72
  Henderson the Rain King, 150–153
  Seize the Day, 153
book trade, 29, 40, 172n24, 192n54
  as burgeoning postwar industry, 4–5, 43, 67,
    94, 168nn14–15
  market-structuring concerns during postwar
    era of, 14, 58, 100, 134–135, 153–154
  See also prestige
Brinkley, Alan, 1, 7, 47, 168n19
Brooks, Cleanth, 44, 46
Brooks, Gwendolyn, 99–100
Brown v. Board of Education, 105–106
Broyard, Anatole, 84
Bulosan, Carlos, 18, 57–58, 76